Butterflies in the Belfry—
Serpents in the Cellar

◆

An Unintended Pursuit for a Natural Christianity

J. MICHAEL JONES

ISBN: 978-0-9977-5910-5 (sc)
ISBN: 978-0-9977-5911-2 (e)

Library of Congress Control Number: 2016921201

Lulu Publishing Services rev. date: 1/6/2017

DEDICATION

As I wrote this book I thought continuously of those, like me, whose prior Christian convictions had faced serious challenges from inside and out. I saw myself as forerunner, with a machete in hand, trying to hack through the dense undergrowth of questions and confusion. I dedicate this book to these pilgrims, with the hopes that my work and thoughts have given them a path that will make their journey a bit less harsh and with a shorter passage to that glade of peace.

CONTENTS

Introduction xiii

CHAPTER ONE 1
The Year of the Rabbit
    The Visit 6
    The Fall 10
    The Nadir 16
    The Crater 17

CHAPTER TWO 21
Postcards from the Post-evangelical Wilderness
    More than S'mores ... But Not Much More 21
    The Student 24

CHAPTER THREE 29
Strangled by My Belt
    The Buckle 30
    Jake the Raper 32
    Arthur and Marilyn to the Rescue 33
    The Eccentric God 34

CHAPTER FOUR 39
The Baptist Bar Mitzvah
    The Loss of Innocence 41
    The Art of Pretentiousness 45

CHAPTER FIVE **49**
What are You Worth?
    The Common Denominator 50
    The Measurement of the Self 52
    A Personal Measure Gone Bad 53
    A Tango with the Reaper of the Worthless 57

CHAPTER SIX **59**
Repossessed Memories
    A Primal Loss 60
    The Stabbing 64

CHAPTER SEVEN **69**
Freakin' Jesus Freaks
    Coach 70
    Enter Aaron, the Disciple Maker 71

CHAPTER EIGHT **77**
Foundation Blocks
    Underpinnings of Chalk 77
    Christ the Cornerstone 78
    The Art and Artifice of Sanctification 79
    The Great Gospel Paradox 81

CHAPTER NINE **83**
Linchpin
    A Bifurcated Foundation 84
    This Worthless World and the Celestial Puppeteer 87
    Dualism's Perspective on a Tragedy 88
    Dualism and the Body 92
    Dualism and the Mind 94

CHAPTER TEN **99**
The Shoulders
    Eschatology and the End of Everything 99
    Inerrancy or Magic 102

CHAPTER ELEVEN. **107**
Utopia?
   A Real Fatalism 108
   Beneath Eden's Green Garden. 109
   Christian Valuation 111

CHAPTER TWELVE **115**
The Great Bifurcation
   Castaways 116
   A Platonic Relationship. 120
   The Persian Mystic 122

CHAPTER THIRTEEN **127**
The Celestial Tango
   Beyond Questions. 130

CHAPTER FOURTEEN. **133**
A Mystery of Cars
   Gnostic Ponderings 136
   Don't Be Taken Captive 139
   The Keys Are Key 140

CHAPTER FIFTEEN **143**
House of Medici: The Midwives of the Renaissance
   Crazy Old Gemistos. 146
   The Rise of the Medicis. 147
   The School of Athens 149
   Averroes the Aristotelian 155

CHAPTER SIXTEEN **159**
The Gnostics
   The Heavenly Hustle 160
   Touching God?. 163
   God Is on My Side ... or Is He?. 166
   Augustine the Platonist. 170

CHAPTER SEVENTEEN **177**
A Divided Present
    Make Love, Not War 178
    The Secrets of Victoria. 180
    A Secular Faith. 182
    Hankering for Love 182

CHAPTER EIGHTEEN **185**
The Summit Ridge
    The Philosophical Tightrope. 186
    The Psychological Tightrope. 188
    A Raw Sanctification 190

CHAPTER NINETEEN **193**
So? The Philosophical Question
    A Metaphysical Repentance. 194
    Neurons or Demons, Take Your Pick 195
    A Substantial History. 197
    The Paradox of the Divine Assassin. 198
    Nature: Finders Keepers, Losers Weepers. 200
    The Loss of Platonic and Aristotelianism Certainty 201

CHAPTER TWENTY **205**
So? The Spiritual Question
    On Plato and the Soul 205
    On Aristotle and the Soul. 205
    American Evangelical View of Spirituality 206
    A New View of the Soul and Spirituality 207

CHAPTER TWENTY-ONE. **209**
So? The Question of Community
    The Community of Christians 209
    Church Defined. 210
    A Perilous Search for the Authentic Church. 213
    Then I Met Dave 215
    The Community of non-Christians. 218

Good Guys and Bad Guys 218
Being Human 221
The Resort and the Landmark 222
Honest Questions Deserve Honest Answers 223

Index 225

Bibliography 233

INTRODUCTION

This book is the culmination of over three decades of deep and personal ponderings. But the word *ponderings* has too soft and subtle a meaning to adequately express my experience. Perhaps a better way to describe this process would be arduous and gut-wrenching—anything but subtle.

Some writers are most productive when they are isolated in a cabin on a romantic windswept beach. Without distraction, their creative minds assemble highly imaginative worlds out of thin air—worlds their readers can escape to and cavort in for days or weeks.

I visualize these writers waking with the dawn, then pouring a cup of strong, black coffee brewed on a wood-fired stove. Sipping their java for hours, surrounded by double-hung windows that face the sea, in this idyllic setting they churn out pages of a mystery novel and artfully weave them into magical books of gold, as if by Rumpelstiltskin himself.

Butterflies in the Belfry, Serpents in the Cellar came about not in peaceful solitude during long walks of inspiration on isolated beaches. Instead, it was conceived in moments of desperation and long crawls in the trenches amid the crossfire of the true war of the worlds—or at least world views. This is not to say that I didn't have my own pleasant walks of solitude, but those were word-finding walks, where, like a journalist, I attempted to select the right words to best communicate and reflect the story that had already been written on the pages of my life.

People write books from different perspectives. Many write as authorities or teachers. I have spent countless nights groping for the truth by studying the Bible from cover to cover. As well, I have studied hundreds of other books on theology, philosophy, and history, but I make no claim of being an authority on any of those subjects. Mine was subsistence research, striving for my own intellectual, emotional, and spiritual survival, not the kind of research that makes one a professional. I write as a humble journalist, an observer and recorder of life, or at least that part of life through which my incredible journey has taken me.

Like many people, I was accidentally swept up in the whirlwind of a troubling experience in the same way as Tolkien's Frodo. I became a participant in a personal and dangerous adventure of the soul. I had no choice in the matter; I was pulled kicking and screaming by the overpowering undertow of events. I wouldn't have believed it before this experience, but there truly are things worse than death. In my storms of life, I almost lost my soul. And then, against all odds, I have inadvertently found it again.

CHAPTER ONE

⬥

The Year of the Rabbit

Click, click, click—*the collapse of my world spread rapidly, with the foundation the first to give way and then everything above it—the whole Church and my entire Christian experience. Had it all been a farce? By the time the sun was high in the sky, I was no more a Christian than my Muslim neighbors in the next flat or the agnostic I once was before I'd become this so-called new creature.*

On the surface of a cheap imitation-bamboo table, a murky pit began to appear before me. The pit was materializing between an assortment of real bamboo chopsticks, each well used and stained with dark brown, soy-based sauces. The pit was a figurative one, of course, but in some ways, it was a real rabbit hole or a portal to another world. I felt the grip of the tight circumference of the hole around my arms and shoulders, the darkness reaching out and pulling me headfirst into its dreadful mouth like a carnivore of the soul.

The force that was drawing me into the pit must have started decades earlier, and, after such a sustained momentum, no mortal power was capable of stopping it now. I fell in and began to tumble in slow motion, head over heels.

Around the table sat two other men, but, as far as I knew, I was the only one falling. And neither the hole nor my fall was the result of any kind of mysterious oriental magic conjured up by one of my dinner partners. It was the simple words of Rod, sitting to my right, that became the last straw, or more correctly, the downy feather that pushed me over the edge. He wasn't even aware of the impact of his words at the time—nor was I.

Rod was my boss. He was a heavily built man on a six-foot frame with a blondish-gray goatee that pedestaled a reddened, sun-kissed face. His turquoise eyes beneath the thinning hair of a man approaching his middle years gave him an intimidating look, whether he wanted it or not—but I suspect he wanted it. The other man, an Arab, was a stranger to me but a friend of my boss. I was in these exotic surroundings as a missionary. We weren't sitting in some out-of-the-way restaurant in Shanghai but in Cairo, Egypt, and the year was 1988. It was the only Chinese restaurant I'd ever seen in the chaotic streets of this dusty, ancient city.

For months, I'd been eagerly awaiting Rod's visit. My wife Denise and our three small children were teetering on the edges of emotional meltdowns, and we'd been in the country for only a little over a year. Culture shock made up only a small fraction of our growing distress. It was situational shock more than anything, precipitated by a chain of events no one could have predicted.

We had volunteered to join a close-knit team of missionaries in Nicosia, Cyprus, with an organization I will refer to as Disciples Inc, henceforth simply known as DI. In Cyprus, we planned to work among Muslim refugees from Lebanon's cruel civil war of the early 1980s. I'd spent two years studying the cultures of Cyprus and Lebanon as well as the layout of the land and city of Nicosia. I had photos and maps of Cyprus taped to the stone walls of my basement office back in Ypsilanti, Michigan. For those two years, I also studied Lebanese Arabic and gradually developed a passion for this people. I dreamed about Cyprus almost every night. There was no place on Earth I could have been more excited about moving to. My wife felt the same—that Cyprus was the perfect fit for us.

As we neared our departure date, with support funds raised and belongings shipped to Cyprus, Rod paid us a surprise visit at the headquarters of DI in Chicago, where we were attending a week-long missionary conference. While we were standing in the breakfast buffet line one morning, he said to me casually, "Mike, the team in the Middle East met recently. We've decided you won't be moving to Cyprus but to Cairo, Egypt." I stood there stunned while he paused to put an ice-cream scoop of scrambled eggs on his plate. "Also, because we know single men do much better in language acquisition, we want you to go alone, without your family." Then he smiled and walked away. It seemed that, at the last minute, without any input from us, Rod had reassigned us, or at least me, to live alone in the enormous city of Cairo. This new development was deeply disturbing.

I quickly found myself in a disconcerting place. My training with DI had emphasized completely obeying one's superiors. We had been taught that God puts leaders above disciples and to disobey leaders is to disobey God himself. But I resented, in particular, his last request—that I should go alone without Denise and my sons, Bryan and Daniel (our third, Tyler, was born soon after we arrived in Egypt). Such a concept was unthinkable to me, and his request would have seemed even more absurd if it weren't for the deterministic view of leadership to which we had all subscribed.

Later that week, I told Rod I couldn't possibly leave my family behind. Despite the ludicrousness of his request, I still felt guilty for opposing his directive. He reluctantly agreed, saying, "Some men don't have the faith to do great things." In consolation, he promised to bring all our belongings—including baby diapers, clothes, books, and cooking pots that we'd already sent to Cyprus—down to Cairo after we arrived. It didn't make sense to me. Why couldn't we retrieve them ourselves? But I trusted him, as he implied that he would be down to help us settle in the exotic city. In hindsight, I should have listened to my intuition. Rod never brought any of our belongings to us, and, during our assimilation into the Egyptian culture, we were on our own. I saw him only once, briefly, before I set eyes on his goateed face again until two years later—in the Chinese restaurant.

We arrived in Cairo with the shirts on our backs and only the basic items that would fit into a few suitcases. To our surprise, as soon as we landed in the Middle East, we learned that Rod had taken a job with the Assad (Hafez Al-Assad, not his son Bashar) government in Syria (while maintaining his missionary status with DI) and had moved from Cyprus to Damascus. When our belongings had arrived in Cyprus, he'd locked them up in his garage just ahead of his departure from the island. After living in Egypt for 12 months, we received only a couple of brief, formal notes from the DI team and certainly didn't receive any of our property.

Arriving in Cairo on our own, without our effects or a resident visa, was only the start of our difficulties. We were also under strict orders from Rod to avoid contact with all other Americans, both those in Egypt and friends and family back home. All letters to us had to come through Rod's hands in Damascus—for security reasons, he said. This process rendered us extremely lonely.

Perhaps Rod had honest motives for our isolation, but, in retrospect, they were misguided. He theorized that our intense loneliness would drive us to develop relationships with Egyptian Muslims, the people who were to be the focus of our ministry. He believed that if we were "baptized by fire," as he used to say, into the Arab culture, we would be better fit for long-term ministry. Rod knew it would be difficult for us to find our way without any assistance, but he sincerely believed that the process would harden us in the way that a steel tool, once forged and hardened, is more useful. But Rod's conspiracy of adversity turned out not to be the issue; our major challenges had to do with our health.

When we arrived in Cairo, our two sons, Bryan and Daniel, were ages four and two, respectively, and Denise was seven months pregnant. As soon as we established a place to live and got on our feet, we had to begin making arrangements for our new son's birth. Tyler came into that exotic world without any complications, but his older brother Daniel (by then age three) soon became quite ill. His illness lasted throughout our two long, arduous years in Egypt, and, during the months leading up to Rod's infamous visit, Daniel had been near to death on one occasion. Based on his symptoms, we believed his most serious illness was typhoid. He became nonresponsive at the worst point, and the pediatrician said there was nothing else he could do for him. He recovered from that terrible experience but still suffered an unrelated chronic illness that started soon after our arrival to Cairo. His background illness was never diagnosed or successfully treated even after seeing five Egyptian physicians and being placed on a bucketful of medicines. But it left him covered in painful itchy sores for our entire time in Egypt, along with fevers and irritability. It was like a case of chicken pox that never went away. Having a seriously ill child while living alone in a strange country was deeply draining on our spirits and emotions. After 10 months, in our desperation, Denise broke Rod's mandate and called her parents for help. They were quickly on their way.

During the worst period of Daniel's illness, I succumbed to illness myself. I'd been doing medical work as a physician assistant (PA) with sickly children in a slum known as the Village of Garbage, where I was exposed to many infectious diseases. Meningitis took over my faculties on the day that Denise went to Cairo International Airport to pick up her parents.

I knew something was wrong when I got up that godawful morning with a terrible headache and fever. By 10 o'clock I had become so ill that I couldn't accompany Denise to flag a taxi and fetch her parents. By the time she returned three hours later, I was on the verge of unconsciousness. It was frightening for her to have her three-year-old son in one room with her, ill and covered in sores, and now her husband in the adjacent room, barely conscious and so sick he couldn't sit up. All this against the backdrop of life in a huge, filthy city with only a broken third-world health-care system for assistance and absolutely no support from our organization. Thankfully, Denise's parents were there to help with Bryan and Daniel while she attended to me.

I spent the next 10 days face down on a foam pad, the place where I had originally collapsed, sequestered in the sweltering boys' bedroom as a makeshift hospital isolation room. Denise had moved the boys into the guest room with her to keep them away from my nasty germs and had given her parents the master bedroom, which was roomier. A dubious Egyptian doctor visited me each morning with cups of colored pills, some of which I actually took, but when I was in better control of my senses I brushed most of them under my pad. As a medical practitioner myself, I knew no pills existed that would treat viral meningitis except to dampen the senses and bring temporary comfort. I wanted my senses to be as acute as possible to make sure the doctor didn't inadvertently poison me with his pills. In the United States, I would undoubtedly have been in ICU.

In the process of recovering from meningitis, I came down with a painful case of shingles across the left side of my face and into my left ear. Daniel simultaneously took another turn for the worse. Denise, fortunately a nurse by training, bounced between Daniel and me, at the same time attempting to provide her parents with some hospitality and orientation to this culture, so radically different from their Minnesotan farming community.

The grand finale in our bad-health saga was the illness of Denise's father. On the eve of his departure back to the States, after I was on my way to recovery, he collapsed. I was back in a real bed, in the guest room with Denise, on the verge of falling asleep when I heard the cry from my mother-in-law. "John! John!" (She called me John, particularly when she was serious about something.) I jumped out of bed and ran out into the dark hallway. Halfway between the bathroom and the master bedroom, my father-in-law lay face down on the cold, tiled floor with Denise's mom hovering over him, distraught beyond measure.

I rolled him onto his back. He was not breathing, nor did he have a pulse.

I was ready to place my mouth over his to give him a breath of air when he took a deep breath of his own. I felt his pulse again—it was thready and irregular, but present. He was apparently having a significant heart arrhythmia, which put us in the middle of another medical nightmare on the heels of mine—and still with Daniel in the other room continuing to decline.

There was no 911-type number to call for Denise's father, no emergency room to drive to even if we had access to a car. I called my one American acquaintance, whom I had met only once a few months earlier. He was a PA working for a private defense contractor over an hour away, and he was kind enough to rush over with medical supplies and an ambulance, which he had commandeered from his company. We managed to get an IV started in his shriveled vein. I pounded a nail into the wall above his bed and hung the glass bottle there. Eventually we transported him to a hospital where he was admitted to a makeshift cardiology unit.

The purpose of our assignment in Egypt was to learn Arabic, learn the Arab culture, and make friends with Muslims, in that order. The eventual purpose of our friendship was to engage Muslims in a dialog that would cause them to want to convert to Christianity. Looking back over the previous 12 months, I think we had succeeded in all of those goals, and additionally I was working in providing medical care to the poorest of the poor who were living in the garbage dump. Denise had a full-time job of trying to maintain a home with three young children, including walking for miles every day in the heavy traffic, with three little boys in tow, to shop for the basic staples of life. But life was hard for us, even from the first day. It would have been difficult for anyone to arrive in Cairo with a few suitcases of belongings, not knowing anyone, and try to carve out space for a life. So even before the series of health problems, we were totally exhausted.

After all the difficulties, what were the few words spoken in the Chinese restaurant that became my breaking point?

The Visit

One day, out of the blue, I had a phone call from Rod. I had not heard a word from him in about a year. Out of the receiver I heard him say, "Hey Mike. I'm in Cairo on business for the Syrian government. I've got your mail from the states, and you need to come pick it up."

Recovering from my moment of shock, I slowly eased down onto the stool beside the phone and answered back, "Uh ... okay ... but we need to talk."

There was hesitation on the other end of the phone. "Well, I'm only in Egypt for a week, and I'm quite busy."

"We can't meet just for an hour?"

"Well," he said, still stumbling in reluctance, "Stay by your phone and if I find an opening sometime this week, I will call you and you can come into Cairo and pick up your mail. Then and we can talk."

Cell phones were a thing of the future, so I stayed in our flat within earshot of the bells of our big, black landline phone. I knew he was leaving the following Friday, and I didn't hear anything until Thursday morning.

"Hey Mike," he said. "Come on in this evening, and we will have dinner together at 6 p.m."

"Okay," I said. Then I got the address and the room number to his hotel.

I was desperate to talk to Rod. Denise and I both felt we were on an unsustainable path, and I was going to seek him out that night asking for mercy. Denise and I had decided that we wanted to finish our difficult assignment in Egypt as soon as possible and rejoin the rest of the team in Cyprus, where we could have some emotional sustenance. We wanted to reunite the boys with their clothes and toys and claim the diapers and other baby equipment we had shipped to his flat a year earlier and desperately needed. Most of all we wanted to connect with our peers, to have someone to talk with to break the grip of merciless isolation.

I took the hour-long train ride into the heart of the city that memorable night, repeating in my mind—and even audibly at times—the words I wanted to say to him. I knew my words were deeply fraught with emotions, frustrations, and confusion. But Rod, an aggressive speaker, left few alleyways between his sentences into which I could park a single word. I was nervous. I had always found confrontations difficult, but it was extremely difficult to go up against the DI leader, something I had been taught never, ever to do. Not only was he in DI leadership, he was akin to a superstar among their leadership.

I got off the metro train in the heart of the city. I followed my hand-drawn map into the dark, labyrinthine streets of old Cairo, southeast of the American University. I knew the path to the university well, as I had spent five days a week there for the past year, studying Arabic. The area beyond the university was unfamiliar. There the buildings, built in the nineteenth century or earlier, were all beige and crumbling and all looked exactly alike, except for small signs here and there—some in Arabic and English and some just in Arabic. Most blocks were accented with identical walk-in-closet-sized mini markets, all selling the exact same products, and each product had only one brand. I finally caught the name of his hotel above its front door. The place had seen its better days. I took the dimly lit and dirty marble staircase to the fourth floor. Fortunately, his room was one of the few that still held its number, "455." I knocked on the old door with my knuckles and waited. There was no answer. I knocked again and still there was no answer. I was puzzled. I looked at my watch: 6:07 p.m.

I went back down the staircase to the small lobby. On my way up, I had seen a thin man sitting in the office, wearing a wife-beater, watching soccer on a small black and white TV. He was swatting flies with a plastic fly swatter, ignoring me when I came in. "Uh, do you speak English?" I asked him. I was prepared to speak Arabic if he didn't, but I knew those Egyptians who did speak English spoke it better than I did Arabic.

"Yes ... we are full."

"I don't need a room, but can you tell me if Dr. Rod Chris is in room 455?" He opened a green book on his desk and flipped pages. "Yes, he is here until tomorrow."

I took the steps back up to the room and banged on the door with the soft side of my fist but this time harder. After a second round of banging I heard a voice ... a faint conversation coming from inside. In a minute the door opened and there was Rod's sleepy face, and he was in pajamas. "Oh hi ... it's you. Let me get your mail."

Looking at my watch again, "Yeah ... you said we were having dinner at 6 p.m., and it is 6:18 now. Did I misunderstand?"

Opening the door wider, he said, "Oh, that's right. Come in, have a seat."

I took a seat in an old French provincial chair beside a small glass-topped table. Only then did I get the sight of another man getting out of bed. Rod spoke to him in Arabic and went into the bathroom to wash up. I watched as he, and eventually the other man, got dressed. Then Rod introduced him, "Mike, this is Ahmed. He is a business acquaintance here in Cairo."

I shook the man's hand. He smiled. Rod then looked at him and said in English for my benefit, "Mike is here to get some mail."

"Yes," I interrupted, looking at Rod, "and Rod and I am going out to dinner … aren't we?"

Rod looked back at me, "Sure. Ahmed and I have some meetings to go to first and you can tag along." Then, looking at Ahmed he asked, "Do you mind if Mike joins us later for dinner?"

Ahmed seemed hesitant and said to Rod, "We do have things to talk about and you are leaving tomorrow."

Rod looked at me, then back at Ahmed, "Oh, Mike will only take a minute."

Ahmed shaking his head, "Well then … I guess that's okay."

I was feeling quite frustrated at this point. The conversation that I wanted to have with Rod was extremely important for me and my family. I realized with Ahmed's presence, the conversation would be severely muted. Rod was a clandestine missionary in Syria, with the stated goal of converting Muslims to the Christian faith, and any conversation in front of Ahmed (whose name made it clear that he was a Muslim) about DI business could blow his cover. I would eventually look at this moment for many years and question why didn't I say, "Hell no! We had an appointment at 6 p.m. for dinner for an important conversation, and I will not accept my visit as just a footnote to your evening plans with Ahmed! This dinner must be in private!" But I didn't say that … or anything. I just stood there as the proverbial deer in the headlights.

A couple of hours later, after following Rod and Ahmed to a few meetings and standing outside waiting, we finally headed to eat. Eventually we were seated for dinner and orders had been taken and served. It was getting late, and I sensed my opportunity to talk to Rod running out, and I may not see him again for yet another year or two. In front of Ahmed, I gave him my petition to move to Cyprus.

Rod looked at me, smiling, and said, "Mike, I actually made a decision earlier this year to assign you and Denise to Sana, Yemen. So really, you won't ever be joining us in Cyprus." He paused for a drink of his green tea, sloshing it around in his mouth, as I sat stunned, at an utter loss for words. Stirring his noodles with a chopstick, he looked at Ahmed, with a grin and then back at me, adding, "But one thing I've learned over the years—women don't handle these changes very well." Now pointing his chopstick at my face and looking serious, he concluded, "Lie to Denise and tell her you're moving her to Cyprus, then surprise her when you arrive in Sana." Then he smiled again, allowing it to morph into a loud chuckle before he took another sip of his tea.

Even before he finished speaking, I'd begun to feel a tightness building in my chest and a warm, flushed feeling suffused my face. My adrenal glands had discharged their venom. I'd known of Rod for 10 years and known him personally for three, but I'd never said an unpleasant word to him. I believed, as a Christian, that it was wrong to do so—to say unkind words to a brother, let alone to harbor anger. But on that night it took every ounce of strength in my body to hold back a flood of vile verbiage, profanities, or possibly even a left hook to his sunburnt cheek. I knew suddenly and for certain that this man didn't care a damn about me or my family.

"I'm fed up with your crap!" I said in more of a whisper than a shout as I trembled. "I am *not* taking orders from you anymore!" My throat was acting like a high-pressure valve on a fire hose, turning gently to let a few, quiet words slip out while guarding against an uncontrolled explosion. Being a "godly man," my intentions were for my behavior to reflect that idealized character of a saint—all part of the evangelical charade.

For a few seconds, he looked flustered. But he quickly composed himself and rose, thrusting a bundle of envelopes tied with a string at me. "Here's your mail." Turning toward Ahmed, he said, "Let's get out of here."

I felt dizzy and the table began to spin—not literally but with a vortex of emotional confusion.

I stood up, too, shaking so hard I couldn't say another word. Rod's parting words over his shoulder were, "If you have a problem with my orders, Mike, write me a letter." He winked at me, and then he and Ahmed vanished into the frenzied streets of downtown Cairo. I didn't see him again for another year, when I flew to Cyprus to repack our belongings, still in his garage, to ship back to the states. It was an awkward meeting over a glass of wine where there were more sips than words. But on this night in Cairo, he had swept in with no warning, dropping a bomb of plans for our lives, as if were none of our business, and swept away into the nocturnal Sahara breeze like a mirage.

THE FALL

The vortex on the imitation-bamboo table kept spinning and its suction escalated. Trying to escape its tug, I exited the small restaurant, stumbling outside, then pausing to catch my bearings. I left the fumes of wok-burnt noodles and stumbled into the dark, dusty air that hovered over the busy night streets of Cairo as one intoxicated ... on bewilderment. It was a thick desert air, saturated with an unorthodox mix of motor exhaust fumes, jasmine, campfire smoke, incense, and rotting—animal, I presumed—flesh.

But even outside, walking along the crumbling sidewalks beneath clusters of date palms, dulled by the perpetual coating of coco-colored dust, I felt myself continuing to fall and lose control as if it were actually happening. The rabbit hole was following me, and, like quicksand, there was no escaping its pull and nothing within reach to grasp, nothing that might arrest my fall. I turned the corner and stepped off the side street into Tahreer Square at the heart of Cairo. Even at nine o'clock at night, it was a perpetual hive of activity with hundreds of walkers and drivers amongst buses, donkey, and camel riders. But in the midst of the chaotic masses, I'd never felt so alone— and terrified. Not just terrified of Rod or of Egypt but of my own darkness, which was beginning to percolate up through the hole, a darkness with claws, scales, and saber-like teeth. What was most scary now was realizing that the hole wasn't in the imitation-bamboo table or even in the restaurant but in the middle of my own soul—and there was no escape. The adrenaline had fermented into a sour, inward-pointing rage. I refused to name the dark force at first, but I knew what it was—it was raw hate. A hate that had germinated while in the breakfast buffet in Chicago and that had been nurtured through Rod's long absences and failed promises of bringing our things and helping us assimilate into this inhospitable place. And I'd allowed the anger to proliferate when Daniel was so sick and I was so scared.

Earlier that year, we had sent Rod a telex saying we were taking our extremely ill boy back to the United States for emergency medical treatment. A sterile, impersonal telex returned the message: "Request denied. Use only Egyptian medical services." All my wrath at Daniel's suffering and near death I now allowed myself to spew at Rod. And at myself. I hated Rod for disrespecting me and my family. I hated myself for having allowed it.

A mile away, I fixed my eyes on the metro train station, which was my portico from the chaos to the relative peace of my home and my lifeline to Denise's comforting arms. I continued walking, but slower, now that I knew I couldn't outrun the void. I heard the sound in my ears ... on the left and on the right ... before me and behind me ... a soft thumping sound. It was my house of cards starting to fall in slow motion, the cards landing one by one. The thin cards, little more than façades, had been carefully but perilously put in place since my conversion a decade and a half earlier. There were the stoic kings, always in control, with a confident sense of purpose. Below them were the princes, serving as the perfect Christians of obedience and order. Finally, at the bottom, were the smiling jokers—the first to fall. The entire house of cards of my Christian persona was toppling. I kept walking, focusing my eyes on the sparks shooting, like fireworks, from the pantographs and overhead power lines as electric trains pulled out from the station, leaving a trail of ozone in the air like an android's perfume.

What was the meaning of those fifteen years of devotion to Christ? When I first came into the fold, my DI mentor had shared with me a verse from 2 Corinthians 5:17 that now I was a "new creation." He went on to explain that all my past was erased, and I was a blank slate of purity. I felt his words so reassuring because as a young man I had a lot of anger. My mentor also taught me a simple formula for Christian maturity, like a magic growth potion: Time in The Word (meaning the Bible) = Christian maturity. I'd spent thousands of hours in The Word—30 minutes of devotional time most mornings. I'd memorized hundreds of Bible verses, not to mention all the other activities of Christian discipleship, such as evangelism and prayer. I'd also attended hundreds of hours of workshops and classes, thousands of hours of lectures and sermons—and for what?

Thump, thump, thump fell the cards before me and behind me as I—in a zombielike state—boarded the faded green train, which listed to one side because of broken springs, a consequence of chronic overloading.

I collapsed into a well-worn red vinyl seat. I rarely had a seat on this train commuting to and from Arabic classes, when it was standing room only. At peak travel times, I was lucky to get into the interior of the train at all. Once, I'd hung on the outside with my toes on a quarter-inch ledge, the fingers of one hand grasping the window's chrome flange and my other hand wrapped around terrified Bryan's neck as the train raced through the crazy maze of Cairo's streets. One slip on that day, and my son and I would have been crushed beneath the train's iron wheels. But on this night a new danger seemed far more vicious. I needed a seat. I could barely stand as the foundation beneath my entire existence slowly crumbled.

I hated Rod that night, with the kind of hate I might have harbored the day before I came into the Christian fold. It was a hate as strong as that of the militant Muslim Brotherhood, who I knew wanted me—an American missionary—dead. There were rumors they wanted to kidnap and behead me. I was always looking over my shoulder, trying to avoid them, taking a different route each time I went out. But on this night, I too felt murderous. If I'd heard that Rod's Egypt Air flight to Damascus had plunged into the Mediterranean, I would have felt some joy. As Jesus in his wisdom noted, murder is hatred's twin brother. I could pretend sorrow and even shed a Christian tear in public, but I knew in my heart I'd take some measure of delight in his demise. This was the real doubt-inducing dilemma that I faced that night. I could rationalize Rod's cruelty, but the conundrum of my own hatred threatened to overwhelm me.

Thump, thump, thump … the cards continued to fall. What was the meaning of all the spiritual training I had received from great men of faith? What was the significance of the six years I had spent at a DI staff training center prior to meeting Denise and moving to Michigan, probably the most disciplined program in Christendom outside of some ascetic Byzantine monastery of the tenth century? What had all that self-denial, discipline, and study gained me? How could I, the *tabula rasa*, still carry that evil nature I'd known so well before I met Christ and thought I'd long put behind me? Why was the magic formula for maturity not working? All those serpents, which I thought I had slain and banished in the catacombs of my mind, were once again raising their atrocious heads. Had I only disguised them in a party dress rather than crushed them with my heel?

Moreover, I felt something must be wrong with me that I had allowed my own family to suffer so much. In my Christian idealism, I'd always wanted to be the most perfect, loving father and husband, but instead, I was finally realizing that my wife, and especially my son, had suffered tremendously in Egypt under my watch. How could I have allowed that to happen? Why hadn't I stood up for them earlier?

I gazed out the window, studying the continuous flow of humanity that lined the old tracks. Shiny plate-glass windows of the fancy dress shops of Roxy were accented with homeless *bowabs* (doormen) that huddled in their dusty *galabeyas* (long gowns) over a campfire fueled by street-trash, with dinner—a single ear of burnt corn—being stirred in the coals. I saw my own reflection on the inside of the train window—faint, almost ghostlike—superimposed over the alien world beyond. My eyes looked sunken, distant, and estranged from myself; by that time, I felt like only a semitransparent shell.

By the time I was halfway home, all the cards had fallen. The Christian Mike was gone. The stoic faces of kings, disciplined princes, and joyful jokers were in disarray beneath my feet on the dirty floor of the listing metro train. But my fall down the hole didn't stop there. Head over heels I fell, with nothing to grab hold of to cease my descent or at least to slow it down, as the hole continued to devour me. The muffled thumping had ended, but I began to hear a subtle sound replacing it—an insidious clicking.

Was the clicking real? Maybe it was the noise of the train wheels over the fatigued joints of the old rails. But the sound wasn't real. Through the haze of my emotions I saw no cards of my persona left to fall, but I did notice that the fabric of the entire Christian world was clicking as it shifted and changed. Tiny threads of that fabric, like a scene from the movie *The Matrix* (Warner Brothers 1999), were turning to ones and zeroes and running downward. What was this? I was confused and horrified beyond fear as I watched my whole world dissolving before the eyes of my emotions. I was experiencing some kind of emotional breakdown that was as real as anything I had ever known.

And my disillusionment had spread, like a virus in a pandemic, outside my own persona—to Rod. Three years earlier, when he'd first invited Denise and me to come to Cyprus under his leadership, I'd felt so honored. I considered him one of the godliest men of faith within the Church. After all, he was the poster child of commitment inside one of the most disciplined organizations in Christendom. He alone had worked as a missionary during a difficult and violent period in Beirut when other Americans were being killed and kidnapped by the score, and all other missionaries had fled Lebanon for their personal safety. Even his own wife and two daughters had fled then had not heard a word from him for over a year because he'd been too busy to contact them. His legend was well known to me long before I met the man in person. He had been my hero—a true champion of the Christianity I'd come to know.

Now my righteous hero appeared to be a monster. How could I resolve this paradox? He was the greatest man of God I'd ever known—and also the cruelest and most savage. Nothing was making sense anymore. My previous boss at my secular job in the United States was an agnostic Jew, a man who was kind and loving to me and my family. He would never have treated us this way. The whole paradigm of my Christian world was disintegrating under the weight of its own erroneous presuppositions, like a paper house under a real stone roof. Those presuppositions were that God was always in total control to bring good and that the Christian society was ethically far above all other societies, where each member cared deeply for the other.

After the hour-long ride, the train pulled into my stop. I had to move quickly or the train would leave again with me still on board. My feet hit the fine Sahara sand beside the tracks, and I started the 200-yard walk down the narrow street toward our flat. On the right was a "green space," an empty block where children played football among the grazing sheep, occasional camels, and rows of food merchant's tents. One for fish, one for yogurt, one for simple pita bread. On the left was a row of concrete apartment buildings of ashen complexion. My home was in the fifth building, and I didn't know if I could make it. *Click, click, click* ... the fabric of my universe was continuing to unravel. I wanted to make it to our third floor apartment and the safety of Denise's arms before I diminished into a mirage of myself.

When I arrived at our flat and our old wooden door squeaked open, Denise appeared in the living room in her housecoat. She was trying to muster a smile on her sleepy face. "How did it go?" With our future resting on the outcome of the evening's meeting, I knew she was hopeful that the end to our struggles was near.

"Horribly," I said softly. I dropped down on the couch and said, more softly, "Just horribly. Everything is a total mess, and we will never be moving to join the team in Cyprus or even getting our belongings." Denise and I sat, for what seemed like a couple of hours in silence, side by side, holding hands and just staring into to space. Occasionally she would ask in different ways something like, "What did he say?" to which I just shrugged my shoulders. As close as the two of us were, I couldn't find a way to communicate what was happening inside of me. It was the beginning of something terrible, and I had no idea how dreadful it would eventually become or the full decade it would endure. I sat up the entire night. Denise returned to our bed to rest, but she didn't sleep either.

THE NADIR

The hours between two and four in the morning were the only times our apartment's interior temperature was bearable during the summer. *Click, click, click* ... the clatter continued into the coolness of the early morning until the sun broke over the eastern desert and the rooftops of the apartment buildings that neighbored ours. Even the face of God was starting to blur and change as though it were melting like wax under the heat of the rising sun. Who was God? Did I really know him? Did he really exist after all?

I'd learned of God as a loving father who was in control of everything, even the very hairs of my head. I'd also learned that he rewards those who do good and punishes those who do evil. Hadn't I done good things? If so, why was I suffering? Why had so much gone wrong on my path of good intentions?

For 15 years, I had believed following God's will was my highest desire. In my secret places, I knew I wasn't perfect, but I was sincere. In my zeal, I'd sought out the toughest Christian disciplining programs precisely because they were hard. I'd given up a good job and, with my family, lived out of an old, brown, diesel VW Vanagon for almost two years while we raised the finances necessary to be missionaries to the Muslims. Then we came to one of the most difficult places in the world, just because it was the most challenging mission field—to serve him and follow his will. So why were we being punished? Had I not pleased him after all? Why was God hiding his face as if he was ashamed of me? *Click, click, click* ... the fabric of all I knew of God was falling apart and falling downward into oblivion. I begged the heavens for someone, anyone, to answer me. I heard nothing save a barking dog in a distant flat and the braying of the donkeys pulling the old two-wheeled carts, where garbage-collecting children rode in the shadowy streets of predawn.

At the break of dawn, the fajr prayer call starts as the first rays of sunlight touch the roofs of the minarets. First at a mosque, to the east. Then they begin to spread westward into the city, chasing the night away until they reached our little street. "God, he is the greatest," came that familiar chant in Arabic, streaming then from all corners of Cairo as an out-of-sync chorus. "Fools ... we are all damn fools," was the insistent thought that echoed back from inside my head.

As the early-morning light began to penetrate the glass doors leading to our balcony, I remembered the bundle of letters Rod had handed me. The parcel was now covered with Egyptian train dust. It had been months since we'd received a single letter due to the requirement that they be sent first to Cyprus then to Damascus. Around the time Denise broke the rules by calling her family for help, I had followed suit and sent out a desperate newsletter directly to our supporters from Egypt, bypassing Rod's censorship. In the letter I had simply asked for prayer—prayer because we were struggling to "cope with some health issues."

From the bundle of letters, wrapped with a simple cotton string and bearing the familiar Cypriot postmark, I removed one with a handwritten return address: Ricky Marriot. Ricky was an old friend who had been at the DI training center with me way back before I'd met Denise. I opened the letter, looking for some comfort in the midst of my pain. Instead of amity, it bore rebuke. Ricky wrote, "When people have struggles it is because they don't have their eyes on Jesus." He added, writing from his comfortable middle-class, air-conditioned American home, "Real Christians don't just 'cope,' they are victorious, and you should be ashamed for asking for less than total success, not that you can just survive." He ended it with the exhortation for me to "repent and shape up." The loneliness I felt at that moment was like the musty taste of death itself.

Click, click, click ... the collapse of my world spread rapidly, with the foundation the first to give way and then everything above it—the whole Church and my entire Christian experience. Had it all been a farce? By the time the sun was high in the sky, I was no more a Christian than my Muslim neighbors in the next flat or the agnostic I once was.

THE CRATER

For any man standing in the center of a total ruin—be it the physical ruin of a bombed-out city, a personal ruin like the loss of a spouse, or, in my case, a spiritual ruin—there are three main pathways out. The largest and most inviting path is that of emotional numbness. The ones who walk this corridor continue going through the motions of their daily lives, working, eating, and sleeping, but develop a thick skin to insulate them from the pain of their reality.

This was my father's response to losing his three sisters and parents to tuberculosis in the early 1940s and then to dealing with his horrors on the beaches of Normandy. He never talked about those things. He didn't shed a tear when his close brother died years later, except when he was alone, beneath his blankets in the middle of the night. My mother told me how she felt the bed shaking and reached over and felt him curled up and sobbing. She pretended to go back to sleep to give him a solitude of grief. Numb people, like my dad, become the kind of rock the great American songwriter Paul Simon sang about in his song, "I Am a Rock." Zombielike, they carry on through the remainder of their lives until a natural death brings relief.

The second path is to extinguish one's physical life by one's own hands. Those who choose this path, I think, do it mostly out of fatigue. I was terribly weary at this juncture. I would become more tired in the subsequent years. Although the first path seems to be the broadest and most traveled, this second path is, in some ways, the easiest and most alluring.

The last and most difficult path is the long, torturous journey to understanding. This path is taken usually out of curiosity and sometimes with the hope that understanding will bring resolution. I was fatigued, but by nature I've always been curious. Thus I stood in the center of my ruin, almost visibly contemplating which path to take. I would flirt with each of the paths over the next few years. But ultimately, my deep disillusionment bred an intense longing to understand. That was why I eventually left on my perilous decade-long journey. But to find raw truth, maybe for the first time, I had to live immersed in truth, or a better term would be reality. This would mean that I had to embrace a level of candor that I had never known before.

I was determined to find the answers and to solve this celestial puzzle of why my safe, Christian world had really been built on un-tempered glass. Why did I still harbor within my Christian soul the worst kind of evil imaginable—rage? Why had the great saints of my spiritual world disappointed me? I would eventually ask, where do I go from here? I also needed to discover whether God was ever there—and if he was, who the hell was he?

Not wanting to be quitters, Denise and I stayed in Cairo for another year but without any connection to the DI mission organization—not that there had been any connection to sever. At the U.S. headquarters this seemed like a huge deal, as if we were stepping away from the security of a mission organization into the cold darkness. What they didn't realize was that we had already been living in the cold darkness, and leaving the organization made, absolutely, no difference to us, except for protecting us from Rod's sudden reappearance and giving us another new direction to our lives.

Initially, I followed the wide path of just being numb. Studying the Arabic language, working in the slum's clinic and breathing were my only purposes in life; the rest of me was a lukewarm corpse. I had no thoughts of God or spirituality. Barely remembering to eat, I lost 15 pounds, and I couldn't escape my fury and confusion about life long enough to sleep. It was a great struggle for me to nurture my wife and children as I knew they needed. By the second half of our second year in Cairo, I saw on the horizon our return to the States. There, I hoped to find myself again, and I hoped my family could find rest, stability, and good health. But such hope would quickly vaporize as being only an illusion.

CHAPTER TWO

――◆――

Postcards from the Post-evangelical Wilderness

After arriving back in the States, we returned to our prior home in Michigan. Old friends were kind to us, loaning us their basement apartment for a couple of months while I looked for a job. I quickly found a position in Duluth, Minnesota.

MORE THAN S'MORES ... BUT NOT MUCH MORE

A couple of weeks before we moved to Duluth, we were invited to a church camp out. It was next to a beautiful but mosquito-infested lake. One evening, as we sat around the campfire with about 30 other church members, the deacon who had organized the campout, asked me and Denise—so-called missionaries—to give an impromptu account about our experience. It was a strange evening, crowding in on the bizarre. I ad-libbed a summary of the story just as it had happened and without any resolution. There was no, "God taught me such-and-such to make it all worthwhile" and no happily-ever-after to tie everything up in a neat rational bow. I just ended with, "Then we flew home."

You could have cut the awkwardness with a surgical scalpel. For about 10 minutes there was complete silence, except for the buzz of insects and the electronic bug zapper going off over at a Winnebago. Everyone just sat and stared into the fire. One kid stirred the hot coals with a gummy, marshmallow-coated stick. They had never, ever heard a Christian testimony that didn't resolve with a happy ending or some higher meaning. The ice was finally broken when one of the teenagers farted loudly, causing laughter from everyone younger than thirty. Denise and I returned to our simple, "two-man," pup tent with our kids, and no one from that church spoke to us again, ever, about our experience. The deacon must have had great remorse about ever asking me to share with the group. He was one of the people who never brought up our missionary experience again. I actually can't remember him ever speaking to us again, at all. His silence, I assume, was not out of any kind of anger or disappointment in us but from a pure feeling, on his part, of social gracelessness.

Arriving in Duluth, we knew no one, and we thought it would be better that way. It seemed easier to start over among strangers than to try to repetitively justify our return to our friends in our old church. I knew I was too muddled on the inside to try to make sense of things to other people. If we had stayed in Ypsilanti, unless I left the church completely, I knew that would I feel pressure to just fake it and resume my previous, pre-Egypt evangelical persona. This would mean taking the broad, stoic, numb path and smile, saying simply, "God spoke to us and called us home." I knew the mores of Christian culture well and that I could always play the God card, putting my words in God's mouth, and no one would question it. On the other hand, I could also be candid and tell people that I was doubting everything. But experience told me that if I had shared my real feelings, it would have been inferred as a personal moral failure ... or maybe me allowing demons to influence my thinking. No one would take my questions at face value and point me toward any hope of finding answers. Then I would be forced to play the role of the poor weaker brother. Pity is adorable and comforting at first ... as is a jackal pup. But when it matures, it scavenges your world from the inside out, leaving you cowering in the corner in a state of total helplessness. I didn't want to play games of any kind anymore, especially Christian games. I was willing to take a gamble, betting everything on reality. I would have been happiest to find a new, but honest, Christianity, if such existed. But finding an authentic life that had no Christianity would be a consolation prize I would accept.

I was quickly disappointed to find that, even in Duluth, I found no peace. My fall hadn't yet run its course. I'd passed through the realms of spiritual discordance, intellectual doubts, and finally into a purely emotional fall. I was experiencing clinical depression for the second time in my life, this time far more seriously than the first. This depression was aggravated by a resounding silence from DI, an organization that had been my family for more than 15 years. I felt—whether true or not—that we were jettisonable ballast to an enterprise that had gone awry. However, the most powerful force shaping my sadness was the fact for those 15 years, everything I had done was in preparation for spending the rest of my life working among the indigent in the developing world. For the last five of those years, this vision was focused on the refugees coming out of Lebanon's civil war. Now, all was lost and I found that inevitability unbearable.

My initial taste of depression had occurred before I was a Christian, when I was a teenager. This time, however, it was much worse, and I was constantly shadowed by sincere thoughts of suicide. The opportunity to end the pain forever was seductive. However, I had more reasons not to do it. I had a wife, three boys, and now a new baby girl, Amy. At times I thought they would be better off without me. In a strange way, it seemed like it could be a noble gesture for me to take my endless grief and confusion out of their life and to set them free. Previously I thought I had known all the answers, but now I was a father who was without confidence about anything. But I also had mentally healthy days when I knew that if they lost their father, even a confused father, it would be devastating.

The entire first year back on American soil, all my—and unfortunately Denise's—energy was spent on me trying to find my way out of my melancholic colliery. Eventually, I did get my emotional feet back on stable ground. Having considered and discarded the first path of numbness and the second of suicide, I was ready to move on, this time to the third path of searching with one quest: finding the real truth. The Christianity I had known for a decade and a half now seemed deeply flawed and nonsensical, like high tea around the Mad Hatter's table in Wonderland. If Jesus was real, who was he and what did he really teach?

I also eventually stumbled upon a seductive fourth path that—unfortunately—many of us fall into after any kind of painful experience. Personal, tragic experiences, leave us in a type of perpetual loneliness. Grief is the hungry wolf that separates you from the herd of humanity, as if you were an injured caribou. To the rest of the world, which had not lived through your experience, there is no human way to convey your feelings or thoughts with any accuracy. From that point forward, it is as if you speak a different language. Maybe, if someone was there with you, the two of you can communicate to a point. That's why foxholes produce bands of brothers like nothing else. While Denise and I shared many of the common experiences in Egypt, such as the health struggles of our family, she had not been part of DI prior to our assignment. She could not, therefore, share in my difficulty of losing the spiritual family, which I had been part of for so long. I was now dead to them, and I could not understand what I had done wrong to have deserved that silence.

This type of isolation is no one's fault but simply the nature of pain. This later track of seclusion can also lead you to being obsessed with one's own pain, a type of self-victimization. In a selfish and destructive way, it is akin to the wounded animal licking its wounds day after day, turning a small gash into a gaping hole. I had wandered onto this path many times, and, once on it, like the enfeebled beast getting caught in a gooey tar pit, it was difficult getting unstuck. Fortunately, my curiosity eventually won out over my self-pity … but not without a formidable scuffle.

Denise still wanted to have Christian friends, and I followed her lead, out of respect for her. The fact that we had been missionaries earned us a lot of brownie points when Christian people first met us. However, when they asked me about our experience, and I didn't give a glowing report of victories and miracles, they were stunned just like back at the church campout in Michigan. I was violating all the rules of the evangelical value system. It is a custom that missionary stories have a happily-ever-after (even after a tragedy) garland wrapped around their ending like the Hudson Taylor and Jim Elliot biographies, which are popular in evangelicalism (Taylor 1987), (Elliot 1981).

THE STUDENT

During our second year back in the States, I joined the Airforce as a medical officer, and we moved from Duluth, Minnesota to Marquette, Michigan. We were hoping that the Air Force would eventually be a means to living overseas again, such as at the American base in Crete or Turkey. We still loved the expatriate life. That overseas assignment never happened, but the move was good for all of us.

Besides being a time of intense study for me, Marquette, Michigan, was a place of healing. Something about the long winters, where the grass and dirt melt into monochromic white, not to be seen again until April and where those snowfalls are measured in feet rather than inches, quietens the heart. We lived there for seven years and had a small farm where we raised sheep ... and five children. Our last, Ramsey, was born at the Air Force base's hospital.

Healing, too, were the crystal-cold waters of Lake Superior, which we could look over from the hill where our farm stood, and that I could feel, personally, softly slipping and churning beneath the hull of my sea kayak like angry silk. In the other direction, from our farm, were rolling hills of paper birch trees stretching out to the southern horizon like brigades of lean, tall cigarettes. In the autumn the tops of those trees, and their maple comrades, would blossom into a golden aura so brilliant that I had a legitimate fear of going leaf-blind. Beneath those trees were those iron-rich streams where, on a good day, I could pull up a chinook salmon from the rusty waters with my rod and reel. It was a glorious time when I could hold all of my kids on my lap at once ... and offer them a father's perfect shelter and at an age when hugs weren't resisted. It was a place in my life that I bookmarked and would return to in a second if only I were a chronovator. Maybe in the new earth that God is restoring, such revisits will be possible.

Perhaps the most healing balm of Marquette were our Air Force colleagues and the new civilian friends that we made. Military people, I think, due to their short assignments, have taken the art of friend-making to a new level. We have never had so many and so dear friends as we had at K. I. Sawyer Air Force Base and in Marquette. Our prior five-year experience, living in a van raising support for two years, then living in Egypt for two years and then living in Duluth for one year, left us seriously wanting in the friend's department. But that base closed and all of our lives were suddenly uprooted.

During our fourth year in Marquette, an old acquaintance, Dana, from my DI days at a Tennessee college, came through town. He had remained with the group and was even working for their headquarters. We had dinner together and he shared that he had heard about our failure due to culture shock and, that for no reason, I had been very rude to Rod. When I explained that there was more to it than that, he encouraged me to try again to meet with the missionary department. They would not speak to me right after we had returned. They had—I later learned—spoken to Rod about our resignation. He debriefed them that I had an anger problem and that he would no longer considered us to be "missionary material." They did not want to hear our side of the story at the time of our return despite my many calls and letters.

However, Dana pointed out that they were probably more open to a meeting now because they had a new director. Also, which I was hearing for the first time, the family that went to the Middle East to replace us had returned home after one year, claiming that Rod had been abusive to them. After a brief investigation, DI fired Rod. Dana had, wrongly, assumed that we had been informed.

We arranged a meeting with the new mission department director at DI headquarters. I asked that the Middle East director be there as well as an independent observer, such as a psychologist. They accommodated my requests. I flew out and Denise joined us by speaker phone. The three men sat in a respectful silence in front of me as I told my—unabridged—story from beginning to the end. There was no discussion. When I had finished talking, I took a restroom break. The men talked between themselves while I was gone. Upon my return, the missionary director simply said, "Denise and Mike, we are very sorry for what happened to you. Our organization has sinned against you. We ask for your forgiveness." In tears we accepted their petition, and I felt a mightily closure had taken place that day and that a sad story of a severe injustice had been rewritten.

After I moved past my clinical depression, during our early days in Marquette, and into my search, I read countless books and listened to hundreds of hours of lectures on cassette tapes. This was before the days of DVDs and the Internet. Dr. Francis Schaeffer became one or my major resources and I read his, *The Complete Works of Francis A. Schaeffer: A Christian Worldview* many times (F. A. Schaeffer 1985). I read every book on Christian apologetics that I could get my hands on, hoping within them I could find some answers.

Schaeffer was my door to philosophy. I spent the next few years studying the classic thinkers and writers. Philosophy was my conduit to history. I read several books on the history of Western culture. General history led me back to the history of the church and then to the study of world religions. I also studied the Bible, and with more fervor than I had ever applied, even at the DI training center, but this time out of a desperate allurement and not as a religious exercise. I studied simply to find out for myself, what did the

Bible really say? I was no longer interested in what certain groups or people thought it said.

Like trying to find the single unifying theory of quantum physics or the Higgs boson, in all my studies my search was to find that one fundamental flaw, a real fly in the sacred ointment regarding my previous way of thinking that, once uncovered, would allow me to make sense of everything. At least as much sense as it is humanly possible to disclose. But, to find this philosophical culprit, I would have to go back through my entire Christian journey, like Sherlock Holmes bearing a magnifying glass. But it would be more like using a telescope where you must apply different filters to enhance different features of celestial bodies.

I knew I would have to start with myself and work outward, like an unwinding of a spiral, through concentric rounds of questions. Each answer would spur more questions. The first filter would be for examining my personal upbringing and psychological makeup to figure out why I was so angry. Rod wasn't completely wrong in his assessment. I knew it would be hard to do this with the required candor. But something was wrong with me, and I had to find out what it was. There was also a reason that had not stood up for my family … and myself … in Egypt. There was a cause to the rage that percolated up out of my soul, once the impasse was breached. It didn't simply start in a cheap restaurant on Cairo's backstreets and over a plate of soggy noodles. It came from a much deeper place, and to complete this journey I had to enter that shadowy underworld of the soul.

CHAPTER THREE

Strangled by My Belt

The Appalachians are a beautiful area, rich in folk history and antebellum architecture. The sounds of dulcimers playing ancient mountain music can be heard echoing in the valleys with lyrics telling of lost loves and heroes found as well as hymns about this world not being important and having a cabin in heaven is better than a palace on Earth. Deeper in the valleys, or what we called dark hollows (pronounced *hallers*), were the ruins of old moonshine stills and even darker family secrets—secrets of affairs, robbery, incest, and murder.

Growing up in those hills, we slept under brightly colored quilts, sewed from old rags, which told of hardships and struggles indigenous to the region. The hardships were a result of the inhospitable land, where the hills, valleys, and hollows were so rugged you could barely scrape out a decent living trying to grow anything in the poor soil.

Despite the poverty, the landscape is rich, with rolling green hills covered by orange-clay cattle tracks that corkscrew up their grassy sides. The hills, in stair-step fashion, take you from muddy creek bottoms in the lowlands up to steep, spruce-covered mountains rising over 6,000 feet above sea level.

Accenting the valleys and hills were villages like ours. The topographical summits of each of these settlements featured old white clapboard churches with steep spires and silvery tin roofs. In some cases, the old churches had been replaced with larger, more modern red-bricked ones. Fundamentalist Christianity, as a culture, had found no better resting spot than here among these hills.

The Buckle

When I was attending university, a sociology professor from out of state fondly referred to our area as not only the Bible Belt, but the "buckle of the Bible Belt." In other words, it was the very heart of American fundamentalist Christianity.

This professor loved living in the area as a social scientist and researcher of culture. His expertise was with a group of backwoods' churches deeper in the mountains, where rattlesnake handling, poison drinking, and playing with fire were routine parts of Sunday morning worship. This church based their services on the Bible verse Mark 16:18: "They will pick up snakes with their hands; and when they drink deadly poison, it will not hurt them at all; they will place their hands on sick people, and they will get well." He often filmed these services with an old eight-millimeter black-and-white Kodak Brownie movie camera on Sundays and showed them in our spellbound class later in the week. He included his graphic footage of the time when the pastor of the church died from multiple rattlesnake bites. The bites and subsequent death were supposedly indicative of the handler's lack of sincere faith—that is, if one took the Bible to its literal extreme.

Our little Baptist church looked as if it had been taken right out of a Thomas Kinkade painting. It was of the white clapboard style, with tall stained-glass windows, except they were not the highly decorative and colorful design you would find in an old cathedral; rather, each separate pane was monochrome, either red, green, or yellow. The church stood at the top of a steep but rounded hill. Behind it, encircled by a lacy wire fence covered with many layers of silver paint and supported by limestone posts, was a cemetery. The oldest gravestones, circa 1800, were made of smooth, weather-worn limestone with wording that now looked as though it had been carved in warm, white butter. Between the black lichens, these messages told of grief and hope from two centuries past. The earliest ones nestled up against the church wall, and the more recent ones, of friends and relatives—including my dear father—were far up the hill in the new section. Who knows, but someday I may find my final rest there.

The church building itself was equally old, from the period of the Second Great Awakening that had swept through the area during the early nineteenth century with circuit-riding evangelists on the backs of mules.

Inside, running horizontally, were white-pine quarter-sawn boards covering the walls and ceiling. Two rows of about 20 dark-oak pews filled the sanctuary with a wide green-carpeted aisle down the middle. The pulpit, made of a lighter oak, sat on a riser and, along with the carpet, was a newer addition from the 1940s or 1950s. It was a wooden monolith, weighing in at around 200 pounds, with a cross carved on its front. That cross stood just above the communion table, which was long and narrow with a white linen cloth draped down the middle lengthwise. Engraved on the front of the table were the words "IN REMEMBRANCE OF ME."

Behind and to the right of the pulpit were four rows of pews facing the congregation. This was where the choir sat during the service and where my uncle Casey Jones, a deacon, taught adult Sunday school before worship. On the wall above the pews was an old dark-stained oak sign with movable black and gold letters and numbers. It listed "SUNDAY SCHOOL ATTENDANCE," "CHURCH ATTENDANCE," "LAST WEEK'S OFFERING," and, simply, "SAVED." On the wall behind the pulpit was a large painting of Christ, in muted tones of brown, moss green, and beige. He had long sandy-blond hair flowing past his shoulders, looking like a Swedish Fabio with a full beard.

Across from the choir pews, on the left wall, was a solitary shelf about 10 feet off the floor on which perched an old clock with a shiny brass pendulum that never ceased swinging back and forth ... *tick, tock, tick, tock*. I found it astonishing that the pastor always stopped the service exactly at noon, not 30 seconds before and not 30 seconds after. It was a mystery to me how he did it without ever looking at the clock. If we had a guest minister, and he went one minute past noon, the church would suddenly become restless as if he had committed an unpardonable offense.

The church roof was made of tin with many layers of plastic-based coatings to try to stop the perpetual leaks. What rainwater didn't leak through the rusty spots and nail holes ran into large round gutters and downspouts that led to a large underground cistern, from where the church drew its potable water. The cistern had a metal door with some kind of lock. I know this because I can remember one of the Parson boys trying to pry it open. He thought it would be a funny prank to pee into the cistern. For some odd reason, he found it hilarious to imagine the tight-laced, blue-haired church women drinking his piss-tinged water from the big, holy porcelain fountain that sat in the vestibule. Fortunately, the padlock served its purpose well.

I can still remember a thick cotton rope that hung through a hole in the ceiling in the vestibule. It led to the old bronze bell up in the towering steeple. My uncle Casey, now buried in the new section of the cemetery alongside my dad, would lift me up to pull the rope on Sunday mornings. I didn't have the strength to make it toll on my own, even if I swung on it with my entire weight of 50 pounds, so my uncle would cheat by slyly pulling on the rope with his left hand, beneath me, leaving me to think I had done it. But I knew better.

JAKE THE RAPER

The earliest thing I remember about church service in the 1960s was nothing as exciting as live snakes; instead, it was a time of confusion and conflict. I must have been about five years old when an episode of screaming between adults opened the worship service. Frightened, I squatted on the floor and crawled under our pew as the arguing continued. It wasn't until I was much older that my mother explained what had happened on that scary Sunday morning.

The Plummer family was the most powerful family in our church. Among the husband, wife, and adult son, Jake—who still lived at home— they held all major posts. Jake was the music and Sunday school director. I think his dad was the head deacon. I was never certain what post his mother held, but she seemed more powerful than both of them—a kind of godmother or matriarch.

On that memorable morning we had new family visiting the church service. The father of that visiting family was well-known in our community, per my mother's later explanation, because he had been arrested a couple of years earlier for embezzling money from his employer. He'd gone to prison and had just been released. I think most people assumed that, once out of prison, he wanted to take a different path for his life and the life of his family, and so he decided to bring them to our church on that day—maybe the first time they had ever darkened the doors of a church.

They came in late—perhaps they weren't sure what time church started—and took a pew. An old hymn was being led by Jake in the usual manner. When the hymn was finished, the church went silent. In the midst of that quietness, Jake's mother stood, visibly upset. She pulled the collar of her flower-print dress up around her neck, looked at the pastor, and announced, "We do *not* go to church with criminals!"

Pastor Short, who was elderly, soft-spoken, and probably one of the sincerest pastors the church ever had, was obviously disconcerted by this outburst. His extreme reaction showed the signs of an opinion that had been a long time coming. Stepping out of his quiet, humble character, he shouted at Mrs. Plummer, "If we're going to talk about criminals, maybe we should start by looking at your own family!"

A nuclear bomb detonation would not have caused more pandemonium in the sanctuary that morning. Everyone knew what Pastor Short was talking about, but the words had never been spoken louder than whispers between friends around their kitchen tables over coffee or between husband and wife in the dark quiet of their bedrooms. Jake, the 30-year-old Plummer "prodigy," had been habitually sexually molesting young boys in the church for years. It is hard to fathom now, but the response had always been, at the least, to pretend it wasn't happening and, at the most, to ensure your own sons were out of reach of his sticky fingers. My mother was the latter.

By the time the church service was over that morning, the Plummer family had fired the pastor, and the search was on for a new one—someone who would never venture into the dark cellars of the souls of the members. Pastor Short had opened the cellar door only briefly, yet that feeble effort caused a fatal outrage—fatal as far as his career went.

ARTHUR AND MARILYN TO THE RESCUE

A new pastor was eventually summoned, and he appeared to be the perfect fit. Arthur (who went by "Art") seemed to be a good man, at least on the surface. He was a hard worker, polite, and articulate. He was also well-educated and well-dressed, but later we would find out that he had some serious flaws.

He impressed the church members because he drove a new metallic-green Cadillac with fins on the back, and his wife was glamorous, in the image of Marilyn Monroe—well, maybe Dolly Parton. She was a spunky bleached-blonde and wore dresses that revealed most of her large, fleshy bosom unless it was covered by a mink stole. She was the closest the people in this out-of-the-way church imagined they would ever get to Hollywood. Most of us boys had never seen that much bosom—at least not in real life.

The pastor accomplished a great deal during his tenure. He had the
church building extensively remodeled, the parking lot paved, and the new
section of the cemetery built. He also started many new programs, including
a major theatrical production every Christmas. His wife, the Hollywood
type, directed the plays. I was a shepherd in a couple of her shows. Their
busyness never afforded them the time to meddle in people's personal lives,
and the congregation liked it that way.

The historic church, ironically, burned down the day Pastor Art retired.
It was surreal. For a decade he had slaved to improve the church building,
and on the evening he declared his job done, it burned to the ground, leaving a huge crater lined by the limestone foundation and the old cistern now
charred. They say the fire started from the electric heater being set too close
to the curtains in the basement. This tragic event forced Art to come directly
out of retirement and oversee a new program of rebuilding a bigger, red-
bricked church on the same spot. The new church had fake wood paneling,
plastic "stained-glass" windows, and an aluminum steeple with electronic
"bells." Everyone saw the plastic and electronics as an "improvement" because they portrayed precision, order, and pretense. But, most of all, because
they were cheap.

Art seemed the perfect man for the pastorate in many ways. He not only
didn't make the time to snoop, he never seemed to have a desire to. I suspect
that he preferred to keep the cellar doors closed rather than peer inside—
and that was because he kept and nurtured his own private ogres down
there. The trade-off, while sounding hideous now that I'm writing about it,
seemed to be typical of the unspoken world of surface niceness over some
ugly behavior. I think Charles Webb captured this world of 1950s and '60s
Americana very well in his book *The Graduate* (Webb 1963).

THE ECCENTRIC GOD

It was in this setting that I first learned about God and Christianity. In a rich
(but not so pure) Christian culture, I came to know God as an absentee land-
lord, or maybe an absentee Lord. What God was to us was the same as what
Genghis Khan must have been to someone in a remote, twelfth-century
village on the Black Sea, at the periphery of his empire. We heard a lot about
God, but he wasn't anywhere close by. He seemed at least 2000 years away in

travel time. He did have a local embassy, our church, which taught us about this mysterious emperor, what he liked and what he disliked. We learned, too, that he was all-powerful and would reward us if we did exactly what he wanted but would punish us if we disobeyed him. Some of the punishments could come in the form of fatal car wrecks, pimples, cancer, or a small penis. The boys all feared pimples because we believed it was a punishment for masturbating. Everyone feared cancer. Additionally, we learned that doing nice things for the absentee emperor would make up for any disobedience—a kind of Protestant penance.

It should be understood that I am not speaking of official Baptist theology here. Most Baptists will be offended at the way I describe these concepts and strongly deny this world I'm describing (wink, wink). As a reporter, I am simply giving an honest account of the "folk" or "colloquial" Christianity most people in the Bible Belt experienced, be they Baptist, Methodist, or Presbyterian.

The main thing that God seemed to like, and the greatest act of penance, was us going to church every Sunday. He liked us to get up, hustle to dress in our best clothes, drive up to the church, and sit on the hard, punishing pews for an hour. We also had to pretend that we were good people while at church. There was no question it was considered at the top of God's list of favorite things. It seemed peculiar in the eyes of a small child.

The whole congregation would sit, tuned out, while pretending to listen to a monotone sermon about Paul Harvey or a Peanuts comic strip that culminated with a Bible verse and an altar call. The lectures used words far out of reach of a preschooler and made no sense until I was in high school, and, by then, they were just plain boring.

My dad learned to sleep during the sermons while sitting straight up. His eyes were closed, and his chest moved slowly up and down inside his neatly ironed white shirt. His skinny black tie seemed to pucker up and stretch out—in and out—like a shiny inchworm. I think mom told me that he'd learned to sleep that way in World War II, sitting behind French hedge rows with his rifle at his side and his finger on the trigger.

Mom, like many of the ladies, kept her mind preoccupied by studying people, noticing who was sitting with whom, who had alcohol on their breath, or who was carrying a new brand-name Aigner purse. She would sit far to the outside edge, where she could look back and keep her eye on everyone. For a while she couldn't keep the corners of her eyes off a young couple who were French-kissing in the back pew each Sunday or a young mother who was chewing up peanuts, spitting them out, and feeding them to her hungry toddler.

After the sermon, we would sing a few songs about this world not being as important as heaven. The *tick-tock* of the clock would continue until both hands pointed straight up and we could go home—penance done for another week.

As a young boy it was always hard to figure out why this ritual was so important to the creator of the 13-billion-light-years-wide universe. It was so important that, even if you had done a lot of things he didn't like, you could erase the negatives on the balance sheet by going to church more, such as on Sunday evenings or Wednesday nights. There must have been something magical about coming in the door wearing your best clothes because, even if God wasn't mentioned there, it still made him very happy that we had shown up.

Our Christian culture also taught us that God didn't approve of lying, unless of course we lied for him. If I said I caught a 15-inch bass that was really only 12 inches long, this absentee God would be angry. But if I said I'd seen a miracle, which I knew in my heart wasn't true, that seemed to make God and everyone in his embassy delighted because it "brought him glory."

It seemed, too, that God hated all forms of alcohol, cigarettes, poker cards, music with a beat, dancing, long hair, and facial hair. An exception existed for tobacco—we believed God had a special dispensation for men, like my dad, who had survived either the Great Depression or World War II. They were allowed to smoke because they had earned the right. The many tobacco growers who attended our church were also exempt. Selling alcoholic beverages, as one of our deacons did on the side, was okay only if you kept the alcohol earnings in a separate bank from your godly money, which you used for church work and tithing. Somehow, any money used to buy alcohol became "dirty" and God, for some reason, didn't like dirty money mixed with his clean money.

The tobacco exemption was enjoyed by all who qualified. Between Sunday school and worship, the steps of our little white church looked like a choir of dragons. Every man over 40 was puffing away. The men stood with their backs to the doors, so as not to blow smoke inside. They all faced the same direction, with smoke sifting out from their nostrils and floating upward into one confluent cloud above them. But, because of their suffering during the Great Depression and the war, God looked the other way when they practiced their bad habits, as if they had a mutual understanding with God. It was as if the war veterans knew something about God, something they promised not to tell if he left them alone. But if one of us kids sucked on a lit cigarette out in the parking lot, God would be really pissed.

Men who had lived prior to World War II also received some kind of dispensation regarding their hair. In bygone-era photos posted for the Sunday school centennial celebration, many of the men in the photos sported long beards and hair. Even the pastor from 1865 looked like Ulysses S. Grant. Our Sunday school teacher explained that God made an exception for those men because in those days razors weren't cheap, so God let them off the hook. However, young people of today (the 1960s and 1970s) had no excuse.

More than any other sin, this absentee God hated premarital sex. Actually, he wasn't fond of sex in any form, even within marriage. It was nasty and disgusting, earthly and animal-like. Anything that brought physical pleasure would be equally suspect, like eating too much chocolate.

God also didn't like any questioning. To believe everything that you were told by parents and especially at church without expressing any doubt was pleasing to him, or so we were taught. He seemed to really like ignorance and ignorance really was bliss. In this type of Christian culture, knowledge and critical thinking were opposites of faith, and faith was considered the greatest of Christian virtues. But this kind of faith would prove to be an unhealthy faith.

CHAPTER FOUR

The Baptist Bar Mitzvah

Turning 12 was a catastrophic event, and it was more than just pimples. Southern Baptists considered this the "age of accountability." I don't know who invented the age of 12 as the magic turning point, but it seemed written in stone, if not on Mount Sinai, then at the headquarters of the Southern Baptist Church in Nashville. Maybe "accountability" was something that sprouted with pubic hair, but it apparently happened overnight.

Somehow, when you went to bed on the eve of your eleventh birthday, you were innocent and accepted by a sweet and loving God. Then, at the stroke of midnight, you were suddenly condemned to the eternal and torturous fires of hell by a wrathful God, and it all happened while you were fast asleep.

The next day, you awakened with an overwhelming feeling of guilt like you had never known before. The only thing that can take the sting of guilt away is to walk up the aisle to "receive Christ." This act of going forward, placing your hand in the pastor's hand and saying that you want to become a Christian was usually not a deep spiritual awakening but a ritual awakening, like taking the test to get your driver's permit. It was something that was expected by the Christian culture. Every Christian culture has had equivalent rituals since the beginning of the organized church. It might be baptism or catechism in other circles.

I remember the Sunday after my birthday, as though it was this morning. I had already been living under the fear of hellfire for 48 hours. That Sunday, the choir sang happy birthday to my uncle and me. Our birthdays were a week apart—his on the Fourth of July and mine on the eleventh, but he had missed the previous Sunday service as he was on a fishing trip. I was hoping no one would notice what age I had attained.

As I was leaving the sanctuary at the end of the service, I followed the tradition of parading by and shaking the pastor's hand. While my parents were telling him about how much they had enjoyed his sermon, I tried to sneak out. I'd done it a thousand times if I had done it once. This time, however, Pastor Art wouldn't release my hand, holding on tightly to it with his right hand while reaching across with his left to shake my mother's.

After my family had passed, he looked at me. "Johnny," he said, "how old are you now?"

I was terrified. I looked up at him, wanting to lie and tell him I was 11, but I knew he would eventually find out the truth. And being so perilously perched above the all-consuming fires of hell, it wasn't a good time to start lying so easily, unless it was lying for God as my folks had just done when they said they enjoyed the sermon. But lying to a preacher was among the worst of all sins, along with premarital sex.

"Uh ... 12," I mumbled.

Pastor Art's eyes lit up. He loved seeing the number of "Saved" on the church's oak sign increase and my salvation was now his personal goal. "Well, I'm looking forward to seeing you making a decision for Christ." I smiled and made a break for the car.

I was a late bloomer in my trip to the pulpit. The honest reason, looking back, wasn't any kind of hesitation about becoming a Christian, because the going forward was so irrelevant it had virtually nothing to do with your own spiritual condition. It offered an instant release of guilt, fire insurance from hell, and getting all the adults off your back forever. No, the real reason it took me almost a year to go forward, which I didn't realize at the time, was that I suffered from a serious case of social phobia. At the time, I didn't know what social phobia was; I only knew that people frightened me beyond belief.

The act of going forward during an altar call didn't simply mean walking up in front of the church full of people. I would also be expected to make a speech and then greet the entire church, one by one. It was only when the intense guilt feeling finally outweighed the intense fear of public speaking that I closed my eyes and made the first step from my pew. It was exactly like the first time I rappelled off the side of a cliff, as I also have acrophobia. It starts as an intense fear, then a closing of the eyes, and finally taking that first step.

I suspect this is the main emotional reason that many people don't go forward during altar call—a simple social phobia. It is the same reason that most people don't volunteer to go on stage during a magic show or comedy improv. Yet the church people don't know how to label the emotion internally so it becomes, mistakenly, a spiritual issue of them feeling they're rejecting their faith. I am sure that there are some older adults who avoid the altar call because they don't want to give up things they enjoy, like sex or alcohol. But I'm speaking for the majority of 12-year-olds who feared going up due to stage fright. In this watered-down version of conversion for a preteen, little was expected for a changed life.

For a few weeks after I went forward and was baptized, I was on an emotional high. I wanted to believe it was tangible proof that God or the Holy Spirit was really there after all. But, as time passed, in my heart I knew it was simply that the load of psychological guilt had finally been lifted. No longer would I feel the hundred pairs of eyes staring at me every Sunday morning as the choir sang "Just as I Am." I wouldn't feel the incredible shame bestowed upon me by that distant, absentee Lord. Now I could move on to the next great landmarks in my life—getting my driver's permit and losing my virginity.

The Loss of Innocence

Another major event that occurred when you turned 12 in the Bible Belt—at least in our small church—was moving up from the grade school Sunday school class into the high school class. Our congregation was so small that everyone between the ages of 12 and 18 was in the same class. There were few between the ages of 18 and 25 in our church because, in the Bible Belt, as soon as you were emancipated from the control of your parents, you didn't go to church anymore. After what I've shared so far, why would you? Perhaps when you were in your late 20s, married, and have had your first child, the pressure of tradition and the desire to be a "good" father or mother might move you to return to church to raise your family. But in my tiny community only a small percentage did return.

High school Sunday school was a completely different world due to one thing: testosterone. The classrooms were in the basement, the walls made of old limestone blocks covered with cement stucco and painted white. Blue carpet on the floor had the musty cellar smell of perpetual dampness. In the winter, we were warmed by a large electric heater with four coiled springs around ceramic posts that glowed red. A small silver fan behind it blew heat across the damp room. More than one teacher used the hot, glowing coils as an illustration of the heat of hell that awaited us if we weren't good people, or if we kept interrupting them while they were trying to speak. In a surreal way, the metaphor came to life. It was the same notorious heater that eventually burned down that old church.

Interruptions were commonplace, not to mention a general disrespect. For those reasons, no adult wanted to teach this group. The boys outnumbered the girls three to one in the high school class. I was never sure why, but the adults said it was God's way of providing soldiers for war. Superstition of the day held that if a lot of boys were born in a certain year, it would mean America would be at war in 18 years. My group must have been the exception because the draft for the war in Vietnam ended when I was 16, and we were at relative peace for two decades, or at least the conflicts that the United States did engage in were supported by an all-volunteer army.

The boys sat across the back row in an L-shape along a corner wall. The three or four Sunday-white-cotton-dressed girls who sat in a short, straight row along the long arm of the boy's L row behind them. The girls rarely uttered a word, their emotionless faces pale and their hands gripping gold-leafed Bibles. They surely hated coming to the class because the boys kept them in a constant state of embarrassment.

I was mortified myself the first day I came into the class. Rather than a nice lady teacher coming in and taking control as they had in the elementary classes, no one was in control. Every Sunday for the following five years, the pastor would spend the entire hour trying to persuade an adult, any adult with a warm body, to come and teach our unruly class. But no one wanted this opportunity, so we were often left alone.

Jimmy Parson was a cocky 16-year-old athlete in the spirit of Sam Malone (of the old *Cheers* TV series). He sat with his folding chair tipped back on two legs against the stone wall. In many ways, he was the teacher, at least for the boys' section. He had his driver's license, and, most importantly, he had a gorgeous girlfriend named Kathleen who went by the name of Kat. Her father and mine had been boyhood friends, but they'd gone their separate ways. Strangely, they had met again on a beach in Normandy in the midst of the chaos of D-Day morning. Kat's absence gave Jimmy the freedom to describe their dates from the previous night in graphic detail.

"I got my hand on her boob last night!" Jimmy would announce at the beginning of class. The older boys would laugh and snicker in excitement. The girls and the 12-year-old boys like me were frozen like statues, in shock. The girls' faces were crimson and my pupils were fully dilated as I listened, enthralled.

Jimmy would describe how he had learned to unhook a bra with his left hand while Kat wouldn't even suspect it. Then he would make his move. She would fight him off, but he was persistent. His plan was to wear her down, date after date, as if she were a bull and he was a Spanish matador. Each week he would give us a play-by-play account, as he methodically moved in on the "kill."

On those rare occasions when a teacher came in and took over the class, he or she would pull out the *Quarterly*, a Sunday school lesson book published by the Southern Baptist Convention Press in Nashville. The class would form a circle, and the booklet would be passed along, each student reading a paragraph. The content was entirely ignored, but we went through the formality, knowing that this was another of those rituals that pleased the absentee Lord. Sometimes we would try to outdo each other, reading in the most monotonous voice we could muster. "Then—Jesus—said—to—the—disciples—" Even more rarely, we would have an adult teacher who did try to create some discussion, but it was a challenge to pull anything more than a wisecrack out of the group.

One Sunday morning, Jimmy's father was picked to lead the class. He did so reluctantly. After we'd read the entire *Quarterly*, he quickly exited to work in a smoke on the front steps before worship. As soon as he had closed the door behind him, one of Jimmy's peers asked, "Well? Did you bang her last night?"

As soon as Jimmy began revealing the details, one of the girls sitting in silence in the front row reached her breaking point. She turned, her face fiery with the veins bulging on the sides of her neck like a cluster of garter snakes, and shouted, "Would you just be quiet!" Then she whirled to face the front.

As I watched in disbelief, Jimmy, along with the boys at his end of the row, started laughing. Reaching to the girl in front of him, Jimmy unhooked her bra through the back of her sweater. The poor girl didn't notice at first, but then she heard the boys' laughter increasing in volume. Looking down, she saw she had a problem and immediately burst into tears, racing from the room as the boys chuckled. She never returned to Sunday school—or church, as far as I know.

Only a few Sundays later, Jimmy also made his last appearance in Sunday school. Right before that, his Kat suddenly broke up with him for some untold reason, and he was devastated. I don't think he had the heart to face his group of admirers with such failure. He continued to come to worship because his parents made him, but he told us, "Sunday school is for little kids."

At first, I felt uncomfortable with the continuous volley of sexual innuendo in the classroom, accented now and then with instructions for making home-brew or pipe bombs, shoplifting tricks, who was selling pot, or news of pending fights. As I grew older, unfortunately, I became used to it.

By the time I was 14, I was invited to join the older boys, between Sunday school and worship, out in their souped-up Chevy Novas or Mustangs. Our rendezvous took place in the gravel cemetery parking lot behind the church, inside the lacy wire fence and well out of sight of the fathers smoking on the front steps. It was there that I was introduced to Pink Floyd, Creedence Clearwater Revival, and photos of naked women.

The strange thing was that I was still learning about God and the Christian culture he supposedly inspired, and that, despite all the negative things I was exposed to at church, I was still taught that I was where he wanted me to be. Imagine if I'd had a Puritan streak in me and hadn't wanted to be exposed to those things and decided to stay home to protect my innocence. If that had been the case, my parents, Pastor Art, and the entire Christian community would have been outraged. I would have been scolded, "You have turned your back on God!" But with my parents' help, I earned several Sunday school perfect attendance pins. Pastor Art pinned them on me with great pride. The whole thing was as perplexing to me as another tea party with a crazy Mad Hatter and a warped March Hare.

So the message was loud and clear, but at the same time, it was befuddling. We were frequently told God hated men with long hair and music with a beat? But he wanted me to go to church every Sunday despite the content of that experience. It didn't matter if at church you attended high school class where all you learned was how to get into your girlfriend's panties. You sat still for a boring hour each week listening to songs about how this material world was not important, followed by an equally boring lecture about a comic strip. Then you had to run a serpentine pattern to keep Jake, the music director, from touching your crotch on the way out of church. What kind of crazy absentee Lord was this? The entire Christian world seemed nuts.

THE ART OF PRETENTIOUSNESS

Another loud and clear message was that appearance is far more important than substance. Jake, the choir director, was a good Christian because he dressed nicely, had a crew cut, didn't swear in public, didn't partake of alcohol, and was a hard worker at church. He was considered the model Christian man for us to imitate. It didn't matter that he was using his position to lure young boys into his parents' antebellum farmhouse to fulfill his sexual pleasures—as long as that was kept in the cellar, figuratively and literally. After a while, I finally figured out that this absentee Lord didn't have the ability to peer into those cellars—or at least that's the way it seemed. Maybe the cellar doors were made of kryptonite and God was a type of Superman.

I was a bright young man and did pay attention when exposed to the Bible by the nice elementary Sunday school teachers. When I read about the real historical Jesus, I was able to read between the cultural lines enough to recognize that he was quite different from the absentee Lord that the Bible Belt culture was espousing. I never saw where he judged people by their appearance or for not following certain rules. As a matter of fact, he was always getting into trouble with the established religion of his day for being a rebel. Rather than hating sin, what he really seemed to hate was pretending. He loved the hookers, who wore their sin on their sleeves, but despised the Pharisees whose secret cellars overflowed with some really nasty stuff, such as killing innocent people because they were a threat to their power. Yet these Pharisees followed the external rules to perfection. But even though I had a glimpse of this real, authentic Jesus, the Christian cultural mores in my community were extremely powerful and overwhelming, and they quickly extinguished such insights.

By the time I was 16 or 17 years old, I was filled with so much confusion about life that I began to wonder whether there even was an absentee Lord. This was in the quietest place of my innermost being, far away from the scrutiny of my parents or any adults. For one thing, I had discovered science

difference is, most people realize they're pretending, but the evangelicals don't."

As I was trying to say to Dan, the same is true in all cultures, not just Christian ones. I believe that Islam has taken the charade to a much higher art form, like rubbing the center of their foreheads to create a deep, dark *zabiba* (raisin) so fellow Muslims will see it and think that they are a devoted prayer (their foreheads touching the ground in prayer five times a day for years) when in reality they don't pray that often if at all. Like I told my son, even the materialists and secularists behave this way. I've known many fine atheists who cannot live consistently with their beliefs because in the hidden places of their hearts they know their lives have true meaning beyond just survival of our species, and that ethics really do matter. Their nihilism is only skin deep.

When I turned 18, I left most of this Bible Belt religious thinking behind me; however, there was a residue left—regarding my concept of God—that would haunt me for years to come. However, I realized that my rage was not rooted in some mischievous theology but in some other psychological factor. Jake never got his hands on me, so while my god-concept had been tainted, church was not my source of anger.

In my next cycle of questioning, I would need to explore my most basic psychological makeup. I would have to smoke out that part of this mystery as well. To thoroughly understand what had gone wrong with me on that abhorrent evening in Cairo, I had to know myself better, and that meant going deeper into the center of the spiral of questions.

CHAPTER FIVE

What are You Worth?

Knowing yourself was an essential step in my journey in the same way that, to understand and trust the output from a computer, you must know how the basic operating system is set up and any inherent programing errors.

This re-passage into a deeper point of my spiral of question would be more difficult than the first because it was personal. It is part of our natural psychological defense mechanism to consider that the way we are, emotionally, is exactly the way we should be. To open the door to other possibilities beyond our normalcy is terrifying. The only thing worse than being blamed for something you didn't do is being blamed for an outcome that is your total responsibility. It was especially horrifying for me, as a well-studied evangelical, to even consider that my fall down the rabbit hole could be partly my own undoing. Tough discipleship invariably breeds a type of arrogance. I wanted to think of it as a push from evil Rod, rather than any kind of a personal stumble or failing. But I did know that something was wrong with me; somehow I was broken, and my intense curiosity after my fall compelled me onward to discover the reasons. The rage that erupted out of the restaurant's pit almost consumed me for the following three years, and I was desperate to find its source.

First, though, I had to establish some kind of universal landmark or grid through which I could evaluate all human behavior as well as that of my own. I spent months contemplating this whole idea, trying to reduce the human psyche down to its fundamental building blocks. Of course, scores of psychologists and philosophers had done this before me, but I needed to do it for myself.

The Common Denominator

I once attended a lecture by a local, retired astrophysicist. Early in his lecture series, he commented that all energy can be traced to one simple source— gravity. That didn't sound right to me and I thought I knew a lot about physics. For the next few days I kept meditating on that remark, trying to challenge it by following every form of energy that I could think of to its ultimate source. I thought about nuclear energy, coal, solar, hydroelectric, photosynthesis, even the Krebs cycle deep within our own cells. Finally, I had to admit that this man was indeed telling the truth. It does all start with gravity. I wanted to find a simple source of human behavior, so basic, that all great views of psychology, and of course scripture, could not contradict it.

My searching eventually led me to conclude that the root of all human behavior is ultimately based on the personal appraisal of one's self-worth. This was a eureka moment for me. I realized I had finally gotten past all the complex theories to the essence of behavior, and I could see us as our naked selves. This discovery became a key component for my understanding of what was wrong with me, in the microcosm as well as the big picture of what had gone wrong with the Church over the ages.

All cultures since the beginning of time have believed that determining your personal worth is central to your existence. I would suggest that most suicide happens only after an eventual self-assessment of worthlessness. I soon realized that the appraisal of determining self-worth, which I will abbreviate as ASW (appraisal of self-worth), was and is an extremely important concept—not just a sidebar to my search. This notion would play an important role in understanding myself and the behavior of people throughout history.

The persona of each individual is made up of our physical desires (the basics need for food, water, comfort, etc.) and what many would call the spiritual. But the spiritual, I believe, is the amalgamation of the reason, personality, and emotions. Spiritual needs are met by feeling valued by God, society, and ourselves. Per my definition, this valuation is determined by our brains through our reason and emotions. This valuation, in turn, greatly influences our personality.

This simplified model of the human soul may fly in the face of the thinking of most modern Christians, who see a great disconnect between the self, which is defined by the structure of the material brain, and the spiritual-self that transcends the material. However, I'm not alone in this view. N. T. Wright, theologian and professor of the New Testament and early Christianity at the University of Saint Andrews, Scotland, writes about this problem and describes how he thinks this modern Christian concept of the separation of the spiritual soul and material body was borrowed from Plato (c. 427–347 B.C.) rather than from scripture or early Christian traditions. You will find some of his ideas reflected in his book *Surprised by Hope: Rethinking Heaven, the Resurrection, and the Mission of the Church* (Wright, Surprised by Hope: Rethinking Heaven, the Resurrection, and the Mission of the Church 2008). I will return, with much more detail, to how Plato has influenced Christianity's concept of the soul and other areas of thinking in later chapters. Hence, for now, I use the terms *emotional* and *spiritual* interchangeably, although they may not be exactly the same, as I think there is a mystery to this concept that no words can fully describe.

Our fundamental emotional hunger is to be loved. While this desire is likely the same for men and women, I think a difference exists between the sexes when it comes to this need. John Eldredge was right, to a degree, in his book *Wild at Heart* (Eldredge 2011), in which he described men as having an intrinsic desire to be loved as a hero (dragon slayer) while women desire to be loved for their inward or outward beauty (princess). I'm speaking in generalities, and this doesn't apply to all men and all women, of course. You could also argue whether this difference is inherent or has been taught as part of cultural expectations for gender roles. I accept that much of this is culturally taught and, in future generations, this may change, but the description does seem to fit. Socialization in different cultures can influence these roles, too; however, generally they form the same pattern. I've visited people on almost every continent, and I've never seen a wide deviation from these basic needs. Another hunger I would classify as emotional is the hunger for knowledge and creativity.

There is also the emotional hunger to be accepted by God and, tied closely to that, the desire for personal value. We don't feel acceptable to God if we feel we have no value, and the same is true in reverse. If God created us, like a potter creating his pot, and if we feel we are defective or of no practical use, this would bring disdain from the artist who made us. This desire to be of value supersedes almost all other hungers, and this is where the concept of ASW comes in. Even the Fall of Adam in the book of Genesis can be explained by this hunger for value as well as knowledge.

THE MEASUREMENT OF THE SELF

ASW cannot exist without a form of measurement. As with material things, there cannot be an appraisal of worth without a standard of value. For used cars, it is the *Kelley Blue Book*. For gold, it is grams and carats.

In determining human value, as with most other things, only one measuring stick exists, and that is comparison. If one person were alone on a deserted island and had never met another human being, his or her feelings of self-worth would probably be high or might be of no concern to the individual. I don't think such a person could have low self-esteem. However, as soon as another person stepped onto your little island, the comparisons would start—at least in your own mind—in order to assign yourself value. If you were of the same height, weight, intelligence, and goodness, perhaps you would still see your value as equivalent. But if person A is slightly taller than person B, giving a person some practical advantage such as reaching for coconuts, then suddenly person A has more value than person B. The concept of value has meaning only if humans can make comparisons.

Each particular subculture arranges comparisons according to a different hierarchal ranking, which is the basis of my concept of ASW. These priorities or values are different from one culture or even subculture to the next and can change over time. However, it is your personal appraisal, how you see yourself fitting within this hierarchy that determines how you appraise your own value (assuming that the society at large is assigning you the same appraisal as you do yourself, which may not be true at all).

It is astounding how heavy an object one can lift with a lever, with the key point of any lever being the fulcrum or pivot point. Comparisons allow you to use another person as that fulcrum to lift yourself up as you push them down. But to make a comparison, you must first differentiate yourself from them. The thinking might go something like, "I'm male and they're female, and, by pushing them down, disrespecting them, I can push myself up." But taken further, this thinking might go, "I'm white and they're African-American, I'm Anglo and they're Hispanic, I'm Sunni and they're Shiite, I'm Aryan and they're Jewish, I'm Northern and they're Southern, I'm in good shape and they're fat, I'm straight and they are gay, etc.," until full-blown prejudice and superiority are occurring.

Friedrich Nietzsche (1844–1900), a German philosopher, believed that the fundamental motive of all human behavior was to gain power over other people. This thinking had its roots in social Darwinism, essentially stating that the strong end up on top. But I take it back a step to the issue of self-worth. The reason you want power over others, by pulling yourself up or by pushing them down, is leveraging for self-worth. I'm not suggesting this is the way things should be, but the way things truly are and even the saintliest Christians still carry this basic modus operandi, at least in the deep cellars of their private world. Of course God has solved this problem once and for all, but we always seem to forget that. Scriptures are clear that he has endowed all of creation with endless value and thus total equality.

Now that I had established my primal basis for human behavior, I could start to make sense of my world and my personal makeup.

A PERSONAL MEASURE GONE BAD

What I had considered relatively happy elementary school years came to an end on a warm Tuesday, September 10, 1968. On that day it was announced to my seventh-grade class that basketball tryouts would start the following Monday. This would put me on the path of some major-league misery for many years to come.

I didn't grow up in what could be called an athletic family, although my older sister played softball and basketball. The week before the Monday afternoon tryouts, I learned that the appraisal paradigm of my whole world and worth was about to change abruptly in a direction for which I was ill prepared.

During my elementary school years, the ASW was based on comparisons of intelligence, appearance, economic class of one's family, brute strength (bullies did well on this item alone), and personality—in that order. I fared reasonably well with the ASW during those years. I was intelligent. I didn't have any major facial deformities. Our family was not rich, but we weren't poor, either. I had no brute force to exhibit, but my personality wasn't too bad. I was kind to other kids and was well liked. I was reasonably comfortable in my self-worth measurements, but it was still a fragile contentment.

Two human activities are most conducive for ASW because they assign numbers to one's value. Comparisons between people are always easiest and most objective with numbers. The two human endeavors that use numbers are athletics and business.

Because I'll be mostly discussing athletics, I will briefly mention business first. I work in medicine, which has become a business like any other (alternative health care and supplements have become an even a bigger business). A phrase often used among my peers is, "What's your worth?" referring to what kind of skills and talents has a practitioner accrued that can be translated into income. All businesses use these same measurements of what are they worth.

It is also interesting that some people can be quite content with a reasonable income, but if they find out that Neil or Rosie, doing the same job, is making more than them, they suddenly become discontent and feel cheated because it is a mark against their personal value.

Athletics are even more easily measured with numbers. In fact, that is what athletics is all about—a system for using numbers to compare human physical accomplishments. The most obvious number is the score of the game. We had 66 points, and they had 64 points; therefore, we are better than they are. But it goes far beyond the score. The whole area of sports statistics is about comparisons used to rank human beings according to their worth.

Some athletes have said they would be willing to die to win a gold medal versus a silver one. Dr. Robert Goldman wrote in his book, *Death in the Locker Room II: Drugs and Sports Updated Edition* (Goldman 1992), that 50 percent of the athletes he surveyed said they would take a drug if it would guarantee them winning the gold medal even if that drug would kill them within five years. However, subsequent surveys have shown much lower numbers. Athletics have become a kind of addiction for some because of the ASW. Even middle-school sports teams practice year-round, the sport becoming the center of the players' lives because winning is everything. Of course the coach's ASW is entangled in winning, too. It's not that sports are evil. But athletics, like everything in the broken world, has its dysfunctional side. More than that, being competitive is a favorable attribute in almost every subculture, including Christian ones, but we Christians just cloak it with other names.

In my junior high school (today it begins even younger), athletics was the number-one endeavor for determining a boy's personal value. I knew boys who were poor, unattractive, and unintelligent jerks, but their heroism on the football field or basketball court catapulted them to the top value of society locally. Some of them maintained their high athletic status well after graduation and that garnered them more opportunities in business and other areas of life. Devastatingly, several female patients of mine were raped by sports stars in high school or college, and, far from being punished, the perpetrators continued to be exalted in society. That was the prevailing attitude in the 1960s and 1970s, and even today such crimes take place and are often not prosecuted.

A good athlete needs three attributes: natural talent, hard work, and the right psychological makeup. As I was one of the taller boys in my class at the time, it appeared I had potential, and when basketball tryouts began I hadn't even thought about learning the basic skills. However, after not making the team on the first try, I became so competitive and wrapped up in my self-worth that I worked harder than any other player in my school for the next five years. My mother was so worried about my obsession that she wanted me to see a psychiatrist. I wish she had. I slept with my basketball. I got up in the mornings and dribbled it for three miles. After practice, I would stay at the gym long after the others had left, shooting hoops for up to eight hours a day—all to little avail. I was desperate as I watched my personal value dropping like a brick down a well of broken dreams as athleticism became the most important measure of my worth.

This drop in personal value was in my own mind, but it was true in the external world as well. While my popularity slumped, other boys come out of nowhere to do so well in sports that they rose in popularity—especially in the eyes of the girls, to whom they became heroes. They were the dragon slayers because they could hit a layup in a game.

Even though I worked hard and had a reasonable amount of natural talent, I never succeeded in basketball because of that third attribute, the right psychological makeup. As I've mentioned, although I wasn't aware of it then, I suffered from general anxiety disorder and, more specifically, social and performance anxiety. At the time, I didn't know what the heck was wrong with me. I only knew I could hit 19 out of 20 jump shots from the key while I was in practice, but put me in a game in front of a crowd, and I would transform from Dr. Jekyll into Mr. Klutz. I remember taking a shot and missing the entire backboard and hearing laughter in the crowd—and it was a home game. I was jerked out of the game when I made mistakes like that, and my playing time would diminish. People who didn't know me assumed I had no talent. But I could beat every guy on the team in a one-on-one pickup contest—as long as nobody was watching.

As a sophomore, for one week, I was pulled up from the B team and chosen to start as the high school point guard by a new coach who appreciated my talent. But as soon as scrimmages started, the nightmares began again. I performed far below my potential and felt helpless to do anything about it. The coach worked with me because he had enough insight to know that my problem was mental. But my frustration magnified over the next couple of years by a factor of 10, as I wasn't equipped to understand the nature of the mental component. I just worked harder on my skills, thinking I wasn't good enough, that it was a talent issue, but sadly, it didn't help.

About this time, I started developing insomnia. At first it only affected the nights before the games, but then it became every night. My social anxiety worsened, and I became wrapped up in a vicious downward spiral. I sat on the bench, being terrified of the crowd, yet at the same time longing for an opportunity to prove myself. When I was finally put in, I would faithfully screw up because my trembling was so severe.

Out of one of the dark corners of my deeper places, an insatiable rage grew. But it was anger without an obvious reference point. I could try to blame others. "The coach wasn't giving me enough playing time. He's not being fair!" I would complain in the locker room, but I knew that argument was unfounded. I didn't understand who or what was causing my downfall despite my efforts. Eventually I grew to detest myself as my most perilous enemy. I forced myself to practice harder and harder, as if I were an angry father disciplining his unyielding child. All the while I continued to feel the value of my identity sliding.

I've heard stories of hostages who believed they were going to be executed but somehow survived. Some of them watched helplessly while others in their party were, for example, beheaded by Islamic extremists or killed by the Nazis during the Holocaust. But when you believe that your entire value, your reason for existing, is measured by your performance—points scored in a game, assists, rebounds, and games won—the terror of failure seems worse than the end of life itself.

By the time I turned 15, the acute distress of low self-esteem seemed to have risen to its highest point. I started thinking about killing myself. Looking back, I don't think I wanted to die as much as get attention for my plight. If I came close, so I believed, I could find someone to help me navigate out of my self-imposed labyrinth of despair.

A Tango with the Reaper of the Worthless

One night, I stayed home from a ball game. The house was empty. I went down into our basement and found two large hose clamps. First drinking some of my dad's hidden whiskey to help me get up the nerve, I tightened one hose clamp around one wrist with a screwdriver. Sliding the second clamp under the first, I put my hands together behind my back and fastened the second clamp around my other wrist—awkwardly turning the screwdriver until the clamp was tight. When linked together, the two created a kind of handcuffs. I was frightened, but at the same time I felt completely hopeless, so worthless that I felt I no longer had the right to exist. I broke a quart jar in the area of the basement where mom kept her canning supplies. Taking a deep breath, I closed my eyes and slammed my wrist down on the broken jar. A sharp pain jangled my entire body.

When I opened my eyes, blood was dripping between my feet, crimson drops on a gray concrete floor. I couldn't see my wrists because they were locked behind me, so I didn't know the extent of the damage. I sat down waiting to die—okay, maybe just to pass out. In retrospect, I know I was hoping to pass out from blood loss because deep down I still believed there had to be answers somewhere to what was wrong with me. I also had some fear of death. My secret doubts about my Bible Belt upbringing were fairly serious by this time—I really thought that there was an appreciable chance that there was no afterlife, and, if I died, I would simply cease to exist.

Time passed, and I neither died nor fainted. I was coming to my senses enough to be scared that I might really die, so I stood up and made my way back to Dad's workbench. There, I took a screwdriver and meticulously began unscrewing the clamp, an eighth of a turn by an eighth of a turn until it came loose. I pulled my wrist around into view. The cut was so superficial that it would have taken a week for me to bleed to death, if the cut hadn't healed over by then. I also didn't understand, at the time, that hose clamps—make good tourniquets. I cleaned up the small dribbles of blood, put gauze around my wrist, and have told few people about the episode until now.

From talking to hundreds of patients over the years, I am aware that many other people have contemplated suicide at some point in their lives, many far more seriously than I have. But the truth is, I've been in the vicinity of taking my own life twice—that time as a teenager and again about a year after I fell into the abyss in the Chinese restaurant in Cairo—both times for the same reason, feeling of a total loss of value. However, this didn't make sense if you followed my previous evangelical way of thinking. We believed that you entered the Christian faith as a spiritual babe. These so-called babes might wrestle with things like depression at first, but then, if you followed the formula of Bible study = maturity, later on your life would be almost perfect. There was no way, we figured, that a true disciple would want to kill him or herself.

During this difficult period after Egypt, I observed that my internal rage had ripened into something toxic. Without a doubt, Rod had some serious flaws in his thinking and behavior, too; however, I was not in the position to examine his psyche, only my own. There were reasons that I had not stood up to him and reasons why he had tapped into my ancient volcano of anger. I was determined to find the ultimate source, and I knew it had to have started long before I ever touched a basketball. This remembering of my difficult teen years did not solve the riddle of the anger. The years of struggling to play basketball embedded a great frustration within me, but there was a social anxiety that pre-existed that story. There was also already a foundation of self-anger that I had to get to the bottom of—before I could move on.

CHAPTER SIX

———◆———

Repossessed Memories

Everyone has a story to tell, and I mean that in the most positive way. Incredible narratives of mystery, wonder, and, unfortunately, grief are engraved on every page of our lives. Mine is no different. The reason I've spent so much time already in this exercise in personal introspection is linked to why and how I fell down the rabbit hole. Like everyone, I had my own baggage that contributed to the narrative, and, without sorting it out, my hopes of resolution would be thwarted.

Delving into one's psychological heritage is a little like walking into a minefield. The repressed-memories movement swept onto the scene of popular psychology during the late 1980s and took it, especially Christian psychology, by storm. Psychologists and counselors who held these views believed that recovering repressed memories was the cornerstone of the patient's healing. While that may be true for a few, I think such positive outcomes are rare. The concept of repressed memories has remained controversial in mainstream psychology, considered by most to be no more than a passing fad.

Yes, healing may be found in those bloody minefields, but more often what's found is uncertainty, if not worse. Those hallowed or possibly haunted grounds can also be a quagmire where one can become caught in a downward spiral of self-examination without any fruit of resolution. I've seen countless patients of mine relive their Vietnam War experience, or their abusive childhood, yet they are not able to get beyond the nightmares, allowing themselves to become defined by those horrible past experiences. The vet begins or continues wearing army fatigues with peace symbols sewn on the pockets, marching in MIA parades, and starting all conversations with facts about their post-traumatic stress disorder (PTSD) or Agent Orange. For some this can be healing and helpful, but others get their feet stuck in the mud and can't free themselves. They eventually die as seniors and are buried in their army fatigues, which they have worn for more than 50 years.

I knew that getting stuck in an emotional quagmire would certainly not be helpful in my quest. There is a fine line that separates finding answers that help resolve and finding answers that excuse. But, at the same time, to untangle the paradox of why my faith had become so easily unraveled, I had to go back even deeper.

A PRIMAL LOSS

I could have let it go with what I'd observed about my early spiritual heritage, or even about my frustrations as a teenager, but I wanted to venture on—into that minefield—still being driven by my life-sustaining curiosity. I tried to heed the warning signs along the field's edge: "TAKE CARE, TARRY NOT."

Looking back into your life is like looking down the throat of a large funnel. The big end, filled with well-defined details, is close to your eyes, but the farthest end narrows and extends into a shadowy world between real memories and imagination.

My life before high school seemed to be an elongated tunnel that extended into a murky infinity. My memories of the really old days are broken up, more like snapshots than a continuous movie. The farther back you go, the fewer the photos and more the haze. As if from an old photo album, the distant past is filled with memories like black-and-white Polaroid snapshots. But it's as though the album was recovered from a flood or other natural disaster because the pages are stuck together and most of the pictures are faded or ruined beyond recognition, with only a few surviving unscathed.

My most substantive memories are from ages four and five. I was the youngest child on my dead-end road, by far. My sister Susan was closest to my age, three years my senior. But the majority of the dozen or so kids were in their teens.

When I first started to venture away from the safety of our yard, enclosed by an iconic white picket fence, it was usually with Susan leading me by the hand. On one of the first of such trips we walked toward the end of our gravel road, down its steep end as it diminished into a reddish-orange clay two-tire track that eventually narrowed into a footpath. The trail was quickly swallowed by a dark hollow of pines, maples, and sassafras trees. Susan had been telling me for weeks about the wonderful clubhouse she'd built with her friends, and I was excited to see it for myself.

Venturing into the dark woods was a real-world rendering of the Mother Goose stories that I was familiar with. I imagined at any moment a lion, dragon, or lost woodcutter with a double-headed ax would jump out and grab us, taking us to some witch's hut—which may have been a blessing in disguise.

When we came into the clearing, my pregnant imagination was not disappointed. I saw a beautiful two-story stone clubhouse with a thatched roof. To my four-year-old eyes, it looked no different from the lithographic prints in my storybooks—and I'm sure my imagination has kept its image inflated and far bigger than life. Thinking back, I don't know how those young kids pulled off such an engineering feat—or again, maybe my memory has embellished the building's characteristics. I recall large stones placed neatly into straight walls, with clay mortar holding them in place. They had used old lumber from a nearby dilapidated barn to create the base of the second floor. A wooden ladder led up to the loft. The windows were open to the outside, but the girls had made curtains that could be drawn shut.

The roof was simply made from stalks of straw that grew in the nearby field. Rising through the middle of the stone house was a functional chimney with smoke billowing out. On the fire below, Lottie, a 14-year-old neighbor girl, was "cooking" mud pies. The local reddish-orange clay gave the pies the appearance of real pumpkin pies, but instead of whipped cream they were piled high with white daisy petals.

It soon became apparent, of the eight to 10 kids at the playhouse, that Larry was the alpha male. As the boss, he was giving instructions to all the others. He was a big kid, both in age and body size. Although he was 10, he seemed as tall as my parents and much heavier. Initially, he gave the feeling of safety in this remote part of the woods.

I don't know what I did that day that changed things, but they did suddenly change for me. When Lottie was finished cooking her mud pies on the small fire, Larry announced, to my disbelief, that I, "the new little spurt," would now eat a pie. I was horrified—but I had no choice. He grabbed me by the shirt collar, handed me a pie, and demanded that I eat, forcing my face down into the mud.

I slowly ate it, bite by nasty bite, as he squeezed the back of my neck more and more tightly. I ate the dried clay, gravel, sow bugs, earthworms, and daisy pedals with Larry hovering over me, grasping my shirt, cutting off the blood supply to my head, while he and some of the others continued to belly laugh. I felt nauseated and embarrassed. I was also confused. My reality was changing, and I loathed it, but there was a deep, unspoken feeling that I somehow had caused it.

This was the beginning of a long and difficult relationship with Larry and several of the other kids on my street. Because I was the youngest of them all, by several years, I became an easy target for their brutality. For reasons that my small mind couldn't understand, whenever Larry found me outside my house he would come over and grab me, drag me through the bushes, and force me to do things I hated. Eating mud pies was just the beginning of the abuse.

During my preschool years, at least, I had some break during the day when the older kids were at school. However, at four in the afternoon, when the old yellow school bus came down the highway, I would retreat indoors to hide. Soon the big kids would come looking for me, and Mom would force me outside to "play with them." Their play was inventing new ways to torment me. When I was five, I always felt like I was doing something wrong that would make these older people want to hurt me. After a glorious early childhood, I quickly came to the point of hating my existence.

When you are five, you have no instinct about the cruelty in the world and injustice, the world is, to you, as the world should be. If you feel shame, then it seems it's because you deserve shame. If people hate you, then you believe it's because you deserve to be hated. This is one of the greatest tragedies of the Fall of Adam: the naïveté of only the very young who are served injustices without hopes of understanding in this cruel world in Adam's wake.

My parents were not in the position to help me sort this out. My mom was only 16 when her mother died of breast cancer, forcing her to drop out of school and become the mother to her four younger brothers. Her late father was cruel to her. No one knew what made him mean; however, I'm sure the stress of losing a wife and raising five children in the middle of the Great Depression must have been part of it. The cruelty didn't end when he eventually remarried. Mom tells me that she was often told by her father and stepmother that she was totally worthless. She added that her stepmother's most gracious and repetitive mantra to her was, "You, young lady, are not even worth the salt I use to make your bread." When you hear something like this as a young girl, especially when it comes from your own parents, the hurt gets kneaded into the clay of your soul as an enduring effect.

Mom made the best of her life as she could, considering the little emotional support she had growing up. She became an anxious woman and taught me fear at a very young age. When planes would fly over, we would hide under the bed because, according to her, "If we are bombing the babies of people in Vietnam, it is only a matter of time before they start bombing our babies."

My father had a very different experience in life. As a teenager, he watched his mother and three of his sisters slowly succumb to tuberculosis and die. Then his father suddenly died of a heart attack. Before he could even begin to grieve, he volunteered to fight the Germans. He made the awful landing in Normandy and survived, at least in body. But Dad's hardships made him an impenetrable fortress, and, in any case, he wasn't involved with the child rearing in our family, especially by the time I came along. I'm sure he was afraid that if he opened even one window to that fortress, the whole damn thing would collapse.

Larry's harassments would take short reprieves if I ratted him out to his mother, but he still bullied and threatened me almost on a daily basis. I think it was around that time that I became an avid reader and practiced escapism via my strong imagination.

But my trials with the bullies weren't over. The next phase came when a little blond girl, Mary, age six, moved to the farm that bordered our lot at the far end. One day we were playing in her barn, and I was having fun until one of the older boys wanted me to kiss the little girl on the lips. The idea was appalling. To a five-year-old boy, girls had cooties. But kissing wasn't enough. The abuse got worse and, of all the humiliation I had experienced, that day in the hayloft of the old timber framed barn was by far the worst. I'm not sure when my rage started, but I clearly remember it being in full bloom during that period.

Some time passed after that, and this is where the pages of the memory album are stuck together. I know I avoided Mary as much as I could. It was helpful the next year when she started first grade, and I was still a preschooler because we didn't have kindergarten in our town. Also, as my birthday came in July, I wouldn't start first grade until I was seven.

THE STABBING

The next thing I recall is stabbing Larry in the head. It was a warm September day, and I was playing in the backyard with my plastic army men near my dad's brick barbecue. I know I was seven and had just started school. Larry had been pulling the same things with me, but now with a different girl named Susie—and to my horror, she was in my first-grade class.

Susie's parents were friends of Larry's parents and would visit them every week or so. It was during those visits that Larry would come to our house. Even if I was hiding in my room, Larry would knock on the door and ask for me. Mom, in her gullibility, would tell me to "go play with Larry and the big boys"—if I didn't, it would be rude. She did not seem to find it odd that these older boys, 12 and 13, wanted to play with a seven-year-old.

Larry would grab my wrist and pull me to either his house or his shed and make me kiss Susie. I hated it, and again, it brought total humiliation on me as well as cumulative rage. If I resisted, he would beat me badly. I knew that he'd eventually would demand more, like what had happened with Mary.

That September day, I was minding my own business, playing. I felt secure because Dad had taken down our old rotting white picket fence and replaced it, in the backyard at least, with a hedgerow. I now sat beneath the hedge, which gave me some camouflage—I thought.

To my shock, I heard Larry's voice at the hedgerow. "Hey creep! Guess who's coming here this afternoon—Susie! Ha! Yum … kissy-face … yum, yum … hey, little Susie creep!"

I felt my chest tighten with as much rage as a seven-year-old's heart can muster. I had just returned from the kitchen with a butcher knife because I was building a miniature swinging bridge for my army men, and I needed to cut the cotton twine in strips. What happened next is seared into my mind not only as a well-preserved Polaroid photo, but the only one that is in living color—red.

I really didn't want to hurt Larry, but I desperately wanted my personal nightmare to end. It had started the day I'd visited the storybook clubhouse at age four, and it seemed it would never go away. Three years to a seven-year-old is an eternity. My only hope was that Larry himself would go away, like when the oldest boys were getting drafted to go to Vietnam, but that would be years later.

I looked at him with what I hoped was my sternest frown and held up the knife. "Leave me alone or I'll stab you!"

Immediately he started laughing. "Give me that knife, you freakin' little queer-faced pervert!"

As he walked toward me with his hand held out, I stood up tall, keeping the knife high above my head with its blade pointing at him like I had seen villains do in the movies.

He shouted again, "Give me the knife, you little shit!"

Three years of fury erupted in my chest. As he bent over to grab me, in a blind impulse I swung, striking Larry on the top of his head. He screamed as blood flooded down his face. He ran to his house, holding his head, and I heard the screen door squeak open then slam shut. I remember hiding behind the hedge and nervously waiting. It wasn't long before the screen door flew open again, and I heard the car start and take off up the hill in a hurry. I was sure he was going to die and—I had watched enough episodes of *Gunsmoke* to know—there was going to be a hanging. For some reason I assumed that my hanging would happen in the school gymnasium in front of everyone. He did not die … but he did need stitches. I was spanked for this, but worse, from that day forward was seen as a sociopath, at least by Larry's family.

But these aren't repressed memories. Actually, of all the things in the old photo album, these events stand out the most clearly and have never needed conjuring up by some repressed-memory guru with a magic flute.

My bad times ended temporarily at age seven, although they would start again, with less intensity, with basketball at age 12. I suppose it could be said that my assault on Larry had worked because he left me alone after that. Being considered a sociopath by most of the community might have been the least of the evils I endured, but it left me feeling alienated. When difficulties happen at a vulnerable age, the impact is more deeply embedded in one's psyche.

I remember cutting down a 12-inch-diameter maple tree in our yard in

Marquette, Michigan, many years later. One section had a strange crook in it, and, when I split it, I discovered why. Incorporated in the heart of that tree was a piece of rusty barbed wire. I suspected the young sapling had grown up next to the fence decades before, then eventually absorbed the metal right into the center of the tree. There was no trace of the fence then, except for the piece inside the tree. The early experiences of that tree affected the way it grew for the rest of its life. When you are young and have difficult experiences, they can be absorbed into your psyche and shape it in profound ways.

I don't know whether the maltreatments I experienced and the great frustration that came along with it were what made my esteem or my self-worth so vulnerable. But I do know that, somehow, I developed the tendency to not only fear rejection but to react in great anger when I perceived I had been rejected. There may have been some kind of genetic vulnerability in my anxiety as well. My very earliest memories were night terrors at age two, long before I had experienced any type of abuse. So, I don't know if all my anxiety was taught to me by Mom or perhaps, some came through to me through her DNA

At this point, I felt I had taken this trail into the past as far as I needed to, and more introspection would probably not have been helpful. I was also wary of using my early childhood experiences as a kind of peg to hang an excuse hat on. Most people have difficulties in their formative years; no one has ever had a perfect family. A whole lot of people have endured much worse than I did. On a global scale, I would be in the top 10 percent of positive experiences. After all, I knew my parents and siblings loved me. I no longer think of the bullies on my street as monsters.

With this new understanding of my past, I felt better equipped to find the real truth of what happened in the Chinese restaurant that night. As the instrument for judging reality, I had to be "calibrated." My examining my past was that calibration. Now I could honestly ask, anytime I faced a challenge, "Is it the situation that's at fault or my twisted perceptions, or both?" I recognized that I suffer from social anxiety, and this was a significant part of the reason I had not confronted Rod long before the situation in Cairo came to a point of crisis. The other part was his intentional elusiveness. Some of my anxiety was likely genetic and some if it—I'm sure—was from early childhood experience. The unhealthy dependency on basketball made sense now. I had based my entire self-appraisal on my ability to succeed but failed due to my performance anxiety. But my broken theology of godliness had given me a false security that those things from my youth were not relevant. However, that concept of godliness was somehow twisted like that old piece of barbed wire. This discovery led me to my next round of questions. How did I get my theology so wrong?

CHAPTER SEVEN

Freakin' Jesus Freaks

I had known Drew since kindergarten. He had weathered the sudden change of ASW, where you were measured by your athletic abilities, much better than I had. We had also attended the same small white church on the hill. Mr. and Mrs. Plummer, whose son was the child molester, were his uncle and aunt.

Rather than continuing to invest time in sports, Drew saw the writing on the wall sooner than I did. He realized it was hopeless for him to ever find popularity through being a sports star, and he shifted toward the drop-out sector of our high school. He transformed his persona into an aficionado of Creedence Clearwater Revival and other rock bands, grew his hair out much longer than what was approved of in the Bible Belt, and wore cutting-edge clothes—you might call them alternative clothes by today's standards— purple silk shirts with large puffy sleeves.

Drew had been even later than I'd been in taking the walk up our church aisle. I recall talking to him in the school library when we were 13. "It's really easy. Just step out of the pew and take a couple of steps, then the whole thing is over. I really think you can do it." Some would call this evangelism, but I wasn't speaking in spiritual terms, of making a commitment to Christ, only helping him get this important milestone out of the way so he could move on and stop feeling so damn guilty.

Drew walked up the aisle within a couple of weeks of our conversation, but his action seemed to take root much better than mine had. He began having some spiritual interests—but not a lot right away.

Three years later, Drew was dating Emily, a girl he really liked. She was a cutie, with strawberry blond hair and pale blue eyes, and intelligent. Following the example, we had from older boys—like Jimmy in Sunday school—Drew felt it was his duty to push the intimacy envelope. Even in our Bible Belt culture, it was considered a real shame for a boy to turn 18 and still be a virgin. Paradoxically, it was extremely important that the girl you married be a virgin. Whoever created this paradox must not have done the math.

Drew was facing a real quandary. Emily was one of the few atheists in our school; she came from an entire family of atheists. Being an atheist in the Bible Belt was about as perilous (and as rare) as being a rabbi in Mecca. Even the wildest guys who partied all the time, smoked pot, committed petty crimes, and never visited a church ... hated atheists. Atheists and gays were some of the most despised people in the Bible Belt, replacing African Americans by only a generation.

Drew's problem was that, although he tried his best to deflower his girlfriend, she had high moral standards and put up a great deal of resistance, more so than his previous Christian girlfriend. The fact that her moral standards were superior to his own, a card-carrying Southern Baptist, threw him into a tizzy. Poor Drew lost a lot of sleep over the situation.

About this time, Drew and I both signed up for a new psychology class offered at the high school. I wanted to go to learn what the hell was wrong with me, not recognizing yet that I suffered from social anxiety. Drew wanted to find out how to handle the situation with Emily.

COACH

The first day of class was a major disappointment. Mr. McConnell, the psychology teacher, had been heavily recruited as the head football coach. He was a superb college athlete who'd had professional football aspirations until they were thwarted by a bad knee. He was the quintessential football player. He wasn't that tall, maybe five-foot-ten at best, but his shoulders were broad, and he had no visible neck. The school board considered him a real catch—but of course high schools didn't employ full-time coaches, only full-time teachers who happened to coach.

On the first day of psychology class, Mr. McConnell called roll, fiddled with his pencil for a few minutes, and then vented his feelings. "Hey, I'm a coach, not a teacher. They told me I had to teach this class because psychology was my minor, but I really don't care a lot about psychology." He walked to the window and looked outside, up toward the sports fields, glancing back at us as he played with the blind's cord. We sat in silence. It crossed my mind that he might be pulling some kind of mental experiment on us. Then he spoke again, "You know, psychology is a bunch of crap. If you've lived to be 17 or 18 and no one has killed you or if you haven't become a lunatic, you already know all the psychology you'll ever need to know." Pausing to look out the window again, then back at us, he continued. "I'll make a deal with you. I'll give everyone in the class well-deserved A's if you keep your big fat mouths shut. I'd rather be out on the football field than in here, and I'm sure there are other places you'd rather be. I have to call roll, but then you can sneak out this window while I head out to the field."

My jaw dropped in disbelief. I, along with Drew, had a true interest in learning something about psychology. But just as Mr. McConnell promised, he took attendance, then walked over to one of the two casement windows in the room. He removed the inside bug screen. Then he turned the crank and opened the window so we could all climb up and slip through. Then he vanished through the door without saying a word or looking back over his shoulder. One by one, we crawled out the window and crept across the parking lot to our cars like foot soldiers trying to avoid sniper bullets. In subsequent weeks, Drew and I made the best of the situation and spent third period at McDonald's, after stopping by the classroom for roll call.

One morning Mr. McConnell called roll in his usual fashion. Then he looked at us and announced, "Kids, I've got some really bad news." He rolled his eyes and chuckled. "Well, at least bad news for you." A soft smile came to his broad jaw and he chuckled once more. "It's good news for me because I won't have to come down here to call roll anymore. I can spend my entire day on the football field. What I'm saying is that we'll be having a student teacher starting on Monday to do his student teaching in this class." A quiet moan echoed across the room. We had student teachers in other classes, and they always took teaching far too seriously.

ENTER AARON, THE DISCIPLE MAKER

On Monday morning, an unsuspecting man with long, curly blond hair and a spotty beard walked into the room carrying a briefcase. Students greeted

Mr. Klein by knocking his briefcase out of his hand, carrying him down the hall, and attempting to throw him into the pool. He didn't know what he was up against with a class that had been going to McDonald's and getting automatic A's before his arrival.

But he had the courage to come back. In a move to maintain control, he arrived in the class well before we did on the following day. As Drew and I entered the room, we noticed Mr. Klein had scribbled three men's names on the blackboard: "B. F. Skinner – Sigmund Freud – Jesus Christ." He looked at the class sternly and announced, "For the next six weeks, we're going to be looking at the nature of human personality from the perspectives of these three psychologists."

I had learned some things about Jesus when I was in Sunday school, but I had never realized he was a psychologist. I was confused and curious about this interesting turn of events, while Drew seemed excited at the chance to learn more about the Christian faith that Aaron seemed to wear on his sleeve.

After class that day, Drew stayed behind to talk to Mr. Klein about his situation with Emily. He felt the new teacher would be the perfect counselor for his mixed-up soul. Mr. Klein made the diagnosis quickly: Drew's problem was that he was still a "babe in Christ" and he really needed to "grow." Mr. Klein (Aaron) invited him to attend a discipleship class that he and several of his college friends were teaching at a church in a nearby city as part of the DI ministry. Neither Drew nor I had any idea that this small gesture would have such a profound impact on our lives for decades to come, eventually leading me to Egypt and Drew to Australia and South Africa as missionaries.

But at the time, though Drew was excited, I wanted nothing to do with this Jesus freak. Even though Drew was my close friend, I had not confided in him that in my heart I wasn't at all sure the absentee Lord was ever there. As someone who loved science, a lot of things just weren't making sense to me anymore. For example, the local pastors interpreted the Bible as insisting that the Earth was only 6,000 years old; moreover, it had been created in just six days. Geology was a hobby of mine, and I collected fossils from ancient forests that my uncle had unearthed 8,000 feet below ground in a nearby coal mine. This didn't even touch on the dinosaur skeletons, which I had seen for myself at the Smithsonian. How could those great beasts have lived only 6,000 years ago, and the forest be buried that deeply—not to mention having their prehistoric world transformed into this time capsule locked in frozen carbon? It wasn't making much sense. The entire mountain range around me was the result of deep-sea deposits that eventually folded up to their 6,000-foot heights. That happened in 6,000 years?

Similarly, there was little evidence of this Lord I kept hearing about in the lives of the people who claimed to believe in him. The TV evangelists were no more credible (actually, much flakier) than the used-car, kitchen-gadget, or furniture salespeople who came on late-night TV right before or after them. I had heard of miracles, but none of them panned out as real. God had supposedly cured several people in our community of their cancer, only for them to succumb to it weeks later. Another thing I couldn't understand was the cruelty of this world. If God were here, he was either impotent to do anything about the pain and suffering or, if he did have the power preachers attributed to him, he really didn't give a damn about us.

The whole church thing still seemed like a farce to me. Most church-goers were really only pretending, and everyone knew it. Why would an absentee Lord be so wacky as to have these strange requirements for his people to please him, but at the same time look the other way regarding the brutality of things done in his name, like Jake molesting church children? Yet God was supposedly proud of Jake as a model Christian—or was he?

Drew was determined not to go to this discipleship class alone. Everyone there would be a college student but him. He hounded me for a week until I agreed to accompany him. But I made it clear: "I'll come for the first couple of weeks and that's it. Then you're on your own. I have no desire to be a Jesus freak!" By that time, I also had an attractive girlfriend, Samantha. I had seen how much Drew had changed during his meetings with Aaron after just a couple of counseling sessions. He had ended his relationship with Emily altogether per Aaron's advice. But I was approaching 18 and still a virgin, and I wanted to leave the *deflower* verb in my repertoire of possibilities. And I was—correctly, I might add—afraid that Aaron would quickly put an end to that ambition.

When we arrived at the large urban Calvinist church, the first thing I noticed was that the college students leading and attending the classes took Christianity quite seriously. They didn't see God as some absentee Lord far off in some distant capital, but as a personable, familiar entity. These people were sharing things that "God had shown me" or, even more directly, "things God had told me," as though he was a real person in the next room, sitting in his boxers, smoking Cubans, and watching *Magnum PI*. But what really got my attention was that this group seemed to be genuinely happy. At least they smiled a lot. They were nice to each other, exchanging hugs and saying things like "I love you, bro!" They were also much cooler than Sammy Higgins, a very religious pastor's kid I had known in elementary school. Rather than being clean cut with a crew cut, dressing in slacks, button-down shirts, and carrying a big black King James Bible, they were hippies. They had long hair and beards and wore bell-bottom jeans. A few even sported seashell beads and carried dark-green padded Living Bibles. A couple of them drove VW minibuses. Collectively, they looked like a rock band (two of them were in fact in a Christian rock band).

Although I found their lifestyle far more attractive than that of any pious people I'd ever met before, it was their sincerity—or, at the time, what I perceived was sincerity—that I found most alluring. This caused me to listen to what they were saying and teaching. Although they were teaching some of the same things I had heard from the nice ladies in elementary Sunday school, these folks were teaching it in new, exciting, and relevant ways.

I continued going on the 30-mile trip with Drew every Sunday night to this discipleship class, pretending to be a Christian. I was even beginning to follow their behavioral examples, giving them hugs and telling them, "I love you, man!" I especially enjoyed hugging the college girls. I sensed the other men did as well. As I often say, we were men before we were Christians.

Back when I first met the Jesus freaks, I began to seriously contemplate the validity of the Christian faith again. But I first had to overcome some major doubts. I eventually opened up to Drew, who was flying high with his newfound religious zeal. I spoke to Aaron as well. He was clear that my doubts were "lies told to you by Satan." He diagnosed that what I really needed was to overcome Satan's lies with a personal, and essentially blind, faith. He assured me, "Once you are a mature Christian, you'll no longer have doubts." So, to him, questions and immaturity went hand in hand.

But being a logical person, I couldn't make a blind leap as he was asking me to. I had to have at least one speck of reason around which my snowflake of faith could crystallize. I started praying that God would show me enough answers that I would have some superstructure on which to hang my faith.

The insomnia that had plagued me since middle school had continued throughout high school. But as a senior, I would lie in bed awake, contemplating the possibility of God's existence and the truth of the Bible. Finally, I had a breakthrough. Like spelunking in dark unexplored caves, at night I would venture deeper and deeper into diverging channels of thought. The one line of questioning I could not answer, apart from a personal God, was my own existence. I now know that psychologists and neurophysiologists would lump this under the concept of self-consciousness and would attribute it to a complex array of neurons. But I knew it had to be more than that. The fact that we exist creates a huge paradox that we must all reckon with, and there are no easy default answers such as the "nothingness" one— that out of nothing and for no reason, the big bang occurred and now reality is here. I am me, not just a complex neuron-based software. I do exist, and that's the great enigma.

It was after a memorable Saturday night of no sleep and deep pondering that things began to jell. It didn't all happen right away, rather, later the following Sunday evening, during the long drive back from the discipleship class. Drew was at the wheel of his sister's Plymouth Valiant with the cool push-button transmission. It was spitting snow, and I was continuing to think. Then, in another proverbial eureka moment, I found the evidence I had been looking for.

Years later, during those first few years back in the states, as I mentioned in Chapter Two, I read many books by the late theologian Dr. Francis Schaeffer. I had read some of his writings even as a freshman in college, but I didn't understand the philosophical verbiage. Later, once I understood him, I realized that he described the exact issue I was dealing with as an 18-year-old: it is impossible for a nonpersonal universe, one without a personal God, to give rise to personal man. He was living in the Swiss Alps at the time of his writing, and he illustrated his idea with the analogy of a high alpine lake. Such a lake cannot feed through an underground channel a pool of water that is at a higher elevation. Likewise, a personal universe (with real, personal people rather than carbon-based robots) cannot have come from a much lower, impersonal universe.

This watershed moment of my life set me on an entirely new path. And, unknown to me, the slide that eventually led to the descent down the rabbit hole 20 years later was also set in motion that night. With this settled, it was now time to move farther back out of the spiral to the questions about my eventual theological formation under the training of DI. This would be key.

Chapter Eight

Foundation Blocks

If you ever have the opportunity to go into the deepest parts of a medieval cathedral or ancient castle, as I have, you will notice an array of massive foundation stones. It has always puzzled me how they could move them into such precise position without modern power equipment. However, if these stones had not been precisely placed, strong, and level, the structure above ground could never have had the stability to withstand the centuries. The same is true with our philosophical beliefs or what you might call our personal world view.

Underpinnings of Chalk

As I began to lay the foundations of my Christian life in the late 1970s, several large blocks would become fundamental to my future understanding of everything Christian. Later, standing in the midst of my burned-out shell of a Christian life in the early 1990s, I looked back through the murk of almost two decades for answers. After my thoughtful and deeply intrusive examination of my cultural and psychological makeup, I also had a sense something was seriously wrong with my theology. I wanted to go beyond simply finding errors—I wanted to understand why I, or possibly all of us American evangelicals, had been deceived.

I had a feeling some foundational errors had been established during my formative years, which eventually led to my downfall. I've already mentioned two: bad faith and a hollow Christianity I was taught in the Bible Belt. Other aspects of my thinking at the time acted as foundation blocks, but in retrospect, although most of them were solid and granite-like, others were only granite-colored blocks of chalk, whose fragility would eventually lead to my downfall and probably to the demise of many Christians' faith.

After Drew and I graduated from high school, we enrolled at the university where Aaron Klein was still the campus leader of the DI ministry. DI was mainstream and evangelical. The organization wasn't an obscure cult or even a product of the Bible Belt. Even Aaron was not from the Bible Belt but from suburban Washington, D.C. DI is endorsed by most major evangelical churches and Christian leaders such as Billy Graham. The point is that, although the organization took the Christian life far more seriously than other campus ministries such as the Baptist Student Union, it wasn't uncharacteristic of evangelicalism.

With Aaron's encouragement, Drew and I moved into a DI "training house" with him and another leader of the ministry. DI houses were where younger DI recruits would move into a house with an older DI leader or leaders with the purpose of training them in the Christian life. This process was called discipling.

CHRIST THE CORNERSTONE

The first foundation block I laid during this early phase of my training was, what I will call, the *Christ block*. Christ himself is the cornerstone or chief building block of anyone's Christian life. Connected intimately to this cornerstone was a second one called the *justification block*. Justification is the concept that our salvation comes by grace alone and not by earning it ourselves—it comes through faith. Virtually all Protestant Christians would agree with these two fundamentals.

Like many Christians, we also learned that faith and reason stood on opposite ends of the spectrum. As I've already mentioned, Aaron encouraged me to take the faith leap. A true antithesis lies between the two concepts of faith and reason, and Christians believe they should live by faith, not by sight. To put it simply, we believed that reason and sight (including all our senses and emotions) came from the brain and faith from the soul (the immaterial part of us) as an act of the will. We believed the spiritual was totally separated from the material. As Calvinists, we also believed that this so-called act of the will to believe in Christ was a gift bestowed on us by God. So we believed that the "choice" to believe was programmed into us at our creation by God. I'll come back to this matter of faith and reason later in more detail and explore it from a philosophical perspective, but for now it's enough to say that it would become an important development in my early Christian life.

THE ART AND ARTIFICE OF SANCTIFICATION

The third foundation block, cemented to the other side of the Christ corner-stone, was what I will call the *sanctification block*. Sanctification was taught to us starting with the premise that, once saved, all of our previous sins are erased, and we begin a clean slate as "new creatures." I remember Aaron and the others emphasizing this concept and having us memorize 2 Corinthians 5:17: "Therefore, if anyone is in Christ, the new creation has come: The old has gone, the new is here!" This verse was interpreted by us as, as taught by DI, that our old sins—personal and the sins of others—no longer having any influence on us, our emotional selves, or on our futures. This block, specif-ically, greatly appealed to me because it meant that all my old baggage, my fears, anger, and tendency toward depression and social anxiety, as well as all my chronic faults, would suddenly and magically be gone. I, the frog, had been kissed by a prince, and now I, too, would be a prince. There was not a trace of webbing between my toes or even a hankering for water. The prob-lem was that we didn't accept this concept figuratively—claiming Jesus's righteousness as our own—but literally. We saw ourselves as righteous, or at least on the road to real righteousness.

Building on this sanctification block was a lifelong process of maturing in Christ. Maturity was the process by which the rate of and tendency to-ward habitual sin would go down. How little a mature Christian would sin was dependent upon your perspective. For example, many in my DI group believed that a truly mature Christian, someone we would call godly, might sin briefly with a bad attitude once a week or less. Looking back, I now realize how dishonest and dangerous this kind of self-assessment is, requiring an individual to live far outside of reality and obliges them to construct secret cellars where the real them can find refuge.

Tied closely to this concept of sanctification was the view of a God in-timately involved with the process. The God taught to us by Aaron watched our behavior carefully and interacted with us moment by moment. We believed God would continually speak to us about such trivial matters as which parking spot to park in, which shirt to wear to class, and whether we should wear colored underwear or plain white (we actually debated this in the cafeteria one day, in 1974, believing colored underwear was part of the gay agenda).

This was somewhat different from the beliefs in my small Baptist church, where people would never ask God to find them a parking space at the mall. They also thought he wasn't that concerned about their trivial behavior like white lies or even major behavior like having a mistress—as some of the good church men did—as long as that behavior was stashed neatly out of sight in the cellar. But this new concept of God assured us that he was concerned about all sin.

As part of God's intimacy with us, Aaron taught that God expected total obedience—anything short of that would disappoint him. If we did sin, our personal relationship with God would be completely broken until we confessed our sins, asked for forgiveness, and repented. This had to be performed daily to keep our relationship with God unhindered. Another verse we memorized was from 1 John 1:9: "If we confess our sins, he is faithful and just and will forgive us our sins and purify us from all unrighteousness." This verse was referred to as the Christian's bar of soap. We had to "wash" every day if we wanted to stay clean and keep the channels of communication open with God. If we forgot to "wash," God would remain angry with us until we did.

The way we were to grow in maturity—and sin less—was by using a simple formula taught by Aaron and the other DI staff people. This principle had its roots in John Wesley's (1703–1791) "methods for godliness," which later became the Methodist Church and was the foundational church for the Second Great Awakening.

There were two great Christian revivals in American history. The First Great Awakening was launched by Puritans and spread across Protestant Europe and the American colonies in the 1730s and 1740s. It left a lasting change to the way that Christianity was experienced in these places. The Second Great Awakening began about 1790 and continued into the early 1800s. It covered the area of the south that is now, and as a result of this awakening, called the Bible Belt. I will mention these movements again and in more detail later, but, to say at this point, if there had been no Second Great Awakening, there would have neither have been a Bible Belt nor DI.

We defined the external measure of maturity by the observable fruits of the Spirit. This idea came from other memory verses like Galatians 5:22–23a: "But the fruit of the Spirit is love, joy, peace, forbearance, kindness, goodness, faithfulness, gentleness and self-control." One other measurement of maturity was ministry. Mature Christians should be surrounded by people to whom they are actively ministering. These parameters together would allow us to evaluate our own state of maturity, but more than that—and something we would have strongly denied—they allowed us to evaluate the state of others. The resulting comparison would, we would hope, help us to develop our own ASW.

People who were naturally disposed to having these fruits, either through genetics or upbringing, did well under this system. People with disorders such as anxiety or depression did poorly under this system. People with borderline or narcissistic personality disorders also did rather well (such people are socially savvy and smart and learn how to disguise their primal motives as spiritual ones). In the DI group, the opportunity to evaluate and compare oneself in a deep, psychological way to another's psychological maturity was vital.

THE GREAT GOSPEL PARADOX

We never fully resolved the two—seemingly conflicting—aspects of the gospel: justification and sanctification. This leads us to another confusing and irrational conversation around the Mad Hatter's tea party table.

Imagine in my hypothetical version of the *Alice in Wonderland* story where Alice might ask, "How do we please the great King?"

The Mad Hatter replies, "Oh, just trust that he is the King and then you will be made an honorary daughter. His son is perfect, and whenever the King looks at you, he sees only the absolute splendor and perfection of the prince. It's a kind of magic. When you look in the looking glass, you see the perfect prince looking back at you."

Alice feels good about this and sips her tea. She slides down in her chair in a comfortable reclining position with a warm smile on her face as her shame dissipates. But then the Mad Hatter, dipping his pocket watch into his teacup and wearing a contorted grimace on his face, adds in a whisper, "But be very careful." He looks in both directions, shielding his mouth with his hand so no one can read his lips, and whispers even softer, "If you do anything to displease the King—and he is somewhat hard to please—he will be exceedingly angry at you and chop off your head." A look of horror comes over Alice's face as she realizes that the loving King is also a murderous monster.

By this point I had carefully reviewed my early Christian development, examining it through my metaphorical telescope (mentioned in chapter two), and had applied cultural, psychological, and theological filters. Now, by applying a philosophical filter, I would discover the crucial block, the key to understanding everything else. It sat somewhat like a dead codfish unwrapped in a tightly closed refrigerator, with its smell insidiously penetrating the delightful bowl of strawberry Jell-O nearby.

A journey that had taken me through three long, Marquette winters was finally bearing fruit. Like gravity is to energy, I was on the threshold of discovering that one source to all that had gone wrong in that winterless land of Egypt.

CHAPTER NINE

———◆———

Linchpin

The next foundation block was the most interesting and difficult to explain, which is why I've devoted an entire chapter to its discussion. It was unspoken and unacknowledged, even on a subconscious level, and it wasn't described in any type of flow chart, doctrinal statement, memory verse, or instructional booklet. However, in some ways, it was written on the underbelly of our entire Christian world like a coating of pitch on the hull of an ancient ship, keeping it afloat. I will simply call this foundation block *dualism* and give a detailed explanation in later chapters and a brief introduction here.

Dualism is another universal block, and one not unique to our campus group. Most people who considered themselves part of the evangelical culture followed this thinking, including everyone in our little Baptist church at home. I would even suggest that the tenets of this block are widely held throughout Christendom, more strongly in some places and in certain periods of history than others. American evangelicalism, since the nineteenth century, is one of the cultures in which it has been most prominent.

After the Second Great Awakening, which reached full strength by the beginning of the nineteenth century, this concept became stronger, especially in the path of the southern component of this awakening. The Second Great Awakening initially took form and energy in the South with the help of Methodist circuit riders, who carried the Gospel message from Kentucky through Tennessee, Georgia, North Carolina, Virginia, and back to Kentucky. The flashpoint of the southern awakening, which was also the birth of the Bible Belt, was located at the Red River Meeting House in western Kentucky in 1800. But how did the new awakening usher in a resurgence in dualistic thinking among American evangelicals? First, I must define "dualism."

A Bifurcated Foundation

If you are familiar with philosophical terms, you will not be a stranger to the term "dualism." If you are not, the philosophical or religious concepts of dualism imply that reality is divided between two major domains, usually defined as the material and the immaterial. A significant part of this book from this point forward will be devoted to what I learned about this philosophical concept, its history, evolution, and impact on how Christians think and how I, personally, thought. I hope to prove that the misapplication of dualism was not only the key ingredient to my personal fall but was central to most things that have troubled Christendom throughout its history. Most things in life don't boil down to one simple issue or flaw, so the reasons for evangelicalism's troubles should not be oversimplified. Yet, if there is a single, unifying theory of Christian error, I believe it can be defined in dualistic terms. It is very tempting for Christians at this point say, "Oh, I'm just a simple Christian, and I live by faith in a Jesus that I know is in my heart. I don't need to think about these complex, philosophical things." I believe that such thinking is a rationalization to justify intellectual lethargy, and there is no longer an excuse for such attitudes. It is another circular reasoning to say that it is not important to study the influence of these philosophies on Christianity because the philosophical influence, which has already penetrated the Church, says that it is not important. Nowhere in the Bible does it say that it is a positive attribute to be stupid, but true discipleship is learning and exploring to expand our knowledge of the real world, which God has created.

I will need to define the term and simplify the way I intend to use it. I must be overtly clear that the real problem is not dualism in its literal definition. There is no harm in the act of dividing things into two distinct sides. The Bible is full of dualistic divides, starting from Genesis 2:9b: "In the middle of the garden were the tree of life and the tree of the knowledge of good and evil." Even Christ spoke of them as recorded in John 3:19: "This is the verdict: Light has come into the world, but people loved darkness instead of light because their deeds were evil." No Christian, or person of almost any other faith for that matter, would argue against the notion that some things are evil and some are good. I hope I am explicitly clear on this.

The real issue is not the view of dualism itself, but the how—or more precisely, the where and, in some ways, the when of it. The problem with my early thinking was that I, like my peers, got it entirely wrong.

The foundation block I'm calling dualism is essentially a metaphysical concept, a line of clear demarcation between what is considered spiritual and what is worldly. Metaphysics, of course, is the philosophical concept of existence, i.e., in what specific forms that existence is a presence. This concept of *worldly*, as used here, is a realm that is insignificant at best or pure evil at worst. We were taught that the spiritual realm was God's kingdom and the worldly (material world) domain was Satan's—plain and simple. Some passages that Christians use to support this notion include 1 Corinthians 3:1: "Brothers and sisters, I could not address you as people who live by the Spirit but as people who are still worldly—mere infants in Christ." The idea of dualism is philosophical and may not appear to relate to practical life, but I hope to prove that it is profoundly related to how we think and live our day-to-day lives, even if we are entirely unaware of its influence.

As I continued my studies, I became captivated by dualism's historical development and impact. Dualism's long saga and its relationship with the Church is riveting, with more twists and turns than a hundred books such as *The Da Vinci Code* (Brown 2003).

Starting in the little Baptist church—but much more so in the DI organization of the 1970s—we were taught that all material things are considered worldly. This term *worldly* was used in the broadest definition. Secular culture was definitely worldly because it was supposedly created by physical beings—humans, in other words—and did not come directly from God. For example, worldly things included all TV shows (except for some Christian programming), most movies, non-Christian music, non-Christian art (if it was possible to define which art was Christian and which was not).

Even history itself was worldly, another product of temporal human endeavors. This was true for all levels of history, both for *local history* and what I would term *meta-history*, which is the grand scope of things over the centuries.

Local history is what I call the daily events of your personal life, the bricks and mortar that eventually make up meta-history. On a cold

Christmas night in 1776, George Washington made a local decision and took action to cross the Delaware River, and it became the turning point of the American Revolutionary War. If the Colonies had not won that battle for Trenton (a victory made possible by the crossing) they may not have won the war. If they had not won the war, America wouldn't exist. Imagine how world history would have been profoundly affected in the two centuries since—and all because of local history.

I was taught early on that meta-history was worldly and thus had no positive significance, so there was no need to study it. Our local Bible-Bel t-Appalachian-white-American-Western-European culture was seen as absolute and pure and the norm, just as every other culture views itself. To consider one's own culture as simply the product of a chain of historical events over centuries seemed, to us in the Bible Belt at least, like sacrilege.

Even the study of Church history was considered worldly. We didn't care about early Church fathers or the centuries of struggles over theological issues, including the major historical Church councils. History, in all its forms, was considered insignificant and a waste of time—and possibly even a harmful distraction.

We were taught that studying secular history—the story of secular people doing worldly things—was especially pointless. In this dualistic paradigm, the stories of ancient peoples, unless they were biblical characters, had no bearing on one's personal spiritual life, and it was therefore inane to take an interest in them. The only human history that should concern us was spiritual meta-history—specifically, God's workings in the Old Testament and world events, such as Israel becoming a nation, that we could relate to something spiritual, like Jesus's second coming.

A few years ago, Mark A. Noll, in his book *The Scandal of the Evangelical Mind* (Noll 1995), illustrated this point well:

> The evangelical predilection, when faced with a world crisis, to use the Bible as a crystal ball instead of a guide for sorting out the complex tangles of international morality was nowhere more evident than in the responses to the Gulf War [Gulf War I] in 1991. Neither through the publishing of books nor through focused consideration in periodicals did evangelicals engage in significant discussions

on the morality of the war, the use of the United Nations in the wake of the collapse of Communism, the significance of oil for job creation or wealth formation throughout the world, the history of Western efforts at intervention in the Middle East, or other topics fairly crying out for serious Christian analysis. Instead, evangelicals gobbled up more than half a million copies each of several self-assured, populist explanations of how the Gulf crisis was fulfilling the details of obscure biblical prophecies.

We were also taught that local history should have no meaning unless it was spiritualized. No simple cause-and-effect reasoning was involved with daily events. For example, if a robber entered your uncle's store and shot and killed him, the only significance would be to show how God had allowed it to happen to teach your aunt a lesson about something, perhaps patience. Sure, you might cry and feel grief, especially if you were not spiritually mature. The fact that the robber was abused repeatedly as a child by his mother's boyfriend, became addicted to crack cocaine to quell his emotional pain, and began robbing people to support his habit would be irrelevant. It might be considered a sorry excuse at best.

This Worthless World and the Celestial Puppeteer

In the context of evangelical dualism, the physical world is considered insignificant and the spiritual world of utmost importance. Even the tiniest event of daily life in the physical world, such as a leaf falling from a tree, must have strings attached to God the puppeteer's fingers up in the spiritual realm. So God, or sometimes angels acting for God, had to have master control over all details of our daily life here in the material world or those details would have no meaning. To support this concept, Christians use passages such as Matthew 10:29–30: "Are not two sparrows sold for a penny? Yet not one of them will fall to the ground outside your Father's care. And even the very hairs of your head are all numbered." Despite its literal meaning, many translations of this passage suggest that God watches over the sparrows and doesn't literally control their every move like a celestial puppeteer. But the literal interpretation is most common among evangelicals. The strings could also go down to Satan, who also resides in the spiritual realm. So every event must be assigned to God or his angels or perhaps to Satan. I will use a real, heart-wrenching example from my years at a DI training center.

DUALISM'S PERSPECTIVE ON A TRAGEDY

After I finished my undergraduate studies in premed and psychology in 1977, I wanted to study medicine at the graduate level. I also desired to further my spiritual training through DI. I eventually found a city where I could accomplish both goals, a place with an intensive DI training center and a PA medical school. A DI training center was a rigorous discipleship program—lasting two to five years—with the ultimate goal of preparing their trainees to either be staff in the United States or missionaries overseas. My desire, at the time, was to take my medical training somewhere in the developing world as a missionary.

In our training center we had five guys living in one "ministry house" and five girls living in another. It was a tough program, especially for someone like me who was attending graduate school during the day time. The DI leaders planned activities five or six evenings every week. These activities included Bible study, evangelism, prayer, service projects and then at least a couple of evenings where we were leading Bible discussion groups in the dorms.

We had no social life outside of these activities. If we did do something for personal enjoyment, such as playing a pickup game of basketball or taking a group to do something outdoors, we had to spiritualize it; otherwise it would be worldly and a waste of time. To spiritualize it, we would use basketball as a means to make contacts with non-Christians and then try to evangelize them. If we couldn't find a non-Christian (as an evangelism target) to join our rock climbing trip to the Red River Gorge, we would have to find some other spiritual reason for going. The attitude was expressed in the question, "How dare we do something just for our own (material) enjoyment, when the entire world was going to hell?" Personal pleasure always resided in the worldly realm, unless it was our pleasure of knowing God.

The leader of the DI training center was Ted, a very nice man in his fifties. He was considered a man truly in "tune with God's own heart" and an example for all of us to emulate. He was well known throughout DI because of his godly character. I admired his reputation, which somewhat sealed the deal that his training center was the right place for me. I still consider Ted a good man although now I don't agree with all of his Christian thinking, at least his thinking of the early 1980s.

I will never forget a phone call on a cold, blustery Sunday night. It was during my third year at the center. It was Ted, calmly asking for a favor, which was not that unusual except for the late hour. His emotional tone was perfectly level as he told me that Karl, his 16-year-old son, had been killed that night. "I just came from the morgue where I identified his body," Ted went on. "On the way to youth group at church he hit a tree, came out the window of his car, and a truck ran over him. But we're okay. We were praying that God would bring him home safely, and God faithfully answered our prayers. He brought Karl home safely to him, in heaven, just as we had asked. Now, Mike, if you could call a couple of people for me to cancel my appointments tomorrow, I'd be grateful. I'm tired and don't want to talk about it anymore, and I can't make my racquetball time tomorrow morning."

I was speechless. Karl had been a close friend of mine; we had played a lot of basketball together. I just couldn't believe it. When words did finally escape my choked-up throat, they were really dumb words. I whispered, "Are you serious?"

"Yes, I'm serious," Ted replied serenely.

With a reputation of being a godly man, a man who had walked with God for over 30 years, he seemed determined to live out what he believed philosophically. Like all of us, he believed that all physical events had no meaning except when they were defined spiritually. God had answered their prayers. He brought Karl home safely. That was really all that mattered. The intense emotions of losing the son you had raised and loved, whom you would never see again on this Earth, simply didn't matter.

During the subsequent weeks, I never saw Ted or his wife shed a tear. Perhaps they did in private or even in public, but I don't remember. Instead, as a courageous duo, they preached the morning service at our large evangelical church the following Sunday. They preached not out of brokenness and grief or even in memorial of their son's life, but out of victory and power, proving they had no need to grieve because of their "spiritual perspective" and, foremost, God was in control. It is my belief now, the couple, for whom I still have much compassion and respect, would not permit themselves to show any signs of sorrow. Grief itself, in their view, being worldly, a function of the physical brain's emotions and not a godly attitude. Without question, Ted and his wife loved their son dearly. How they were able to bury the pain so deeply within the cellars of their hearts amazes me to this day.

Only once, a year later, did I see an outpouring of the raw emotion that must have been pent up inside Ted for so long. I and several other campus student leaders were with Ted on an all-night prayer vigil in preparation for an evangelistic thrust in the dorms. We were deep in the woods at a now defunct Bible camp. About an hour into the session of conversational prayer, I heard a thump on the cabin's old pine floor next to me. I opened my eyes a crack to see Ted's 50-year-old, white-haired frame lying face down on the floor, quivering and sobbing. Suddenly the shocking words poured out of his mouth in a high-pitched, desperate cry: "Oh, God, why did you let my Karl die? Oh, God, he was my baby! Oh, God, why? Oh, God," he moaned, "I want my baby boy back! Please God! Please!"

Sadly, we were all in such a state of shock that not one of us said a word. Not one of us reached over and put a hand of compassion on his deserving shoulder, let alone gave him an urgently needed hug. We were overwhelmed with a sense of embarrassment, as if Ted was cursing God for having stubbed his toe on a dresser. But our embarrassment was relieved as Ted quickly composed himself. He sat back up in his chair, cleared his throat, and continued to pray in a much stronger voice, "God, I am so sorry for giving in to Satan's lies. Please forgive me. Please forgive me!" The next morning, none of us mentioned the incident, even though a deep discomposure could be read in everyone's expression.

I had felt so much grief and loss in my own heart for Karl when he died. As a pallbearer at his funeral, I came close to crying. The silver casket seemed to weigh far more than I expected with his fit 16-year-old body. As I carried him, I felt intense grief knowing my friend's dead body was only inches away. I would miss him terribly, and I had known him for only three years. But how could I cry if Karl's own father, my mentor, had never cried, instead he believed the events of that awful night were entwined with strings running up to the heavens and directly into the hands of God himself? To doubt or to grieve was to question God's spiritual meaning in what had happened, to question his control of it. And this kind of doubt was considered sin.

I recently had coffee in Madrid with Antonio, one of my old roommates from the DI training center. He is a dear friend, and we share a lot of common thoughts and ideas. However, he had a very different perspective on this event, seeing it as a tremendous example of Ted's deep faith. But faith in what? Faith in a presumed notion that God precisely controls all events from heaven and human grief is an act of doubt? This material world is real, with real consequences—some of which are horrible. Loss is tangible hurt and deserves a gut-wrenching mourning. This shows no disrespect for God ... but does show a contempt for grief. Because we are material humans living in this material space we only have two options. Feel the pain or pretend the pain isn't real ... even when it is. Because God dwells within reality, the more detachment we have to reality the more the face of God will be obscured.

I can't count the number of funerals in the Bible Belt, including my own father's, where at least one well-intentioned person didn't say something thoughtless to the bereaved like, "Now don't cry, honey, God did this for a reason." But the idea of seeing it as a simple tragic event, or chain of tragic events caused by circumstances, would be considered worldly and not to be pondered by any good Christian.

This evangelical perspective of dualism even viewed the physical Earth itself as worldly. Bible Belters at that time believed that the physical Earth— what some would call nature—had little value. This is not to say a good Christian couldn't admire the beauty of the sun setting in violet hues over the rolling Appalachians and give thanks to God the creator. But, at the same time, the Christian would believe this physical world was completely ruined by sin entering into the world and was destined to be destroyed by fire in the end. In other words, it was pretty much worthless.

As I've said earlier in this chapter, the problem with dualism is not the concept itself but the way it is applied—or misapplied. The mistakes often have to do with where and when dualism is applied. In the case of the low view of the Earth, the misapplication had to do with *when*. In some ways, there was a feeling that the physical world was created inferior at the start and then became totally wretched after sin entered it. Fortunately, this attitude is changing, but that change may be more of the influence of a pantheistic view of nature on our culture than on than Christians finally coming to their senses.

With this background, people in the Bible Belt didn't hesitate to dump their trash in the woods, sinkholes, or lakes. They also welcomed, with open arms, all sorts of heavily polluting industries. As long as the companies provided jobs, there wasn't much concern about what they were doing to the air and the water. God didn't care about the Earth, which he had abdicated and which became Satan's domain, so why should we? A common expression, when talking about damaging the environment, was, "Don't worry, it's all going to burn anyway," which was usually followed by a chuckle. This is the central reason that many evangelicals don't accept the scientific evidence of global warming. They either believe that God will override the cause and effect of carbon emissions or they frankly don't give a damn.

The early Puritans also saw nature along these dualistic lines. William Bradford, the early Puritan leader, spoke of the new world as "but a hideous and desolate wilderness, full of wild beasts and wild men," (Bradford 1736). The Puritan preacher and leader John Cotton referred to nature as "a wild field where all manner of unclean and wild beasts live and feed" (Ed. 1997).

DUALISM AND THE BODY

Like nature, to us the human body was also on the worldly side of the line of demarcation. People in early medieval history took this block to the extreme level—abusing their bodies for spiritual value through self-flagellation—and there are remnants of that thinking even today, especially in strongly Catholic areas of the world. Instead, at least we in the DI group felt we should be good stewards of our bodies and not abuse them as we did the planet.

José Rivera, the screenwriter for the movie *The Motorcycle Diaries* (FilmFour 2004), was describing his Catholic upbringing on National Public Radio's *Fresh Air* with host Terry Gross. He described coming home from preschool one day when his mother noticed blood on the soles of both his shoes. Alarmed, she had him remove his shoes to find that between his feet and the insoles were several soda bottle caps with the jagged edges cutting into his bloody socks. Shocked, she asked, "José, why are you doing this?" He explained that his grandmother, a devout Catholic, had instructed him to do it for a "mortification of the flesh." The thinking was that by punishing the evil flesh physically, sin would be less likely to take residence there.

Like many Christians, we believed all products of the body—including its desires—were worldly and directly "from the pit," as we used to say. In other words, the human flesh was Satan's domain. So all elementary pleasures or bodily functions—eating, drinking, enjoying visual art, going to the bathroom, sex, all emotions, and even back massages—were worldly. That was why, when I was a kid, we had to pretend we didn't have a bathroom when the pastor came for dinner. My parents would never have expressed it in such complex philosophical terms—the bathroom was simply considered dirty, and we had to keep it closed if the pastor was in the house. This same attitude was expressed two-and-a-half centuries earlier by the Puritan leader Cotton Mather:

> I was once emptying the *Cistern of Nature*, and making *Water* at the Wall. At the same Time, there came a *Dog*, who did so too, before me. Thought I; "What mean, and vile Things are the Children of Men, in this mortal State! How much do our *natural Necessities* abase us, and place us in some regard, on the same Level with the very *Dogs!*" (Mather 1681-1708).

When I first became interested in missions, I wanted to go to a mountainous, rural, and cool place. I couldn't tolerate heat. I disliked large crowds, and I loved mountains. Yet my DI friends made it clear that all personal desires and tastes were from Satan. I should consider only spiritual issues, such as where the greatest need was. This was how we ended up in the Middle East, a place in which I had no natural desire to live. I had even applied to be a missionary in Iceland and Nepal, places I deeply loved, until a Christian friend pointed out how selfish it was to want to do missionary work in places I desired for only "nonspiritual" reasons.

The biggest problem with the concept of the body being worldly was that the brain—as a physical organ—was considered worldly as well. The belief that reason was the antithesis of faith came directly from this line of thinking. Reason, emotions, and even mental health were not taken seriously, as they were considered functions of the physical brain. Faith and all mystical experiences were spiritual, functions of the soul, and thus respectable. So emotions were bad, however, spiritual experiences were good. But take the same emotions and dress them up in spiritual clothes—for example, turning feeling happy into being "moved by the spirit"—and they were suddenly elevated to the top of the spiritual value hierarchy.

Dualism and the Mind

The root of my interest in studying psychology in college had its origins in that time of turmoil in my early adolescence through high school period. I still wanted to know what made me tick and why I had failed at basketball. At the time, I had no insight into the nature of my problem, and I believed that by studying psychology I would figure it out.

Before I became interested in medicine, my plan was to become a Christian psychologist. What we called "secular psychology" was in the worldly domain because it dealt with thoughts, emotions, and the mental health of the brain. I wanted to work in a similar field but on the other side of the line of demarcation, the psychology of the soul or what was called Christian psychology.

But first, in order to earn a living, I had to major in secular psychology to get a degree that the state would acknowledge and then license me. I believed nothing that I studied, knowing it was written by non-Christians. And I was not alone. All my Christian friends in college considered their majors at our state school as being on the worldly side of the line of demarcation. Thus, unfortunately, I—and they—did not take history, English, math, or science seriously. We felt that studying anything except the Bible was a waste of time. Because of this, it now seems to me that all the students in our organization were academic underachievers. We truly believed that if we studied the Bible rather than our class materials, God would bless us by giving us A's. If we got C's or D's it had to have some spiritual meaning, God punishing us for lusting too much ... or God kindly redirecting our careers.

At the time, books were being written by Christians on psychology. Christian psychology—specifically the Biblical Counseling Movement—was a new field. I read all the Christian psychology books I could get my hands on for insights I could use in my future professional life.

The most popular Christian teachings in psychology looked at humans strictly from the spiritual angle. One school of thought I ascribed to was called *nouthetic counseling*. The term was coined by the Christian psychologist Jay Adams and means "confrontational counseling." Nouthetic counseling, based entirely on the Bible, is simple. Every so-called mental health problem is either demonic possession or personal sin, and the cure is confrontation and repentance. There are no shades of gray. We considered secular psychology as *humanistic*. The Institute for Nouthetic Studies gives this definition: *nouthetic counseling consists of lovingly confronting people out of deep concern in order to help them make those changes that God requires* (What is Nouthetic Counseling 1999).

I now believe that sin has three levels, which correspond quite well the three "persons" of personal pronouns. What I would call new, personal sin, parallels the pronouns "me" or "I," and it represents the failures for which I am personally culpable. The next state is the second person sin, responding to the second person of "you." This was sin that was done to us by other people and their sin left real consequences in our lives. Adults with lingering mental illness, as the result of childhood abuse, is a tragic and typical example of this kind of sin.

The last state is the third person sin, analogous to the pronouns "he, she, and they." This is the fallout of the sin of humanity as a whole or what we say in theological terms, "the Fall," or "the Fall of Adam." This is where sin entered into the world and caused systematic, but not comprehensive, ruin to all of nature. The aftermath of this sin is expressed mostly within the material, such as in physical suffering and death. It is also expressed in our genetic flaws, including congenital flaws of the brain, which result in wrong behaviors and thinking. Many of these errors in thinking would also fall beneath the label of mental illness. With third person sin, we all share in a collective responsibility, but the individual does not hold a personal blame. The only obligation the individual has in relationship to this sin is to spend his or her life struggling against it rather than just giving up. However, the onlooker has to be very careful not to assign fault in these second or third person sins. This second and third person sins are the most jumbled by dualistic types of thinking because the repercussions of such sins reside, for most part, in the material.

You can even make the argument that the spectrum of political ideologies is based on the understanding of these three levels of failures; however, they would call it "responsibilities." The Republican and even further right-wing thinking places the responsibility of actions all on the first person. The Democrats and more left or liberal thinking tends to place the center of responsibility on third-person. Evangelicals favor the Republican Party because of the consistency with their dualistic thinking, which they have inherited along with their faith. Spend some time thinking this through, and you will see that this is not an oversimplification.

Nouthetic counseling proponents refer to all sin as first-person sin. Thus, because the sin is one's personal act, confrontation makes sense. However, if the sin is second- or third-person sin (not easy to change and not your personal responsibility), confrontation seems cruel, if not moronic.

One Christian psychologist, in the 1970s, claimed that his team was emptying out psych wards in Philadelphia by marching through and confronting each patient. If they perceived that the patient was demon possessed, they would perform an exorcism. The person, according to them, would be instantly healed and discharged to a new, productive, mental illness-free life.

If these patients weren't possessed by demons, then their problem was the direct result of their personal (first-person) sin. The counselor would point out their failures, then get them to confess, ask for forgiveness, and repent. If they did so, they would be instantly healed from any emotional baggage and released. The catch was that those who continued to sin would continue to be mentally ill. With this mindset, there was an incredible motivation to bury one's problems deeply out of the sight of the confronter.

Our dualistic view of human psychology forced underground many—what at the time we considered unscrupulous—emotions. If you were seriously depressed, and you agreed with the nouthetic counselor that your depression was your fault, then you would pray for forgiveness and repent. If your depression continued, it would have to become subversive, moving into the cellar, as it were. You could no longer speak about it or show any signs of it. If you did, it would prove that you were still disobeying the loving God who created you. So you would keep it a secret as long as you could, until it really did improve or until they found your body and your suicide note.

The problem, as I've noted, was that the brain is a physical organ. Most Christians at the time accepted that the heart pumped blood through the body and the kidneys excreted waste water, but it was impossible for many to believe that the brain, also an organ, was involved with emotions, our personalities, and our mental health.

Having spent most of the past 35 years working in neurology, I've seen the overwhelming evidence of the brain's control over not only thinking and memory but also mood and personality. The 1991 movie *Regarding Henry* (Paramount Pictures 1991) dramatically portrays the effects of brain damage on personality. After being shot in a store robbery and loosing oxygen to this brain, Henry—a ruthless businessman—became a gentle, loving man. Henry's story was fictional, but in my office, I've seen hundreds of cases like him. Unfortunately, in most of my cases, mean people didn't turn into nice guys after a brain injury like with Henry; in fact, just the opposite. But when dualism's divide is placed squarely between the physical brain (and emotions) and the spiritual soul, then a good Christian, if that person were to live honestly and consistently with his or her beliefs, would have to disregard the whole field of mental health and most of neurology.

CHAPTER TEN

⸺◆⸺

The Shoulders

As an extension of the philosophical concept of dualism, there were shoulders on each side, strengthening and extending their presence deeper into the heart of American evangelicalism. These shoulders were the last two foundational blocks.

ESCHATOLOGY AND THE END OF EVERYTHING

The concept of the physical Earth being part of the worldly domain, as dualism would affirm, was tied closely to one's *eschatology* as well. This was the first of the two shoulders. Eschatology is the part of theology concerned with death, judgment, and the final destiny of the soul and of humankind. Specifically, the most popular eschatological view in American evangelism is the pre-tribulation, premillennial, dispensationalist view. These precise beliefs, which are based on abstruse scriptures in the books of Daniel and Revelations, are that all Christians would be raptured before the coming tribulations (pre-tribulation), but Christ would return to Earth before his thousand-year reign (premillennial) and that God has worked in different ways during several distinct periods of history (dispensationalism). Some Christians held that they would have to endure the tribulation and then be raptured (post-tribulation). The crucial belief of dispensationalism is that God gave up on Israel as his chosen people during one period of history but is planning on using them again to save the world and usher in Jesus' second coming—and that is happening very soon (imminent return of Christ).

How one thinks theologically has a profound consequence in human history. It is beyond this book to argue, but only to suggest that, if dispensationalism had not been so popular in the United States and the United Kingdom in the nineteen century, Israel would not be a nation today. To explore this topic further, I recommend Irvine H. Anderson's book, *Biblical Interpretation and Middle East Policy: The Promised Land, America, and Israel, 1917-2002* (Anderson 2005). It also begs the question for the dispensationalists after 1948 to point to Israel becoming a nation as proof that dispensationalism is true. I will point out, however, that none of these tenets of the new eschatological block had been part of Church beliefs before the Second Great Awakening.

The First Great Awakening held a profoundly different view of eschatology. The particular eschatology that developed after the Second Great Awakening, which permeates modern evangelicalism, is a relatively new development in Church history. It may have been a product of the despondency that arose from the American Civil War and the wars of the twentieth century. However, in American evangelical circles, if you even suggest that some of these things are not true, you are quickly branded as a liberal or heretic. This is despite the fact that you would be standing side by side with most Church scholars from the previous 1800 years.

Jonathan Edwards (1703–1758), the great preacher and theological thinker, is considered by most as the father of the First Great Awakening. Like most of his peers, he was a postmillennialist, believing that, rather than Christians being raptured out of this failing Earth, God would use the Church to overcome the evils of the world and restore it, then Christ would return and reign—here, not in heaven. But the brutal nineteenth- and twentieth-century wars removed this optimism.

The First and Second Great Awakenings held antithetical eschatological positions, and this change had enormous implications on how one was to live one's life here in the material world. The First Great Awakening did not place the divide of Christian dualism between the physical world and heaven as deeply and precisely as did the second because it taught that this physical world and its associated culture were still worth saving. Throughout its history, the Church has been most dualistic during periods of earthly troubles: plagues, wars, and political unrest.

During the First Great Awakening, the first major institutions of higher learning were built in America, now known as the Ivy League schools. At the time, evangelical Christians did not consider the brain and human culture to be on the worldly side of the line of demarcation, nor did they believe that human history would be ending within a few years. They believed they would have centuries to improve and restore the Earth to a place of peace and glory and then Christ would return (postmillennialism), so it made sense to invest in universities and culture. Many of the early Puritan fathers (and mothers) brought trunks full of books to the New World, as if they were treasure chests. These were not just Christian books, either, but most of the secular classics.

John Harvard (1607–1638) was one such man. Harvard didn't live long in the New World, but he donated his book collection and half of his estate to start a college for higher learning. He did this because he was a Christian, not in spite of it. A few years ago, my daughter Amy and I walked under the large cloth banner at Harvard University with their motto *VERITAS* across the top—Latin for "truth." I felt as if I was standing on hallowed ground. *This* should be the theme of all Christian endeavors—truth. An honest truth. Christianity now uses the word *truth* to mean their view on a particular theological or moral issue.

After the Second Great Awakening, on the other hand, many Christians believed Jesus was coming back within a couple of decades, and soon afterward the entire world, including the physical Earth, was going to be completely destroyed.

If you were going to build a new civilization on a distant planet, it would make a profound difference if you thought the planet would last thousands of years (as did Jonathan Edwards and John Harvard) or it was going to collide with a star or explode within a decade. In the latter situation, you would not bother to create libraries, institutions of higher learning, governments, art, music, or even a sustainable garden. You also would not spend 10 years building a house of worship with real stained glass, huge beams and stones, and precise workmanship of talented artisans. Instead, you would throw up imitation cement rocks with epoxy on pressboard backing and colored-plastic windows in a matter of a few weeks, which may last 50 years at best.

I am a physician assistant today, rather than a physician, as a direct result of my eschatology in the 1970s. After becoming interested in medicine, I had a discussion with Aaron about which direction my future should take. He pointed out that it would take seven more years to become a physician but only four more years, after college, to become a PA, so he suggested I take the shorter route. He doubted the world would still be around in eight years. I agreed with Aaron. My jeep bore a corny bumper sticker with the message that at any moment the jeep could become driverless as I became raptured. I don't regret being a PA. I've enjoyed the profession, but my point is that what you believe deeply impacts the practical choices that you make in your personal life, making these ideas far more than just a cold academic discussion.

These twin foundation blocks of dualism and eschatology were not only part of our little DI world; they were universal throughout Christendom of the twentieth century. Hal Lindsey's book *The Late Great Planet Earth* (Lindsey 1970), which promoted the three tenets of the end times—pre-tribulation, premillennialism, and imminent return—had an enormous impact on both American Christian and secular cultures. For the 1970s, *The New York Times* even called it "the no. 1 best-selling non-fiction bestseller of the decade." That book may have had important influences on Ronald Reagan's and George W. Bush's foreign policy approaches, at least when it came to issues in the Middle East. A serious argument could be made that if Lindsey had never published his book, there might never have been a Gulf War I, the terrorist attacks of September 11, 2001, or the subsequent wars of Iraq and Afghanistan. The indirect sequels to that book, the *Left Behind* series (Tim LaHaye 1995-2007), unfortunately each were bestsellers among a Christian audience.

INERRANCY OR MAGIC

Cemented on the other side of the dualism block is the *Bible inerrancy* block. Dualism does not influence the concept of inerrancy per se but the interpretation of it. If you divide the world into the important spiritual world and the unimportant evil physical world, then reading about Jesus eating breakfast has no value but his transfiguration has great meaning. You would also not engage your physical mind—reason, in other words—to understand scripture's meaning but only your spirit. But how, indeed, can the two be separated? And how is it possible to understand anything without using your mind?

Some examples of relying only on one's spirit to interpret scripture are the fundamental churches whose pastors are not required to have any formal training, only to have been "called by God." In their extreme form, these are the kinds of churches that involve snake handling in the Appalachians. I recently saw a television evangelist who was only a child of perhaps seven or eight years old. He was preaching on TV, imitating the long tradition of shouting with a lisp and pounding a black King James Bible, but his Bible was a little smaller of necessity. If one holds fast to the dualistic view, this would make perfect sense. The brain, including all knowledge and wisdom, has no significance. Everything must derive from the spiritual, and spiritual things can happen instantaneously to anybody at any age.

Within our DI group, the super-spiritual exegesis (interpretation) of scripture was the standard. Every day, God was giving us specific instructions, communicating through precise Bible verses with spiritual, even mystical interpretations—in other words, with an exegesis that had absolutely no relationship to the original intention of the verse. It didn't matter what Matthew, Luke, or Paul was trying to say within their historical context. It only mattered what God was saying to us—personally—on that particular morning and in that particular place. We used the words of the verse in the same way that an animist might glean mystical messages from a falling star or an albino buffalo. At that precise point, scripture stops being a book of knowledge and instruction and becomes a book of black magic.

One example of this use of scripture in the DI group was a rash of engagements that sprang up overnight. This was a group that held sexual purity as high as an ascetic monastery would. Most of us didn't date. There was no romantic connection between any of the men and any of the women. You could have crushes on girls from afar, but you dating or even obviously flirting with them would not be accepted. We believed solidly in the concept of the soul mate, which was one partner created specifically for us by God. Dating wasn't necessary and only caused problems. The men knew they couldn't even hold a girl's hand without some level of sexual arousal, so why bother. At least we were honest about that part.

The older group, made up of Aaron's peers, was just graduating from college and was certainly in a position to begin contemplating marriage. But the whole idea of engagement and marriage was an unexplored territory. No one had figured out how God was going to work out the process. Maybe a beautiful girl would simply approach and say, "I'm the one you're looking for."

Aaron, as the official DI leader, took the lead in this matter as well. He kissed a girl ... and he liked it. The famous kiss came after several nights of intensive counseling with a new convert in the ministry named Tanya. Puzzled and uncertain, she had asked Aaron for help because she was engaged to a fellow she didn't think was a strong Christian. Aaron had convinced her to break it off. Then, during one of her post-engagement counseling sessions with Aaron, somehow he kissed her—on the lips. I will never forget the night when he came home, floating on helium yet expressing it as a spiritual experience.

His roommates, including me, were skeptical about this development, which sounded a little flaky. But the next day, God supposedly gave Aaron a verse during his morning devotions. The verse was Exodus 23:5: "If you see the donkey of someone who hates you fallen down under its load, do not leave it there; be sure you help them with it." Aaron believed that God had given him a sign from that verse that if he didn't "fall down under his load" that day, in other words trip over something at work, God then wanted him to ask Tanya to marry him.

Later, the four of us—Aaron, Drew, our roommate John, and I—sat around the kitchen table, all of us looking confused except for Aaron, whose feet were 10 feet off the ground. Well, guess what? Aaron hadn't "fallen down under his load" that day, so he'd done the obvious thing—raced over to Tanya's immediately after work and asked (more likely told) her to marry him. He made it clear that God had spoken to him directly, and she needed to either obey God or not. That was a tremendous pressure for any new convert to deal with, a form of manipulation and mind control that we all used effortlessly. The great value to the individual of using this mystic message from God is that no one dares question it, and thus they have license to do anything they want under the auspices of God's doings. I've heard good psychologists say that the Church is a great hiding place for the mentally ill. They didn't say this because they saw the Church as being forgiving and accepting, it was because they saw church people as being naïve and easily manipulated.

Like many of us, I was skeptical of Aaron's engagement. Weeks later, I was riding in his hippie van with his fiancée. Since we were alone, I couldn't resist asking, "Tanya, how do you feel about marrying Aaron in a few weeks?"

She seemed a little more confused than I would have expected from a girl so close to her wedding. "Well, I'm still in a state of shock. I always thought I would be marrying someone very different from Aaron. Like someone better looking—and with a real job." Aaron was working for a painting company at the time, as he was looking for a teaching job.

Aaron's engagement was soon followed by the rapid engagements of three more couples, under similar circumstances. One engagement was broken off by the woman, who seemed to come to her senses at the last minute. The two other engagements led to marriages that have actually done remarkably well ... by God's great grace. Amazingly, Aaron and Tanya's marriage lasted for over 20 years, but it eventually ended. I have to admit that even my own marriage had some of this sense of divine calling, as Denise and I dated only once before we got married. We met in Oman, but then corresponded as friends a thousand miles apart for a year, until both of us felt God's calling to get married. God has been gracious us to us, too, despite, what some would call, an impetuous approach to tying the knot.

The foundation blocks I've described above were the basics of the American evangelical Christianity that I knew and specifically of the DI ministry with which I was involved. However, the dualism block had far more influence than the others. It penetrated the core of all that we believed and that many Christians have believed throughout the ages. It was an unnatural separation between the material world and the realm that is seen as spiritual. It continues to not only separate but to devalue the material to the point that nothing in this world has value unless it is connected with some event in the spiritual. This kind of dichotomy gives permission for all kinds of mischief, including the denial of behavior having clearly selfish motives and instead believing they have some higher, altruistic meaning. It is a blank check for total hypocrisy.

CHAPTER ELEVEN
Utopia?

The original *Back to the Future* movie (Amblin Entertainment 1985) is one of my favorites, partially because the bulk of it played out in the year I was born. I thought the storyline was brilliant. The writers, Robert Zemeckis and Bob Gale, were Oscar nominees for best writing and screenplay for that flick, and I thought they should have won. The story was about a boy who accidentally went back in time to the week his parents first met. His subtle interferences in their lives in 1955 would cause major consequences in his life 30 years later. The movie revolved around him contaminating the past and then trying desperately to fix what he had accidentally interfered with. Like this example, any kind of philosophical trend or small change in thinking can have a greatly magnified result over time. Take a subtle liberty with truth, and years later, unless corrected, you can end up miles off course. A dualist, at this juncture, would be tempted to push the mute button, turning away and claiming that none of this matters because God overrides history with his sovereign control. However, I will challenge that notion.

Despite the fact that some good things happened in our DI group in the 1970s, we were obviously making some serious mistakes. As I explained in the last chapter, dualism, and the way in which it was applied, was the universal culprit I had been seeking. This error—the misapplication of dualism—had only a small impact on our lives at the time. As the years turned into decades, however, the misconceptions were amplified, taking many us far off the intended path and taking me, at least, down a terrifying rabbit hole.

Yet, in some ways, my four years in college would turn out to be the greatest Christian experience of my life. The majority of DI students were sincere, which was a departure from my Baptist upbringing. Most of the DI people honestly wanted to please God and mature in their relationship with him. There was a sincere "cellar cleansing," as each person came out of the Bible Belt culture and into a more serious relationship with their faith. I've already mentioned how Drew wanted to clean up his act. I had many of my own serpents to excise and even more so, regrettably, would eventually have to slither into hiding.

In a more general way, some wonderful things happened on that campus and in our lives. For example, if a student's car broke down, and he or she had no money, suddenly and mysteriously an envelope of cash would appear under their door. The person giving that cash may have gone without food for several days to do that. This group honestly did care about one another in a way I had never seen before and, sadly, that I have rarely seen since. But these were the butterflies of Christianity's belfry, a real hope of a utopian society, yet built on a foundation where real serpents fester.

A REAL FATALISM

The first one to face hardships was Lenny. His difficulties emerged even while he was living in our Christian utopia. He would lie awake for hours in his dorm top bunk pondering how God, the puppeteer, had tiny strings running to every single hair of every head—indeed, to every atom in the universe. Local history, simple cause and effect—these were completely irrelevant in his paradigm. Yet, at the same time, he could not escape the material. He tried, with all his might, to believe that there were no real laws of physics, no coefficient of friction or Newton's laws, because these were not "spiritual." If you dropped your pencil, it might fall to the ground, but God might decide to pull it up to the sky the next time. God could pull the strings in one direction at one time and a different direction at another. All behavior, from that of subatomic particles to that of your grocer, was precisely controlled by God—or at least that was what we were straining or perhaps pretending to believe. If the behavior of the grocer was under God's sovereignty, so reasoned Lenny, then the thoughts inside his own head were likewise God-mandated and precisely controlled.

Lenny became confused about the Christian life—trying to mesh what he was learning in Bible study with what life itself had revealed. We criticized and labeled his obsession as "hyper-Calvinistic." But the truth was that Lenny, like the handful of other men in our group, was simply taking what most people within evangelicalism claim to believe to its logical conclusions: Christian fatalism.

Lenny was a good friend. He stood tall, well over six feet, with a soft smile beneath a Beatles' haircut and a Fu Manchu mustache. He spoke with a soft voice and possessed a gentle spirit. His future looked bright. He was to graduate the following spring with honors with a degree in environmental health, and he had just married his lovely, petite fiancée, Patricia, back home in Memphis.

In desperation, on a cold, rainy December night, Lenny intentionally leaped in front of a Norfolk & Western freight train and was crushed to death. The momentum of the massive locomotive could not be halted by the sudden application of its brakes on such short notice. The coefficient of friction of its iron wheels on the wet iron track couldn't save Lenny. He had clearly believed that the only definitive answers he could ever hope to find would be on the other side of the dualistic divide, in heaven itself. Maybe he saw the leap as the one attempt to break the strings or as an act of self-actualization. Looking back now, as a father, I know that Lenny was someone's precious son and not just my good friend. The errors in thinking we were making had huge ramifications. You couldn't think that this material world was worthless except for God's direct tinkering, without it influencing everything. Thinking of Lenny's parents and his wife Patricia, I asked God to have mercy on our confused souls.

BENEATH EDEN'S GREEN GARDEN

Years later, there were a few divorces in the group besides Aaron and Tanya's. This included the divorce of Andrew and Jen Anderson. As I was organizing a college reunion in 1999, the Andersons were the most difficult to find, and when I did find Andrew, he informed me that he and Jen had been divorced for a few years. In some ways I was dumbfounded, but in other ways it made a lot of sense.

Andrew and Jen were considered to have the perfect Christian marriage that we all should emulate. A few years older than Drew and me, they had been married for four years when they first showed up on campus as graduate students. As though in a verbal tennis match, they would constantly serve positive superlatives to each other along with a volley of smiles.

I can remember seeing them every Friday night at our fellowship meetings, which were held in the living room of an old Victorian home, just off campus. Jen, small, thin, and pretty, would play the guitar, and Andrew, tall with aviator sunglasses, would sing and lead us in hymns. He would pause, his perpetual huge smile strung across his face, point at his accompanist, and announce (as if everyone didn't already know who she was), "This is Jen, the most beautiful creature on this Earth, and she's mine!"

Jen would blush with her resonant smile and say, "And this is my husband, the greatest man on Earth! He's my hero. God gave him to me, and God is sooooo good!"

Andrew was always opening the door for Jen, giving her little hugs—not kisses, though, which could cause us single men to "stumble" (which meant we would wish we were the ones kissing Jen on the lips). He brought her flowers and cards, giving them to her in the front of the group. They were so much in love that it made me and several other men hastily sign up for their Bible study, "Preparing for Godly Marriage."

One day I joined Andrew for a ride in his red VW Beetle, the old style with a cloth sunroof that folded back like an accordion's bellows. Andrew cranked the sunroof open, and the fresh fragrance of autumn leaves filled the air. As we pulled out of the dorm parking lot, I noticed something odd: the front windshield had a new break in it. Pointing at the series of spider-web-like cracks, I asked Andrew, "How did that happen? It wasn't there last week."

He shrugged his shoulders and mumbled, "I don't know."

I didn't mean to be so persistent, but I was honestly puzzled. "Do you think you hit a bird?" He remained silent. "Did a rock hit your windshield? Maybe some non-Christian jerk saw your Christian fish sticker on your bumper and broke it on purpose while it was parked?"

Without warning, Andrew turned to me and screamed, "I hit it with my damn fist! Don't you get it? Jen made me so angry that I punched the damn windshield instead of her, with my fist. Now shut up!"

It was one of those brief moments when you have an unintentional glimpse into someone else's dark cellar—a glimpse you know they don't want you to have. So I just clammed up. I never brought it up again, nor did

I mention it to anyone. I hardly thought about it again, not until that day 25 years later when Andrew called me from his Iowa office. "I got your message, Mike. I can't make a reunion—nor can Jen. Actually, Jen and I are divorced, and the last I heard, she is living with a guy in Ohio."

After my rabbit hole experience, I went back and studied those college days carefully. In the midst of the utopia, I wondered what else could have gone so wrong. The answers didn't come easily at first, but after some spelunking—torch in hand—deep within the vaults of the foundation, they did finally come.

CHRISTIAN VALUATION

Only the artist can determine the value of his or her painting, whether it is worth showing or whether it should be painted over with something new. Sure, others can inflate the value of a painting, but that is more of a psychological matter. Famous artists fetch huge amounts for their work, regardless of its aesthetics. I'm sure if Jackson Pollock smeared his fingerprint over a piece of canvas it would have sold for tens of thousands of dollars, but Van Gogh would have just sneered and shook his head.

To exploit this point, the Italian artist Piero Manzoni canned his own feces in 90 30-gram tins and sold them as *Merda d'artista* (Artist's Shit) for the same price by weight as gold in 1960. The last time a can sold, in 2007, it went for $80,000. The point that he was trying to make, how fame values art rather than its intrinsic virtues, was well taken.

As I said in Chapter Five, the assignment of value to one's self is based on comparisons. On a deserted island, where there were no peers, it was likely difficult to feel worthless. Lonely? Definitely. Bored? Absolutely! But worthless? I'm not sure it is possible without others around with whom to compare ourselves and impress. My zeal to become pleasing to God was at the same level of intensity as my desire to be a basketball star and, oddly, for the same reasons, but within a different system of self-worth appraisal or mores.

With those things said, now imagine that the doctrine of sanctification within your Christian subculture is contaminated. What happens if your group really believes that when you accept Christ, you immediately start with a clean slate on the same level as everyone else? That there are no consequences from your years of sin, the sins of your parents (second person sin), or the sin of Adam (third person sin). That—*hocus-pocus-wham!*—it is all gone, wiped clean. Now you have the opportunity to mature, to move toward that elusive goal of perfection at the same rate as everyone else. Others in the group can measure your growth by the litmus test of the fruits of the spirit—how peaceful, kind, happy, and patient you appear, with *appear* being the operative word. In our group especially, how many people we helped to become Christians carried a lot of weight in determining our personal value.

I would speculate that 80 percent of our motivation for going out to try and convert other students to Christianity each week was to increase our sense of personal value. Just going out released some of the guilt, which was our constant companion. If you won someone over to Christ, it would give you the same elevation of self-value as scoring the winning basket in high school. Of course, we were also happy that the person had come into a personal relationship with God, but if we'd been able to be honest with ourselves, we would have had to admit that was probably only 20 percent of the motivation. I would have strongly denied this at the time, though, claiming our "pure" motives as being 100 percent. I expect if any of those people in our group were to read this book now, they will strongly disagree, but I stand by my point.

The influence of dualism on the concept of sanctification is to compartmentalize evil. We start to see the world where good is sequestered to one metaphysical place, and that is within Christendom, and everything outside is evil. It becomes a kind of us-versus-them, dark-versus-light situation between those inside and those outside Christendom. Many of the evangelicals that I was associated with believed that evil among Christians exists but is trifling when compared with the other side. They believed that sometimes new Christians make bad choices, but mature ones rarely do. They also believed in a finite process, flow chart, and series of exercises that can methodically remove the influence of evil over time—and it could be a relatively short time. If you work hard enough, in a few years you can go from being a sociopath or psychopath or drug abuser to a Christian to a mature Christian who rarely does anything wrong or who carries no psychological baggage. Some believed it can happen overnight, literally.

Thousands of people have experienced the idealism of Christian goodness in their youth. Then they experience disillusionment as they catch glimpses into the cellars of their spiritual idols. I suspect many of them left Christianity entirely or at least drifted into a strange place of ambiguity after this disappointment. This was a part of what was happening to me that night in the Chinese restaurant. I was experiencing a tremendous disenchantment, first related to Rod my hero, then of myself.

I kept tracing our theological troubles back to dualistic thinking as the common font from which all ills flowed. The time had now come to move to the next round of questions on the great spiral. How did dualism become such a powerful movement in Church history? History is the scaffolding on which culture is perched. Culture, in turn, is the milieu to every act of our lives. To know why we act, I had to understand the culture. To understand the culture that I was part of, I had to understand the history thereof.

CHAPTER TWELVE

The Great Bifurcation

The effects of dualism on my personal life ended in a bottomless pit. But, in some ways, this story of dualism begins with a tunnel, but a real one cut through almost 4000 feet of solid limestone beneath a mountain called Kastro.

It might be tempting for me to create a story about how dualism was started by one single individual, in one single place and time, and then passed on through the ages by some secret society or well-planned conspiracy to ruin Christianity. I could make the story as entertaining as any fictional story of malice and collusion because dualism's narrative is even more intriguing and enthralling. However, to create one lineage or secret society of dualism would be a gross oversimplification and distortion. Instead, I've chosen one of several possible starting points to tell the story accurately.

Thinking in dualistic terms is often a logical choice and thus has been around as long as humankind. Its origins are diverse. It wouldn't be surprising if young children placed on a deserted island instinctively thought in dualistic ways at times. They would simply perceive some things as good and others as bad. But, in Christianity, as I've stated, dualism itself was never the problem. The Bible is dualistic in places. Unlike some forms of pantheism, which view both good and evil as coming from the same divine source, true biblical Christianity divides between good and evil, light and darkness, and God and Satan. It is the misapplication of dualism that is the problem.

I will now start using the term *Dualism* with a capital *D* to label this particular form of Dualism that greatly (and negatively) influenced my personal faith and, I believe, the faith of many Christians throughout history. In its simplest definition, this Dualism divides reality along metaphysical lines: the physical visible world being lesser if not evil and the unseen spiritual realm being vastly more important and good.

CASTAWAYS

I'll begin my story about Dualism on an island, not a deserted island but a well-populated one called Samos. Samos is in the news today because it is one of the landing places for Syrian refugees coming out of Turkey, and it has been a staging place for cultures moving from the east to the west for millennia. On Samos, Mount Kastro is an important geological feature that is tied intimately with the development of Western thinking. It is an unimposing mountain that stands on the eastern edge of the small island in the eastern part of the Aegean Sea. This island is so far east that most good swimmers (and some of the refugees, from Syrian arid lands have not been) could swim across the Mycale Strait from the mainland of Asia Minor. The geographical good fortunes of this island made it a place of significance in the ancient Greek world.

The weather systems of the Mediterranean and Aegean Seas run northwest to southeast. Moisture picked up by the hot sun is only lightly deposited on the dry mainland of Greece and Turkey to the north and even less in arid North Africa to the south. However, the eastern parts of the Mediterranean, such as Lebanon and Israel, especially their highlands, get substantially more precipitation. Samos's easterly location increases its highly desired rainfall. The abrupt climb in elevation from sea level to its Kerketeus Mountain range, reaching over 4000 feet in height, quadruples the needed rain and supplies the lowlands with an abundance of wonderful springs. Even the name *Samos* is from an ancient Phoenician term meaning "a high place above the water." The lush greenness of Samos makes it stand out among the hundreds of dry, brown Greek islands. (I've flown over many of them, and from 30,000 feet they look like chocolate-chip cookies floating in dark purple grape juice.)

On the eastern side of the island, facing the coast of Asia Minor, is a natural, well-sheltered harbor. Around this harbor grew the fortified city that was also called Samos. The good fortune of having ideal weather, a position close to Athens and Asia Minor, a well-protected port, and fresh water gave Samos enormous wealth.

As this city-state grew in the seven centuries prior to Christ, it began to face a crisis. It did not have enough fresh water locally to support its growing population. A smaller mountain, Kastro, separated the flourishing port town from the plentiful springs that lay to the north in the valley between Mount Kastro and the higher Kerketeus range.

In 540 B.C., Polycrates, a ruthless dictator, came into sole power after murdering one of his brothers and sending another into exile. Samos continued to thrive under his power. He fortified the walls and created the greatest navy in the Mediterranean at the time. But his dwindling fresh water supply continued to frustrate him and limited what he could do with the city, whose population had risen to 20,000 souls. With this many people in such a small space, the city was vulnerable to outside armies if it did not have an endless source of potable water within the walls.

Samos had already attracted a group of mathematicians from around the Hellenic world, but these were abstract mathematicians. Polycrates "commissioned" (compelled, in other words) a group of them, led by Eupalinus, to apply their newly formulated principle of geometry to the real world by finding a way to get the water from the springs to the town. This was like a transition from pure mathematics to civil engineering.

The result was a remarkable water tunnel that cut through almost 4000 feet of solid bedrock. The tunnel started from each side of Mount Kastro and met exactly in the middle, missing a perfect alignment by a couple of inches. Even though the diggers had to navigate around weak veins in the rock at times, the two tunnels rendezvoused with a precision that would be extremely difficult to duplicate today, even with modern surveying equipment incorporating GPS and laser guides. It is still considered by some as the eighth wonder of the ancient world. This application of mathematical theory in a real-world situation was a leap that rivals Armstrong's step onto the moon.

One of Eupalinus's colleagues was Pythagoras (c.569–c.495 B.C.). Pythagoras is most noted as a mathematician, after which one of the principles of geometry—the Pythagorean theorem—gets its name. You might say that Pythagoras was struck by the fingerprint of God on the entire universe because he was captivated not only by the order he found in numbers and their application to the real world but also by music. One of his most famous quotations was, "There is geometry in the humming of the strings; there is music in the spacing of the spheres" (Aristole unknown). He saw the same order throughout nature. It was a supernatural kind of order, the type of order that would allow men, using math, hammers, and chisels, to dig a tunnel through a real mountain from two sides and meet precisely in the middle. This was the same kind of consistency that, two millennia later, allowed Einstein to discover the relationship between mass and energy and eventually nuclear energy—not by fiddling around with uranium in his garage but by mathematical equations, using a piece of chalk on a two-dimensional blackboard. This orderly process screams of a God who creates in an order that reflects his perfect nature. Pythagoras saw patterns everywhere he looked. Because no one else had noticed these patterns before, he may have either been a genius or, in my opinion, holding some of that special gift of seeing mathematical patterns, which some Savants possess.

Pythagoras, as a free thinker, didn't like the control of Polycrates. Twelve years before the start of the tunnel, he left the island, taking a ship westward to one of Samos's new colonies in what is now Italy. With its large navy, Samos had conquered much of the coastal Mediterranean area by this time, including the Italian Peninsula. In Italy, far away from Polycrates, Pythagoras had the freedom to create a school and to continue his thinking, observations, and lectures.

Mathematics isn't my strong point, although my sons Daniel and Ramsey are now working on their doctorates in mathematics-related fields and can put my head in a spin when they speak of mathematical theories. I have read a good deal of the writings of modern mathematical theorists, such as the string theory of the universe. It isn't a great leap to move from talking about numbers to talking about metaphysics and philosophy. Pythagoras did just that.

Pythagoras's philosophical background consisted of an immersion in Greek mythology. However, he soon realized that, within that framework, he could not find the answers of the order, which was bigger than the Greek gods.

As we continue to explore the roots of philosophical dualism, especially that brand of Dualism that had a powerful influence on the early Church, we must keep in mind that ancient Greece is known as the cradle of Western civilization. The Greeks recognized there is more to life than what is visible. They developed a complex polytheistic belief system. In that system, a group of humanlike gods ruled the heavens or spiritual world, beings with superpowers who were much closer to our modern concepts of superheroes than the Christian God. They fought among themselves like men and even had families, parents, and siblings. They were imperfect, made mistakes, and were deceived by one another, much like human behavior. However, to the Greeks they were more powerful than mere humans, yet it was never clear if they controlled fate ... or did fate really control them?

To compensate for the failings and impotence of their gods, the Greeks created more and more of them. Eventually they developed a system of 12 major gods and many lesser gods. The polytheistic system evolved into such a convoluted story that, by the time of Paul, the people of Athens even had altars prepared for still unknown gods (Acts 17:23).

It was obvious to the Greeks that the deities didn't live in the same realm as that of humans because they were never seen. This probably was the first hint of the need to have a dualistic universe, one seen and one unseen. The Greeks could see or visualize things they assumed were consequences of the gods' actions: lightning, thunder, erupting volcanoes, storms, rain, wind, chance, and even human behavior. These mystical gods interacted within this earthly realm but lived somewhere else.

The home of the more important gods was assumed to be upward. Older Greek mythology placed their original home on Mount Olympus, which was the highest point in their known world. If the Greeks had known about Mount Everest, they would have placed the homes of the major gods there. In the skies were stars, the sun, and other godlike celestial bodies as well as closer objects such as clouds. Mount Olympus was the nearest point to these celestial bodies, where heaven and Earth supposedly met.

Hades was a god who drew lots with two of his brother gods, Zeus and Poseidon, and lost. He was subsequently relegated to the underworld, down below the clouds but still out of the human realm. To be below the clouds but not visible led to the assumption that they lived below ground. Even early in Greek mythology, it was assumed that upward was better because Hades went to the underworld only because he lost.

As great as Pythagoras's colleague Eupalinus's tunnel was, the two ends still didn't meet with exact perfection—they were a couple of inches off. Therefore, Pythagoras reasoned, the domain of perfection must be in the heavens where tunnels always met with precision. As a mathematician, he

Thus the word *platonic* is common today in a generic sense, but its historical roots stem from Plato's philosophies over two millennia ago.

The problem, which would soon influence the emerging Church in the first century, was simply that the division between good and bad was defined along altitudinal lines. The Earth was only a poorly reflected image of the ideal or heavenly. As this idea leaked into early Christian thinking, it began to divide things, not along God's divisions, but along a Greek philosophical division between earthly and otherworldly or, using Christian terms, worldly (earthly) and spiritual (heavenly). While the Hellenistic concept of heaven is quite different from the biblical concept, the two became inextricably entwined over time in an unholy marriage.

Plato died 380 years prior to the birth of the Church. His influence was felt strongly throughout the learned Hellenistic world at the time of Christ. This Greek world would become the canvas on which the Church would eventually be painted. The apostle Paul surely studied Plato in his schools, as had many of the Greek converts at Pentecost. I think Paul knew of the dangers of mixing Greek philosophical thoughts with biblical concepts, and that's why he spent so much time warning the new churches not to participate in such devilry.

THE PERSIAN MYSTIC

Before moving on to the fascinating things I learned studying Church history, I'll look at one more point of the extra-biblical origins of Dualism. It concerns the experience of a Persian mystic with a funny name—Zoroaster. If Pythagoras and Plato formed the first source of Dualism, Zoroaster was a second, independent source. It was like two separate springs or watersheds leading to the same river.

Zoroaster (meaning old camel) was mystical in more ways than one. First, it is difficult to pin down when or where precisely, in Persia, he lived. One writing suggests he was alive up to 300 years prior to the conquest of Persia by Alexander the Great in 334 B.C. This would mean he lived just prior to Pythagoras, but several hundred miles to the east. However, his major writings, *Zend Avesta* (sacred writings) and the *Gathas* (later hymns) reflected a language that was in use c.1200 B.C. A few Greek sources claimed he lived as far back as 6000 B.C., but that doesn't make historical sense to the majority of scholars. Most authorities place his life in the seventh century B.C. and assumed he was using an old, traditional language (much like the Catholic Church writing in Latin up until a few decades ago), rather than the Persian language of the time.

Where he lived also was confusing. Certainly it was in the area we now know as Iran, but it is not clear whether it was in the northeast, near modern Tehran, or in the southeast, near what is now Balochistan, Pakistan. Tradition suggests it was in the arid southeastern desert where Zoroaster had his moment of epiphany. When he was in his 30s and experiencing a midlife crisis (the 30s were considered midlife or even late-life in 1000 B.C., that is, if you were lucky enough to have survived childhood), the story goes that he took off into the dry mountains in the proverbial search for the meaning of life. After an overnight vigil on the top of a rugged mountain, the sudden burst of the morning sun gave him the answer he was looking for. All reality was sharply divided between light and dark.

From that supposition he built his entire systematic theology of Dualism—the battle between good and evil, between this world and the next. Unlike biblical Christianity, he taught that the choice between good and evil was made at an early age. Once you choose your "camp" or kingdom, you stand counterpoised to the other side for all of eternity.

On a hot predawn morning in August, I boarded a plane in Dubai en route to Rawalpindi, Pakistan. The year was 1981, and I had just finished a summer working at a mission hospital on the Omani border. I had just met Denise for the first time … and had just said our first goodbye.

The plane was soon airborne over the Persian Gulf and, within a moment, over Persian land. I sat in my window seat with my eyes fixed on the black ground beneath me in great anticipation of the appearance of the morning sun. I was not disappointed. I witnessed the most incredible sunrise I've ever seen—and I have seen a lot of them.

It began with a thin red line forming in the east, beyond which stood an infinite lake of black, like nocturnal ink. Within a minute or two, a brilliant burst of light came from the center of the red line, catching the pinnacles of the rugged mountains sweeping out in all directions. It was as if the brightly glowing peaks were slowly emerging from the black lagoon. Once the blood-red disk of the sun was fully above the horizon, the mountains stood like a cluster of crimson islands whose steep edges dropped abruptly off into tar-black valleys with no visible floors. It was in this same place in southeast Iran that many believed Zoroaster caught his vision of a dualistic world divided equally between light and dark, with a hope that light would eventually win.

Some critics of biblical Christianity promote the scenario that Jewish, Islamic, and Christian faiths actually are evolutions of Zoroaster's premises (these teachings of Zoroaster are sometimes collectively called Zoroastrianism). This is not true. However, there seem to be many indications that Zoroaster's Dualism, along with Plato's, did infiltrate the early Church and all the way up to my little corner of the Bible Belt. But as strong as Zoroastrianism's influence was on the Church, I believe it had a far greater impact on the development of Islam. I think a reasonable argument could be made that, if Zoroaster had never been born, there would be no Islamic terrorism today. This is because Islamic fundamentalists see the world in only black or white. They place full value in the Zoroastrian idea of this physical world not being important at all compared with the heavens. This world is a mirage at best, so blowing up a group of innocent people, or even yourself, pales in comparison with the eternal realm. Indeed, if you were to take this form of Dualism to its sociological extreme, you would end up precisely with the quagmire seen in Iraq after the U.S. invasion, with the extreme violence of people like members of ISIL. Real, physical human life has absolutely no value in that group. It is nothing to pour gasoline on a five-year-old boy and light him on fire like a torch if you think it accomplishes something good in heaven. It is nothing to drive a truck loaded with explosives into a nursery school, destroying your own physical life as well as the lives of dozens of innocent children, if you think you are doing it to please God in the far-more-important spiritual realm.

Similarly, I will argue that there would be no vehicle or motive for Islamic terrorism today had Plato not had such a strong influence within the Christian Church. Platonic Christians also see world affairs in terms of light and dark kingdoms, and history is only important as it relates to eschatology. The abuses and injustices applied to people and groups like the Palestinians are often ignored by American evangelicals, sadly, because they can only view such issues within some heavenly eschatological context. In the Christian-Dualistic perspective, the Palestinians stop being human beings and become pawns in some great spiritual quest for the end times and the return of Jesus ... and the selling of books. This attitude has created an incredible bitterness toward American evangelicals by both Muslim and Christian Arabs.

As I followed the breadcrumbs from the ancients into our modern world, I began to see Dualism's profound influence on evangelicalism, far beyond eschatology. My wonderful days of study in Marquette were drawing to a close. As I moved forward, I knew that I would have to connect the remaining morsels to find how seemly isolated historical events set the course for American evangelicalism, including my own experience.

stuff is happening all around us! There're rumors the Clinton administration is secretly building prisons in every region for the coming internment of Christians." The others all nodded their heads in agreement.

Things have not changed much in the past 19 years since that meeting. Just two weeks ago I saw a post on Facebook by an evangelical friend stating that the Obama Administration, as part of Obamacare, is requiring the implantation of a tracking device in the back of the right hands of all who sign up for the benefits, without them knowing. It often appears that the evangelical culture has given up the search for honest truth in exchange for melodrama.

Do we not serve a God of truth and honesty? Isn't lying for Jesus still lying? I doubt if this elder was intentionally lying about the computer chips, but I believe some Christian somewhere was. This kind of sensationalistic lying is the bread and butter of many TV evangelists. These elders in Michigan were in error by not questioning the report. Now, with Facebook and Twitter, the spread of these types of evango-conspiracy theories is commonplace especially during election seasons.

It is difficult to criticize anything Christian without looking like a person without faith. My point is that the Church may actually be far more vulnerable to deception than secular institutions. I can't imagine any non-religious institution, be it a business or nonprofit, insisting that, if you don't do things in a certain way, you are disappointing God. They could accuse you of being an idiot, but that is would be the extent of it.

The Church is also vulnerable because of the teaching that it is a Christian principle not to judge someone else, even when they say or do things that raise eyebrows. It should not surprise anyone that extra-biblical ideas have been incorporated into Christian thinking from the beginning. Could the Church have grown up in such rich cultures as it did without absorbing some of those cultures' ideas? Scripture inerrancy aside, a study of the history of the early Church shows that such influences were major issues for them. Some cultural absorption is inescapable.

The job of the thoughtful Christian is to determine which surrounding cultural particulars are innocuous, having no harmful effects, and which ones distract from biblical truth. Because the fundamental belief of Christians is that humans are sinful by nature, the heart is deceitful (Jeremiah 17:9) and reason is imperfect, we should be the most skeptical people in our society ...

not the least skeptical. However, Christians often get distracted over the surface cultural features, such as music, language, bathroom use, but fail to understand the various philosophies that the Church has adopted, which are not Christian at all. The philosophies are far more destructive than the T-shirts, tattoos, or toilets, but they slip into the Church unnoticed. Our battles are truly not against flesh and blood, like a real war, but between ideas and philosophies. I will now move on to describe what I learned about those philosophies during my five years of study in Rochester ... with more clarity and with more practical implications.

CHAPTER FOURTEEN

---◆---

A Mystery of Cars

There are great differences between a Lamborghini and a Volvo. I spent $3500 on eBay for an old Volvo for my teenagers to drive a few years ago. It died one day with coolant mixed into the crankcase. It wasn't pretty. I would never have bought my teenagers a Lamborghini. My entire annual salary couldn't pay the insurance premiums for one teenager behind the wheel of a Lamborghini, let alone three. But beyond the simple cost of the car, I would always choose a Volvo over a Lamborghini for my kids. I would also choose an old Mercedes rather than a Ferrari.

So why would one of those cars be more appropriate than the other for my teenagers? The reason is intimately tied to the fascinating development of philosophical perspectives within Western culture as well as within the Church. I truly believe that if Aristotle had not existed, there would never have been a Volvo or a Mercedes because his philosophical premise, which I will explain later, was that logic was supreme. Volvos and Mercedes are built on logic, translating into reliability and safety. If Plato hadn't existed, there would never have been a Lamborghini or Ferrari. The philosophy of Plato evolved, as I will demonstrate, to place the emphasis of thinking (and eventually car building) on the emotions.

After moving to Rochester, Minnesota, I turned my attention from Church history to secular philosophy and its influence on the Church, trying to better my understanding to make more sense of things I had learned previously in Marquette. The Gnostic movement within the early Church was the major introduction of dualistic thinking among the early saints. I will also discuss this group in much more detail later. But what transpired, philosophically, within the Church between the arrival of the Gnostics and our modern world? Francis Schaeffer wrote extensively about the relationship between Dualism and the Church and between Dualism and Western civilization. In Rochester, I could sit among his peers and friends (not to mention his wife) and listen as if I were listening to the man himself. His most comprehensive writing can be found in his trilogy *The God Who Is There* (F. Schaeffer, The God Who Is There 1968), *He Is There and He Is Not Silent* (F. Schaeffer, He Is There and He Is ot Silent 1972), and *Escape from Reason* (F. Schaeffer, Escape from Reason 1968).

Two things strike me about Francis Schaeffer as an author. First, I am convinced, barring some other intervention by God, I wouldn't be a Christian today if it weren't for his writings and lectures. At the same time, his books aren't the easiest to read or understand. I had to read *Escape from Reason* three times before I understood his message. The book is an excellent saga following Western civilization's on-again, off-again love affair with Platonic Dualism. But rather than call it Dualism, Schaeffer points to an enormous divide between Nature (with a capital N) and Grace (with a capital G). Nature represents the material world, or cosmos, as Plato referred to it. Schaeffer calls the heavenly, spiritual aspect Grace, which corresponds to Plato's ether.

Plato also differentiated between man's physical self, *soma*, and spiritual self, *psyche*. But don't confuse Plato's notion of psyche with the modern concept of psyche. Plato's psyche eventually became the Christian concept of the soul—us without material substance.

By the fourth century, according to Schaeffer, Grace literally ate up Nature and became the predominant arena of life based on Plato's belief that the ether and psyche were superior to the physical realms of cosmos and soma. The Dark Ages were the first great cultural experiment with Platonic Dualism, and, in some ways, it was a catastrophe. Some modern evangelicals are attempting to rewrite all of human history, including the Dark Ages, with narratives that imply that this period was the actual zenith of human culture. They say this to contrast it with our present post-Christian society because in the Dark Ages, unlike today, they believe spiritual matters were paramount. This is a greatly oversimplified, and misleading, view.

I will admit that some previous descriptions of the Dark Ages, such as by the philosopher Voltaire, writing during the French Enlightenment, exaggerated the darkness of the Middle Ages because he had an axe to grind against the Church. Until recently, many Protestants had joined in that chorus because they, too, had an anti-Catholic bias. However, those who now attempt to dismiss the hardships and suppression of the arts and sciences of the Dark Ages, especially in the first half, really don't understand the realities of living in that age. Somewhere (depending on where you lived) between 30 to 50 percent of the people died before age five. The life expectancy in Europe averaged between 25 and 30 years old. Life as a common serf was extremely hard. While human creativity continued—and yes Geoffrey Chaucer did write his *Canterbury Tales* toward the end of this period—it was greatly inhibited by the culture of the time.

Schaeffer insightfully uses the evolution of art and music through the ages as surface markers of the underlying philosophical changes. During the Dark Ages, there were no serious drawings, paintings, or sculpture of anything physical such as landscapes or even a flower. Only "spiritual" content such as biblical stories had enough merit for a decent artist to spend his or her God-given talents on. But usually it was *his* talents because the Gnostics also believed that women, the bearers of babies, were earthlier and inferior to men. Landscapes are shown in paintings but only as inferior backdrops to a spiritualized foreground of biblical themes. The depiction of people, at least good people, was spiritualized by the characteristic halos of the period, represented by a circle of a slightly lighter hue than the background color. These important, spiritual people are always portrayed as larger than life—literally. They are disproportionately larger than other people, animals, structures, or even the landscape.

Several examples of the art of this period are the paintings on canvas or wood titled *Madonna and Child*. In the Metropolitan Museum of Art in New York City hangs the painting by that name by Berlinghiero (created c. 1230). Studying it, one can see that the Christ child depicted in that beautiful work is no child at all but actually a miniature man. This idealized child has no normal baby fat.

If the soul or psyche was otherworldly and the physical body and cosmos were material, even the value of real babies was in question. They didn't talk. They were totally dependent. They threw up, urinated, defecated on themselves, and were just, well, human. Moreover, they didn't have the value of independent children or young adults who could communicate. During the first millennium, many Greeks, including some Christians, didn't believe the soul descended into the physical, earthly body until the child was several years old. That was why it was not uncommon to toss one's baby in the woods if she were a girl when a boy was really wanted.

GNOSTIC PONDERINGS

Gnosticism was the door that Plato used to enter the Church. He, of course, died centuries before the Church was born, but the spirit of Plato was still in the Greek soil and needed a new home in which it could bloom and flourish. Gnosticism was an early Christian movement in which people believed they were spiritual beings, and their knowledge didn't come from learning but directly from God. I will examine the Gnostic history in more detail in a later chapter. Some Gnostic Christians held such a dualistic view that they didn't believe Christ, the son of God, could have entered human flesh until Jesus was at the temple as an adolescent. Gnosticism was little more than a palatable form of Dualism, at least in the Church's eyes.

Some Gnostics suggested it wasn't until Christ was baptized by John, or until the transfiguration, or even not until the cross that he became God. Some went to extremes believing that God would never stoop to enter a dirty, physical human body. To them, Jesus, the physical man, was a mirage or an ancient type of hologram.

On the other side of the coin, some Gnostics argued that indeed Christ lived in the flesh of Jesus, but, because he took on inferior, human flesh, he therefore couldn't truly be divine. To them, God dwelled in the superior heaven and thus could never descend and appear in this inferior, filthy, earthly world. The Gnostics also attempted to sharply divide the evil, seen world from the good, unseen world. Some (like Zoroaster) went so far as to assume that this seen world was created by either a lesser god or Satan himself.

The Church historian Robert M. Grant says of this period, "This kind of gnosis was in the air [the early Christians] breathed, and some of it entered their lungs." (Grant 1967). A little later, the second-century Church father Irenaeus said of the growing Gnostic influence, "The Gnostics were sprouting out of the ground like mushrooms." (*Against Heresies* by Christian bishop Irenaeus of Lyons c. 160 A.D.). At the time of Irenaeus, people had no knowledge of spores and assumed that mushrooms literally sprouted from nothing.

Gnostic beliefs infiltrating the Church were what led to the first Church-wide meeting and official statement in Nicaea, Greece (now Turkey), in 325 A.D. Constantine, the emperor of the city of Constantinople, set up that meeting to reach a consensus regarding theology and to resolve the cultural differences in church practice between the eastern Hellenic and the Western Latin cultures. Constantinople became the philosophical epicenter of this debate that carried on for one-and-a-half millennia.

In some ways, the Nicene Creed was an attempt to place an iron brace across the crack of Dualism, which was raising its ugly head immediately after the beginning of the Church, as described in the book of Acts. The Church came precariously close to adopting the extreme dualistic views of the Gnostics: Manichaeism, as taught by Mani of Persia (216–274) or Marcionism, taught by Marcion of Sinope (c. 85–160 A.D.), another dual-istic false prophet. The message of these early Church heretics spread like wildfire and almost consumed the entire Church during the first three cen-turies A.D. All those fires were kindled by one match: Dualism. If they had succeeded—and they would have had it not been for some wise early Church leaders—the Church today would look profoundly different, and the Dark Ages would have been far worse and, I believe, continued for much longer.

Just by reading the English translation of the Nicene Creed, you can see how the early Church fathers were attempting to address this primitive Gnostic problem—making it clear that Christ was truly a physical (soma) man but of the same substance as the divine God. In Platonic-Dualistic thinking, the invisible was the same as the spiritual and therefore more im-portant than the visible. The words in the brackets are words that appeared in some, but not all, translations.

> We believe in one God, the Father Almighty, maker of heaven and earth, and of all things visible and invisible.
>
> And in one Lord Jesus Christ, the only begotten Son of God, begotten of the Father before all worlds [God of God], Light of Light, very God of very God, begotten, not made, being of one substance [essence] with the Father; by whom all things were made; who for us men, and for our

salvation, came down from heaven, and was incarnate by the Holy Ghost of the Virgin Mary, and was made man; he was crucified for us under Pontius Pilate, and suffered, and was buried, and the third day he rose again, according to the Scriptures, and ascended into heaven, and sitteth on the right hand of the Father, from thence he shall come again, with glory, to judge the quick and the dead; whose kingdom shall have no end.

And [we believe] in the Holy Ghost, the Lord and Giver of Life, who proceedeth from the Father [and the Son], who with the Father and the Son together is worshiped and glorified, who spake by the prophets. In one holy catholic and apostolic Church; we acknowledge one baptism for the remission of sins; we look for the resurrection of the dead, and the life of the world to come. Amen. (Wording from First Council of Constantinople, 381 A.D.)

The meeting in Nicaea did not completely suppress the debate about Gnosticism, which continued through a sequence of seven councils. This first meeting, while not settling the issue, did clarify the main doctrines of the Godhead, which Dualism was attempting to erode. At the Fourth Ecumenical Council, the next generation of Church leaders met to discuss this same problem and issue the second statement of the Church, known as the Chalcedonian Creed of 451 A.D. It, too, was an attempt to bridge the Dualistic chasm with reinforcement iron before Dualism tore the Godhead apart.

The true Christian Godhead straddles, without conflict, the Platonic-Dualistic divide, with the good God dwelling in the ether on one side, and his divine son dwelling in the inferior, dirty, human flesh—soma—that lived in the earthly, dirty cosmos. The point is that, were it not for the Hellenistic-Platonic influences, this tension would never have existed in the first place. In the truly biblical view, a seamless continuation exists between the ether and cosmos, the material and the so-called spiritual. To support this point of a secular origin to this point of tension, I will use the Platonic term *ether* interchangeably with Christianized terms such as *heaven* or *spiritual*.

DON'T BE TAKEN CAPTIVE

The verse I allude to several times in this book, Colossians 2:8, warns the early Church not to be taken captive by philosophies of the surrounding culture. This passage is often misunderstood and used to support the notion that we should not study philosophy at all. But pure philosophy is simply the love of wisdom or knowledge (*philo* = love; *sophia* = wisdom, knowledge). This is an honorable goal, to which Solomon aspired and God approved and blessed.

The part about being taken captive is where we apply a secular philosophy and, almost without knowing it, set it up as the grid on which we must fit our Christian theology. The original Greek word for "take captive" in this context is συλαγωγέω (pronounced *sulagogeo*), used when one empire captures and loots a city-state, carries many off into slavery, and forces those left behind to submit to the empire's religion or philosophy. The people of the age knew this scenario far too well. So the warning isn't to avoid all philosophies that aren't purely biblical (which would be almost impossible to do) but not to allow these nonbiblical philosophies into your world and dictate the framework of your thinking.

Dualistic thinking was a problem in that it did not come from a biblical source, and it conquered and dictated the Christian way of thinking. Early Church fathers were concerned and attempted to stake out the boundaries. As you read this English translation of the Chalcedonian Creed, notice the tension between the physical and the spiritual. This tension dominated all serious discussions of theology for a thousand years. The words in the brackets are words that appeared in some, but not all, translations.

> We, then, following the holy Fathers, all with one consent, teach men to confess one and the same Son, our Lord Jesus Christ, the same perfect in Godhead and also perfect in manhood; truly God and truly man, of a reasonable [rational] soul and body; consubstantial [co-essential] with the Father according to the Godhead, and consubstantial with us according to the Manhood; in all things like unto us, without sin; begotten before all ages of the Father according to the Godhead, and in these latter days, for us and for our salvation, born of the Virgin Mary, the Mother of God, according

to the Manhood; one and the same Christ, Son, Lord, only begotten, to be acknowledged in two natures, inconfusedly, unchangeably, indivisibly, inseparably; the distinction of natures being by no means taken away by the union, but rather the property of each nature being preserved, and concurring in one Person and one Subsistence, not parted or divided into two persons, but one and the same Son, and only begotten, God the Word, the Lord Jesus Christ; as the prophets from the beginning [have declared] concerning him, and the Lord Jesus Christ himself has taught us, and the Creed of the holy Fathers has handed down to us.

Before I understood Dualism and its struggle to penetrate the early Church, these creeds appeared to me as ancient gobbledygook. Now they make perfect sense. In many ways, these intuitive and proactive early fathers succeeded in squelching the power of Platonic Dualism in the formation of the Church. However, while the lion was stopped at the front doors of the Church and put in its crypt, Dualism, like termites, crept in and insidiously ate away at the Church's foundation.

Throughout the Middle Ages, the spiritual realm was confined to the institutional Church and clergy, as well as to the King, whose position was considered to be divinely appointed. But this grouping of power made up only a small percentage of the population of the period.

THE KEYS ARE KEY

The Christian Dualism of the Dark Ages created the ultimate environment for extreme spiritual manipulation. If the physical world—such as reason, your own body, and everything you did, including your occupation—was of an inferior or even evil realm, and the Church held the keys to heaven, the important realm, the Church had immense control over you. When the Church actually sold for money the temporal removal of punishment for the sins of yourself or a family member (process referred to as selling *indulgences*), it was only one symptom of this awful disease. The Church and its leadership and institutions became hideously corrupt. It was Platonic Dualism that made such an unscrupulous Church possible, and its leaders thus had no intentions or motivation of shedding Dualism's influence as they had a vested interest in it.

Imagine that the entire known world was confined to a small island surrounded by a salty sea, something like the island of Samos. On this island was only one small freshwater spring. Rather than building a wondrous tunnel through the mountain to bring water to everyone, one small group—for example, the blacksmiths' guild—controlled the spring. The blacksmiths built an iron cage around the spring with a large padlock securing it, and a group of blacksmith-appointed sentries patrolled the cage. Now the blacksmiths' guild controlled the lives of everyone on the island—whether people lived or died—and in time became rich and held every position of power. If you wanted water, it had to be paid for—in money, obedience, support, passion, and devotion.

If the only thing in your world that was important was the spiritual, and the Church held the keys to the spiritual world, you would be at its mercy. To secure its claim to power, the Church taught that you, as an individual, had no direct access to the spiritual realm. This is analogous to building an iron cage around the spring with one door and one key—the key only those in power held. The Church would then control your wealth, your obedience, and your loyalty. This is exactly what happened.

There were a few dissenting voices through those dark centuries, but they were quickly snuffed out. It wasn't until the overall social and cultural climate of Europe had changed that Martin Luther and others were able to break that stranglehold.

I must state at this juncture that, of course, even the Medieval Church had some positive influences on Western civilization. This can be expressed as at times seeking justice when there was none, charity, caring for those who society had rejected, and the commissioning and preserving the arts. I have already spoken about the key role that Church leaders played in the milestone Church councils that met throughout the ages. The list could go on and on, but those good things have been promoted and written about extensively in other places and is not the purpose of this book.

The story of the Medieval Church takes us up to the threshold of the Renaissance. While the Church has faced many Dualistic threats to its foundation, the Renaissance will take a sudden turn in events and put Western civilization on a new—while maybe no better—path.

CHAPTER FIFTEEN

House of Medici: The Midwives of the Renaissance

The Renaissance that started 200 years before Luther was simply a swing in the balance of the dualistic worlds. For the first time in about 500 years, this physical Earth, knowledge, science, art, and simple humans had significance again, being pulled out of the dualistic sewer, piece by piece.

It would be nice to say this swing was prompted by Church leaders who had come to their senses, finally realizing they had been hoodwinked by Plato's ideas and that this earthly dominion was, indeed, important. Once they realized Greek culture was determining the expression and shape of Christendom, rather than biblical truth, they repented. But that is not the way it happened; instead of being caused by the remorse and turnaround of the Church, the Renaissance, like Platonism itself, had its roots outside the Church.

Although Luther and the Reformation would benefit from the change in philosophical tone, the extra-biblical source of the Renaissance would have extreme consequences during the second half of the second millennium. The pendulum would not simply pause in a state of biblical balance at the midpoint but continue in the other extreme—leading to the modern and ultimately the postmodern and the post-postmodern world in which we now live.

The Renaissance movement was widespread, with the Medici family of Florence, Italy, at its epicenter. The Medicis were first mentioned in recorded history in 1230 A.D. The origin of the family name is not known, but *medici* means "medical doctor." Their early ancestors came from the region to the north of Florence, and they made their first money trading Italian dyed wool with France and Spain. Eventually they became powerful, even controlling the regional wool board. In 1400, they were so influential that the city council of Florence, afraid of their power, banned all branches of the Medici family but two from Florentine politics for 20 years. At that time in history, the city of Florence functioned much more autonomously than modern cities, like a small country, so being banned from the politics of the most powerful city of the area was of great significance. One of the brothers, Averardo de' Medici, had conditional permission: if he gave up his involvement with the wool industry, he would be permitted to participate in politics.

Averardo clearly felt the access to power was worth it, but he would have to find a new means to wealth. He began to dabble in banking, but it was his son, Giovanni di Bicci de' Medici, who really started to make money in the new business. Giovanni's son Cosimo di Giovanni de' Medici (1389–1464) would eventually become the "godfather" of the entire Medici empire. Even though his ancestors had been banned from Florentine politics, he eventually became the city "boss" (but with no official title) in 1434. Soon, poor Cosimo was faced with a real moral dilemma. Personal wealth had been frowned upon by the Medieval Church, and the loaning of money for interest was strictly forbidden. Because banking was his livelihood, he began to actively seek a moral and philosophical center outside the traditional Church.

Cosimo was not the first Italian to embrace the old Greek philosophers for this new basis for life. Because the medieval culture was failing, the climate was ripe for change in Europe. Also, the writings of the Greeks were becoming increasingly popular in the same way that Hare Krishna became trendy among artists and musicians during the 1960s.

During its first millennium, the Roman Catholic Church had ignored or even destroyed the original writings of the Greek philosophers. However, the eastern branch of the Church (in Constantinople and Alexandria) held on to many of these original Greek manuscripts, as did the encroaching Islamists. The Fourth Crusade (1202–1204), while commissioned by Pope Innocent III to reclaim the city of Jerusalem from the Turks, turned its war machine on its Greek brothers instead—for the smell of gold. In a complicated story, Venetians were contracted to build the Crusade's ships for a large sum of money, based on the expected number of crusaders to man the ships. However, the brave knights of landlocked France and Germany didn't like water. A significant number of them bypassed Venice and hightailed it as far south on the Italian Peninsula as they could. This left a much smaller number encamped outside of Venice, a number too small to pay for the ships as the Church was paying the Venetians for each passenger. Once they departed the lagoon, their Venetian creditors, who demanded immediate payment from the cash poor crusaders, pushed them to first sack a Catholic city, Zara, for riches and then the Orthodox city of Constantinople. The beautiful Byzantine city was almost completely destroyed and looted. Many of the treasures were carried off to Italy, including the old Greek manuscripts. This vicious attack weakened Constantinople, making it even more vulnerable to the Turks, and the Fourth Crusade was considered a total disaster for the Church, when compared with its original purpose.

The turning point came in 1439, when Cosimo Medici was one of the forces behind moving the great Ecumenical Council (*Ecumenical* meant it included both the Roman Catholic and the Eastern Orthodox Churches) that started in 1431, to Florence. This meeting would eventually last another six years. One hopes they had lots of coffee.

History is interwoven in ways to which this book cannot begin to do justice, and I am only writing a brief summary of what I learned during my days in Rochester, Minnesota, and since, including a week of study in Florence in 2009, and a week of study in Istanbul (Constantinople) in 2014. This Florentine Council was deeply tied to the atrocities of the Fourth Crusade in several ways, including the now weakened city of Constantinople being in dire straits—an island in the middle of Muslim culture, a Christian city almost surrounded by a sea of Turkish turbans as far as the eye could see. The only hope the city could muster, ironically, was to turn to the very people, the Catholics in the east, which almost destroyed it during the previous crusade.

This council was attended by John VIII Palaiologos, the emperor of Constantinople, who had the pragmatic ambition of forming an alliance with the Western Church. That culture had the steel (armor, swords, and arrowheads) as well as the ships to save them. The pope, with an opportunistic glimmer in his eye, wanted to bring the eastern part of the Mediterranean back under his control, doubling his "kingdom" with a stroke of a quill.

The important assembly opened in Basel, Switzerland, but moved south of the Alps to Ferrara, Italy, on January 8, 1438. The bubonic plague, which ironically first entered Europe via rats on Asian ships landing in Constantinople, had spread to the ports of Messenia and Genoa. As the dreadful disease moved across northern Italy toward Ferrara, Cosimo agreed to finance the council if it moved to Florence in January of 1439. Bringing such an important meeting to Florence was a real coup, akin to a modern city being selected to host the Olympic Games.

The hopeful agenda of the meeting was to lay the foundations for a possible reunification of the two Churches. The split had come over the Nicene Creed—the Eastern Greek Church, being even more favorable to Platonic thinking, did not like the term *filioque*, meaning "from the Son," because it pertained to the Holy Spirit coming from both the Father and the Son. To the Eastern Church, Jesus, being of the flesh of this inferior material world, still could not be fully reconciled with God in the spiritual. They came close to reaching their reunification goal with the holdout of only one Orthodox bishop, Mark of Ephesus.

If it were not for the formidable walls built in the fifth century by Theodosius II, Constantinople would already have been overrun by Islamists. While Emperor John VIII Palaiologos was eager to make compromises for the sake of his city, many of the Orthodox clergy, in their theological idealism, would turn out not to be as ready to make concessions. The clergy members' great courage and confidence came from their eschatological viewpoint. They were postmillennial, believing that their city and empire was the millennial Christian kingdom that would last on Earth until Christ came back, assuring their eternal rule. From their viewpoint, they had nothing to fear because Constantinople could not fall—or could it?

But despite the confidence of the Greek clergy, Pope Eugenius IV saw an opportunity to take advantage of the precarious standing of Constantinople to double the size of his spiritual kingdom through unification. The Greek emperor shared the same goal as the Pope but for totally different reasons. John VIII Palaiologos wasn't zealous for spiritual reconciliation but yearned for the armored swordsmen of Germany, the archers of England, and the armadas of the powerful city-states of Genoa and Venice, or otherwise his great city would surely fall.

CRAZY OLD GEMISTOS

One of the scholars who came to represent the Eastern Orthodox was Gemistos. He had recently changed his name to Gemistos Plethon in honor of Plato (*Plethon* is spelled almost the same as *Plato* in Greek). Gemistos was an 84-year-old Greek Orthodox scholar who had devoted his entire life to studying Plato and Islamic/Zoroastrian teachings. He was invited because he had already crafted many contracts and laws for the Byzantine Empire and Orthodox Church, as a scholar of law. Just before his death, he even went so far as to leave the Church completely and attempted to create a new mystic religion combining Platonism, Zoroastrianism, and Christianity.

During the Florentine Council, Cosimo didn't sit through all the formal, stuffy theological discussions as he had intended (he probably had little personal interest in them in any case). Once he met Gemistos, he became obsessed with the gray-haired, flamboyant old teacher in the same way the Beatles had become enthralled with Maharishi Mahesh Yogi. The two men spent many long hours over drinks and rich food served in Cosimo's palace Villa Medici at Careggi.

By the time the Florentine part of the council was over six years later, Cosimo seemed to have found the answers he was looking for—a philosophical center outside the established Church. But, at first he wasn't sure whether Plato or possibly Aristotle would be his new prophet. He knew Gemistos favored Plato, so he commissioned him to write a summary paper on the difference between the two great Greek philosophers and to explain why he favored the teachings of Plato.

In his paper, Gemistos made a clear argument that Plato's thoughts were far superior to the Aristotelian premise that reason was the highest of human virtues. Platonic thinking seemed more compatible with Christian thought, according to Gemistos. However, they didn't fully realize that Platonic ideas seemed more attractive to the medieval Christian because the Medieval Church had already been greatly influenced by Platonic thought for 1400 years. It was simply Narcissus seeing his own reflection and taking a rather fond liking to it.

THE RISE OF THE MEDICIS

Toward the end of the thirteenth century the Medicis began to gain wealth through banking and trade; however, they didn't reach their zenith until the fifteenth century, at which point Cosimo began feeling morally unhindered. They were able to become rich through these avenues because banking, using interest, was essentially forbidden by the Church, and no one else was doing it, at least not in a big way. A few Jews were involved in banking, as they were exempt from the Church's restraints.

The Church forbade loaning money for interest based on such scripture as Exodus 22:25: "If you lend money to one of my people among you who is needy, do not treat it like a business deal; charge no interest." The genius of the Medici family was in creating a complex system for essentially loaning money for a profit. They did this by exchanging currency at one rate with a written guarantee to exchange the money back to the original currency at a later date at a set rate. In practical terms, this meant traders from north of the Alps could come to Italy and exchange their currency for florins to buy Italian goods with a guarantee to buy back their currency later but at a cost. This served the same purpose as loaning money for interest.

When the Medicis' coffers began to fill, the jingle of the coins caught the ear of the Church in Rome itself. Oddly, the Church eventually conspired with the Medicis to become their principal business partner, and the Catholic Church has been deeply entangled in the business of banking until this day. This system resulted in the Medicis becoming not only the richest and most powerful family in Italy, but in Europe as well. By some measures, they may have been the richest family that ever lived. This family, through their great financial influence, eventually produced four popes and two queens of France.

Back in Constantinople, the Greek emperor's new theological alliance with the Western Church fell on deaf ears as the Greek-leaning Church found it unpalatable for the same reason as before—that dirty flesh cannot contain the God of the immaterial and the Catholic Jesus was just that. There were plenty of psychological and social reasons as well. After all, it was the Catholic Church that had sponsored the Crusade, which destroyed Constantinople in 1204 and engendered a hatred for the Western Church that, subsequently, only intensified in the cobblestone streets of the Byzantine capital. This theological and personal inflexibility sealed the doom of Constantinople as well as of the Roman Empire. On May 29, 1453, the city fell to Mehmed II, and the ancient Sophia church, on that day, became a de facto (and later a genuine) mosque. I stood in Sophia in March 2014, and I felt, emotionally, the death cry of an entire culture echoing in the silent 182-foot-tall dome of brick. To help point out how history is connected, this fall led to a major disruption in the Silk Road, which had one terminus in the Christian-friendly city. Therefore, an Italian businessman and explorer, Christopher Columbus, began to look for a new route to trade with the Far East, and, just 39 years later, he thought he had found it when he came ashore in The Bahamas.

As in many areas of Europe at the time, loyalty was not cleanly divided between political entities but rather between large family groups. As the Roman Empire dissolved, the city-states, like Florence, became micro-kingdoms it its place. These city-states were dominated by the rich and wealthy clans in what resembled a Mafia style of law and order. If your family was gaining power, you might put out a hit on the controlling family, as the Pazzi brothers did on the Medicis. The absolute power of the Medici family ebbed and flowed with enough murders, mistresses, plots, and pretense to fill several fascinating HBO series.

As the Byzantine Empire was collapsing, the churchmen of the east began sending precious ancient manuscripts and artifacts (those that had not been looted either by the crusaders or the Muslims) westward out of harm's way toward Rome—with Cosimo's help. He was elated with each new text that arrived.

These manuscripts, which had previously been banned on the Italian Peninsula during the early phases of Christianity's rise, ended up back in Italy, including the complete works of Greek philosophers. Some of them came from remote Orthodox Christian monasteries, where they had been spared from the destruction of fires kindled by Church candles in a previous generation. Others came directly from the Muslims, taken by force during the dynamic give and take between Christendom and Islam. But many came as a result of peaceful interaction and the exchange of ideas between Christian and Muslim scholars. While historical works were being neglected in the Platonic-Christian world, farther east in the Islamic world, they thrived. Many great Greek writings were translated and preserved in their Arabic form.

THE SCHOOL OF ATHENS

Aristotle was a star student of Plato, just as Plato had been Socrates' star student. Plato and Aristotle had similar viewpoints. They were good friends, spending countless hours together, and a deep love and admiration existed between them. Many Athenians, including Plato himself, anticipated that Aristotle would be his successor at the helm of the Academy, which was the major school of philosophy of the known Western world, in Athens. By the time Plato died in 347 B.C., however, his views and those of Aristotle had bifurcated to the point that the school's elders elected Plato's nephew, Speusippus, as Plato's successor instead of Aristotle. So their differences were real and serious, yet not antithetical. But the elders of the Academy knew, just as Marty learned in the movie *Back to the Future*, that one subtle difference could lead to a huge variation in the decades or centuries ahead.

Plato illustrates his metaphysical view of reality best in his allegory of the cave, which appears in his book *Republic*. In this allegory, life on Earth is like being a prisoner inside a deep cave. True reality is the world outside the cave. We can't see that reality directly, and never have, because we are chained down in a position where we can only see the back of the cave. Shadows from the true reality outside are being cast on the rear wall of the cave and that is all we can see. So in simple terms this material world is a dim silhouette of the actual.

Many Christians have equated Plato's cave allegory to Paul's statement in 1 Corinthians 13:12. There Paul writes that we only see things dimly now, like looking in a bad (the type they had during Paul's lifetime such as polished bronze or copper plates) mirror, but some day we will see things face to face. Those are fundamentally different concepts. In the cave allegory, Plato suggests that this material world is only a shadow without real substance, not the same as true reality, which resides in the heavens or ether. But Paul is saying that, in this material world, we see true reality but not as clearly as we will one day. A similar difference might be between seeing a mirage (not real) and seeing a real oasis but through dirty glasses. In the former, Platonic view, this material world is of no significance except as a kind of projection screen onto which the shadows of the true reality can be cast. In Paul's view, this material world is of enormous significance, as it was created real by God, outside of himself. The problem isn't a metaphysical problem, about the material having substance, but a problem of perception by us humans, whose senses have been dulled by the Fall of Adam.

Aristotle continued with the more traditional view that reason itself was complete in this material world. He believed one can reason perfectly with the mind (what we now know as the brain), collecting information through our senses, and, if this empirical reason is followed to its ultimate end, society would be taken into a utopian world. Plato envisioned the philosopher-king, or an idealistic society in which the most brilliant people would control and lead. Aristotle criticized this idea because he believed that, in reality, such a king would be impossible to find. But he modified this idea to a king that has a panel of philosophers to advise him. However, the Platonic concept of philosopher-king is often attributed to Aristotle. From this concept comes the term *aristocrats*, referring to the ruling elite who were in control in France just prior to its revolution. While Aristotle himself thought of the elite as the smartest, over time the term began to mean the wealthiest members of society. This evolution occurred because at one time it was assumed that the smartest, most educated people were also the wealthiest. Just as Italy became obsessed with the teachings of Plato, France would soon become obsessed with those of Aristotle.

After his split with Plato, Aristotle didn't drift off into anonymity but eventually married the niece of a king and moved northeast to what is now the coast of Turkey. Then, with the threat of a Persian invasion, he moved back west to Macedonia. There, he was fortunate enough to meet a local leader named Philip who asked him to tutor his little boy, Alexander. This little boy grew up and conquered the entire known world by the time he died at age 33. Alexander, by then known as Alexander the Great, remained faithful to his tutor until the end, spreading Aristotle's philosophical views along with Greek culture.

The painting by Raphael (Raffaello Sanzio da Urbino; 1483–1520) titled *The School of Athens (Scuola di Atene)* in the Vatican's Room of the Signatura, a papal library, depicts this difference between Plato and Aristotle in a highly graphic way. In the painting, which was completed between 1509 and 1511 at the height of the Renaissance, Raphael portrays Plato pointing upward and Aristotle pointing downward. Plato believed that absolute truth or the perfect ideals reigned in the ether. Aristotle believed that truth rested within earthly, human reason, which was based on perception through the senses and this truth was undefiled. It is not a coincidence that Raphael was appointed to complete this painting by the Church in the very room where the Pope would be doing most of his studies and framing his theology. Raphael didn't pick the content of the painting ... the Church authorities did.

Raphael knew exactly what he was painting. He began studying Greek philosophers as young as age 11. Thanks to the Medici family, Greek philosophy was fashionable at that time, taught at larger private schools throughout Italy. Raphael eventually moved to Florence and expanded his artistic skills under the direct support of the Medici family. He was drawn to the fair city after hearing about the wonderful works of Michelangelo and Leonardo of Vinci, a suburb of Florence. While the artwork was commissioned by Pope Julius II for his private study room, it is no irony that the first pope to enjoy the finished work was Pope Leo X, who was a Medici himself.

With guidance and financial support from the Medici family, not only did art flourish but so did knowledge and philosophical study. For the first time in hundreds of years, learned men could study the actual writings of Aristotle and Plato, which the Medici family had helped transfer from the East to Florence and translated from Arabic and Greek into Latin. They eventually set up the major school of philosophy of the Western world, the Platonic Academy of Florence, which met at the Villa Medici at Careggi.

This "academy" was an informal discussion group that met for about 60 years. Besides translating all the great works of Greek philosophers into Italian, the group members were instrumental in introducing these studies throughout Italy. Giovanni Pico della Mirandola (1463–1494) was one of the scholars who met with the group. His "Oration on the Dignity of Man," written at age 23, has been called the manifesto or charter of the Renaissance. It is worth reading in its entirety but is beyond anything but a brief mention here. It could be said that this speech was the wellspring to the headwaters of humanism, which has been the dominant philosophy of the Western world for the past 500 years.

The titanic shift at this juncture, which changed the Western world, was in the way we viewed of the material world, including our own minds and bodies. During the previous 15 centuries, the marriage of Christianity and Platonic mysticism caused the physical human form, including the mind, to be seen as insignificant and dirty. It was emphasized that we humans are made of dirt from this inferior material world. We also ate, had sex, peed, and pooped. These bodily functions caused us to be spiritually debased, and our only hope was to keep our eyes on God in the real, spiritual realm.

However, this low view of humans throughout the Dark Ages wasn't working. The study group at Careggi reinterpreted Plato's writings. Plato saw the soul as part of the perfect immaterial human aspect that was encapsulated, unwillingly, within the material body; however, in his oration, Pico makes the case that physical human beings are higher than all other creations, and our sensual perceptions are the ultimate measure of all that exists in the material world. This is the essence of humanism. This is also the source of such preposterous questions such as, "If a tree falls in the forest and no one is there to hear it, does it make a sound?" Of course it makes a sound because human experience doesn't define reality ... reality shapes human experience.

Interestingly, during my week of study in Florence a few years ago, I asked every Florentine I met where the old Platonic Academy of Florence had been located, and not one had any idea what I was talking about. While being intimately acquainted with the major museums and works of art in that beautiful city, it seems even many Florentine residents don't realize how humanism started. However, later when I was studying and writing in Malta, I was staying in the apartment of an Italian architect who was born and raised in Florence, and he knew exactly what I was talking about.

On my last night in Florence, in a small Internet café I was able to track down the present location of the Villa Medici at Careggi. It had fallen into obscurity as one of a thousand beautiful houses around Florence and is now owned by a hospital and not open to the public. I wanted so much to make a pilgrimage to this spot, the peripeteia of all that we know as Western civilization, but my son and I were catching a train the next morning, and it would have meant several miles of walking at night to get to that old building.

In one of his films, Francis Schaeffer mentions that the essence of the Renaissance was Aristotelian humanism. That is incorrect and one of the few times I've disagreed with Schaeffer. In fact, the Renaissance had more to do with a deliberate turning away from Christianized Platonic Dualism to pure, unadulterated Platonism or Platonic Dualism. This didn't happen by accident but by a deliberate choice by one single man in history, Cosimo Medici.

In an ironic twist, as Christianity had evolved deeper into Christianized Platonic Dualism during the first couple of centuries A.D., it neglected, discarded, or even burned the original Platonic writings because they were of this world. Plato's teachings had been stripped from the actual man and Christianized during the formation of the early Church. The Renaissance was simply the act of returning to the man himself. I will explain more about that early Christianization of Plato in the next chapter.

As the Medici family and their students rediscovered pure Platonic ideology, they began to interpret Plato's writings in a secular light rather than within the Christian framework. As Cosimo grew older and approached death, he bought the entire works of Plato and became infatuated with the philosopher's thoughts on eternity (much more so than the Church's views). While Plato was still a novelty during Cosimo's early days, only a couple of generations later, Lorenzo, his grandson, wrote, "Without Platonism man can be neither a good citizen, nor a good Christian" (Parks 2006).

The new Platonism (Neoplatonism) began to include more human-centric concepts such as the emotions—love, beauty, hate, sadness, and joy—rather than biblical themes. In the city of Florence, it became acceptable and then chic to enjoy the beauty of a rose growing out of the dirt in one's garden as much as the circular stained-glass, rose-styled, windows of the Duomo had been enjoyed before. A musical piece about romantic love could be appreciated rather than one only about love for God, Jesus, or Mary. The concept of "romantic" feelings is from the root word *Roman*, which was analogous to anything Italian at the time. A better term might have been *Florentine* because the ideas of romance were rediscovered in Florence.

Thus, the new or Neoplatonic view was still otherworldly, but it no longer held a Christian definition. Now this other world wasn't seen or just seen as the place where the Trinity and the saints dwelled, but the place that your own personal emotions inhabited. This was a great shift in thinking, a philosophical, spiritual, and humanistic revolution that is difficult to overstate.

A thoughtful Christian at the time of the Renaissance would have taken some pleasure in the changes because experiencing natural human emotions was once again important. It was acknowledged that God delighted in the creative abilities of man, which were, once more, an essential part of life. However, that joy was short-lived because the Renaissance didn't have its feet planted on a foundation of biblical Christianity but on the back of Plato himself. It is akin to a man dying of thirst crossing the Sahara and seeing a spring of cool water. He drinks and drinks with great joy. Only when his belly is full does he realize the water was brackish and will soon result in his demise.

AVERROES THE ARISTOTELIAN

Complicating this situation was the discovery of Aristotle's philosophies by other cultures. Neglected in the Christian world, Aristotle's writings had been translated from Greek into Arabic and preserved by Muslim scholars throughout the Muslim world, which now included northern Africa and Spain. The Arab philosopher Averroes (1126–1198), born in Moorish-controlled Spanish territory, became a great student of Aristotle. The writings of Averroes, and thus of Aristotle, eventually made their way east over the Pyrenees to Paris, where Thomas Aquinas (also known by his Latin name, Tommaso d'Aquino, 1225–1274) became intrigued with them. Aquinas eventually became one of the greatest theologians of the Middle Ages, and, in the areas north of the Alps, he had a powerful influence on Christian theology from that point forward.

Aquinas attempted to inject reason—a perfect unfallen Aristotelian reason based on the empirical senses—back into Christian thinking. This movement within Catholicism was referred to at times as "scholasticism." It was a powerful movement in the pre- and post-Reformation Catholic Church.

This brings us up to the virtual doorstep of the Reformation. By this time, the Western world was divided among three main watersheds. The first was the old Medieval Christian-Platonic Dualism, the second was the new, secular humanism of the Renaissance based on the rediscovery and direct influence of Plato, and the third was the new Aristotelian-Scholasticism of Thomas Aquinas. These three belief systems formed the three watersheds from which the rivers of the next thousand years would flow.

To elaborate and review, the first view's tenets hold that the universe is divided between the material and immaterial worlds, and only things of the immaterial world are important. Some of these Christians would argue that the cosmos was decimated by the Fall of Adam. However, many sensed an unbiblical aspect: that God had made the cosmos inferior even before the Fall, a view strongly held by the Gnostics. Certainly mankind is subordinate to the Godhead, but were humans and all the material created in a debased state even before the Fall of Adam? I think not; otherwise it would reflect negatively on the creator.

In the second view, the secular humanists, coming from the pure Platonic source, state that the unseen world is the most important realm. But rather than being defined with Christian labels, this view is defined in human terms. This unseen world includes the intangible human emotions of love, happiness, faithfulness, honor, beauty, etc. In this system, which was at the heart of the Renaissance, man's senses became the measure of all that was important; thus the term *humanism* was born.

The last system of belief, following Aristotle's original concepts, states that reason is the only absolute and, fully trusting our senses, can lead us to all truth. If the second system was the foundation of the Renaissance, then this third system was the foundation of the Enlightenment and the great age of discovery and science known as the Age of Reason. The historical impact of these two philosophers, Aristotle in northern Europe and Plato in southern Europe, was that the Renaissance occurred in the south and the Enlightenment in the north. Aristotle's high regard for reason was also the philosophical foundation for the French Revolution (1789–1799).

The French Revolution deposed the Aristotelian aristocrats and slaughtered them in the Reign of Terror, also known as the reign of the guillotine. Estimates put the total killed as high as 40,000 aristocrats, including clergy and government sympathizers who were killed in a matter of days. At the climax on November 10, 1793, the rebels marched into Notre Dame and crowned Sophie, the wife of the pro-revolutionary printer and bookbinder, Antoine-François Momoro, as the new goddess of France. She was dressed provocatively; some say as a prostitute. She symbolized this new goddess of France, as reason. Reason—that is, perfect Aristotelian reason—was the new religion of France. Atheism and Aristotelian reason were now in vogue and would quickly spread westward.

The rebels didn't grasp that reason was indeed fallible and, unlike Aristotle's hope, wouldn't lead to bliss. It wasn't until the horrible wars of the early twentieth century that this new hope in reason would finally run its course, ending in a terrible despair and the suicides of many philosophers who held hope in Aristotelian reason. Out of those ashes of despair rose the postmodernists, who swung the pendulum the other way by greatly devaluing reason, basing truth on a personal feeling rather than logic. One extreme was exchanged for its opposite. We bemused humans are so often unable to find middle ground but instead must frolic in the extremes.

The American Revolution differed from the French one because of the positive influence of the protestant Reformation, which held a deep-seated belief in the fallenness of man, including man's reason. So when the American Revolution took place, although Jefferson himself may have been under Aristotle's spell, most of the founding fathers recognized the need for checks and balances. No one could be fully trusted—not the aristocrats, the king, nor the people, and certainly not the Church.

Following the legacy of these earlier European philosophical threads into Protestantism, an almost geographical distribution of the influences can be observed. In those days, travel was on foot or horseback, and information was not instantaneously exchanged as it is today. Philosophical or Christian thinking could suddenly end at a river's bank or where mountain ranges impeded travel. The Alps were a natural barrier between the romantic Platonics of the south and the logical Aristotelians of the north.

The previous chapter began with a riddle about cars, and now we will return to that riddle as a practical example of how philosophy can greatly influence a culture. The Catholic Scholastics' high regard for reason moved northward and eastward from Paris into England, Scandinavia, and Germany. This included Gothenburg, Sweden (the birthplace of the Volvo), and southern Germany (the birthplace of the Mercedes). Those cultures were deeply influenced by rational thinking and became the springboard for the Enlightenment. They also became the springboard for the deep-thinking forms of Christianity, such as Calvinism. However, Protestant Christianity didn't simply divide into those denominations heavily influenced by Aristotle and Plato. The entire Church had been heavily influenced by Plato from its inception, so all parts of the Church saw things with at least a little Platonic-Dualistic tinting in their spectacles. In addition to this ancient Platonic influence, denominations such as Lutheranism and Calvinism were greatly influenced by the Catholic Scholastics, especially what is called the High Scholastics (in contrast with the early Scholastics) and thus by Aristotle.

The more dualistic and mystical thinking of Plato, both in the old Christianized Platonism and the purer Neoplatonism forms, had its greatest influence within reach of Florence, including the Italian villages of Renazzo di Cento, the birthplace of the Lamborghini, and nearby Modena, the birthplace of the Ferrari. This influence would cover the area we know as the Latin cultures of Italy, Spain, France, and Slavic areas of central Europe. In a convoluted manner, it worked its way into modern Protestant thinking through the Moravians, people like the Czech Jan Hus, and later Jacob Arminius, who were the fathers of several modern protestant denominations.

The motto of the Volvo car company is "Quality and Safety," and the motto for Mercedes is similar. It isn't much of a stretch to see how such values are based on Aristotelian concepts of logic and reason. In contrast, the Ferrari and Lamborghini appeal not to reason (consider the cost!) but to the senses and emotions, which are stimulated by their sleek, sexy lines and the adrenaline rush of speed they can produce. The concept of the "other," in this car example the emotions, as being higher or better than reason, was taken directly from the Platonic-Dualism playbook of the Renaissance.

When I began my discovery of this fascinating aspect of history, I knew it wouldn't be a sanitized account of basic facts but would intertwine with my own life in intimate ways—and indeed it did. Before I discovered that personal connection, however, I was puzzled by how the concept of Dualism first got a toehold in the early Church. After all, much of the New Testament was made up of apostles' writings that warned of these unscrupulous non-biblical influences on the infant Church. After learning the basics of the Renaissance, my curiosity still wasn't satisfied as new questions were raised, especially about how did the Church allow this toehold?

During my last years in Rochester I returned to bookstores, looking for the ancient texts I would need to fully solve my riddle. I knew I had to first take a step back and spend another year researching the earliest points of Church history. I had to know how this whole mess started in the first place. My aspirations were finding enough answers that I could then rest and start to imagine what the Church was really meant to be in its natural form. I want to tell this fascinating story in as practical and organic terms as possible, so the reader could actually taste the consequences within their own lives.

CHAPTER SIXTEEN
The Gnostics

I mentioned in chapter eight that, during my freshman year of college, I lived with Aaron in the ministry training house. The next year my good friend Drew moved into the dorm with me; our plans were to start a ministry among our fellow residents. It was an old red-brick three-story structure with a neo-classical appearance complete with white columns topped by scrolled capitals. While the dorm may sound lovely, it was anything but. It had been condemned and was scheduled for demolition, with our small group as the last residents.

The cornerstone of such a dorm ministry was a Bible study held in our room each week. Through that Bible study, I met many interesting characters, some with no Christian background, and some with a mix of church affiliations. The most memorable was a nerdy-looking fellow named Steve.

I found Steve fascinating because I couldn't pigeon-hole him. He said he was Catholic but didn't fit any of the Catholic stereotypes my Baptist upbringing had taught. He attended mass at the big Catholic cathedral in town, but his primary spiritual input came from a small group he was involved with that went by the unsophisticated name of "The Full Gospel Group at Hank's House." Because Steve had been attending our Bible study faithfully, I felt it was only polite to respond to his many invitations and finally accompany him to the gathering at Hank's.

J. Michael Jones

The Heavenly Hustle

Hank was an interesting middle-aged gentleman with an obvious toupee that gave him a perfectly styled haircut for the mid-1970s. He wore uncool dark green polyester pants with a matching jacket with a white dress shirt, which—along with his personality—fit with his daytime job of some kind of traveling salesman. He spoke in a booming, confident voice, his words accented with "Praise God-*da*!" or "Jaeeeesus!" in every breath. He lived in a humble wood-framed home that stood just off campus, the living room of which was packed with many more people than might be at a fraternity party during rush week. Hank wasn't a tall man, but it didn't matter—I heard him well before I saw him.

It was clear to everyone present that Hank was much more than merely the host of the meeting. He was the teacher, song leader, motivational speaker, dictator—and the incessant centerpiece. The man intimidated me so much that I kept my distance. When he called the meeting to order, most of the crowd immediately took a seat on furniture or on the floor at Hank's feet. I remained standing in the arched doorway of the dining room, inconspicuous because much of the crowd was forced to spill into other rooms of the house, and still others, like me, chose to stand.

Hank began with a chanting prayer of praising God. This was followed by verbal nonsense meant to give the impression he was speaking in tongues. Immediately the entire room, except for myself and perhaps a few other visitors, burst into chaotic chanting and nonsensical verbal pandemonium, as though someone had flipped a switch. The tongue-speaking session soon evolved into completely uninhibited expression of emotion. Some people stood and shadow danced—hands held above their heads—while others fell over in trances. Some laughed hysterically while others cried uncontrollably. Mixed with the gibberish were occasional outbursts of intelligible words such as "Praise Jaeeeesus" or "Praise God-*da*."

As if turning a switch back off after the gibberish, Hank said, "Amen" and raised his hand to quiet the crowd before launching into a sermon. The oration consisted of him reading 2 Peter 1:17: "He received honor and glory from God the Father when the voice came to him from the Majestic Glory, saying, 'This is my Son, whom I love; with him I am well pleased.'" After that, he closed his big black Bible, removed his reading glasses, letting them dangle on a thick gold chain from his reddened, leathery neck, and told us a story.

"I made a sales trip to West Virginia this week," his story began. "While I was in one of the offices, a man looked at me and, unrelated to anything we were discussing, remarked, 'You must be a Christian. I see the glory of God in your face.'" Hank smiled and continued. "Then I called on another customer across the state line in Virginia. The receptionist in that office looked at me and said, 'I can tell you have the joy of God in your life.'"

Hank smiled again, adding, "You see, I got in trouble a few weeks ago for preaching the Gospel during my sales calls, so I promised my boss I would try to refrain. So this week, I didn't say a thing about the Lord to see what would happen. But the glory of God is so full in my life that it can't be hidden, no more than trying to hide a flaming torch under a paper bush. I sensed God was saying to those customers, regarding me, 'This is my son, whom I love; with him I am well pleased.'"

The mob crammed into the little house that evening seemed impressed with this thinly veiled self-adoration. Looking over the group, Hank decided it was time for God to heal their afflictions. A couple of men, who I later learned were deacons, placed a dining room chair directly in front of the leader, facing the crowd. Hank stood and looked across the group, asking, "Who's sick?" One by one, people came forward and sat in the chair, whereupon Hank made an immediate diagnosis of each individual, and it was the same—one leg was shorter than the other. This was despite the fact that they complained of a wide variety of symptoms. He then kneeled in front of each one, lifting their legs so one ankle was clutched in each of his palms, and in an obvious sleight-of-hand, pushed up their pant hems on one side with his thumb, exposing more and more of the sock and making it appear that leg was growing. It was a simple kindergarten illusion at best, but the crowd was completely mesmerized. "Praise Jesus ... Praise Jaeeeesus" was mumbled throughout the group. After each "healing," the patient jumped up and shouted, "Praise God-*da*! I've been heeeealed-*da* ... I feel great!" I felt a little sick myself but for different reasons.

When the healing session was finished, Hank looked around the room and asked, "Where's Mildred? I've heard she's been in the hospital."

A minute later, a middle-aged lady appeared from one of the overflow rooms. She walked with a limp, holding an aluminum cane in her right hand

and being helped by another woman on her left. Hank grabbed Mildred by the shoulders and turned her around to face the crowd. "Now tell your brothers and sisters what's wrong with you."

Looking uncomfortable, the woman described a serious back problem; she'd just had surgery to remove a disc but was still in a great deal of pain. Hank sat her on the chair and asked for prayer and the laying on of hands. He anointed her forehead with Wesson Oil from a Dixie paper cup. Next he knelt in front of her, took her ankles in his hands, which alone caused a grimace on her face, and began to do his leg-lengthening trick. When he was finished, he told her to stand, then jerked her up, which produced another grimace and a high-pitched squeal. And it still wasn't over. He then tried to force her to bend over and touch her toes, causing her to bellow in pain. He seemed frustrated, pushing her back down in the chair with his right hand on her head, in an aggressive manner. "There's sin blocking this healing," he said. "Does anyone have a word of knowledge?"

One of the deacons rose and raised his hands above his head. His eyes rolled to the back of his head as though he was in some kind of trance, and he spoke in a monotone. "The voice of God says that Mildred has unconfessed adultery in her life." To this announcement, poor Mildred began to sob. Hank looked quite happy, as if his failure to heal had been vindicated. He asked some of the women to take Mildred into a bedroom and to pray with her for repentance.

Before the night was over, Hank unfortunately also selected me for an involuntary healing. He announced to the group that God had revealed directly to him that I suffered from severe back pain. I denied it publicly, which seemed to annoy him; still, he sat me in the healing chair and tried the same leg-lengthening trick. As he pushed up the hem of my jeans on the left side, making it look as if my ankle was growing longer, I pushed it back down with my hand. When he realized I wasn't buying his trick, he abruptly ceased his exercise and gave me a hateful look. He spun around so fast that the inertia of his toupee caused it to twist on his head, moving the part to an oblique line across his scalp. When he again called for a word of knowledge, the same deacon repeated his trancelike posture and announced, apparently directly from God, "This boy doesn't have faith and has grieved the Holy Spirit." I didn't sob, but I felt sad—sad about everything I had seen that night. I believe this exact same story could have played out, save the polyester leisure suit, among the Christian Gnostics of the first century.

TOUCHING GOD?

When I discovered how the medieval Church had been influenced by Platonic Dualism, I wanted to go back even farther and learn how this secular philosophy had entered the Church in the first place. My search eventually led me to the Gnostic Gospels.

With the Gnostics came the first expression of dualism in the early Church. At this point, my journey intersects with the fictional book *The Da Vinci Code*, though only briefly. The book was based on some of the writings of the first- and second-century Gnostics. One of the Gnostic Gospels—the Gospel of Mary—implied that Jesus had a deeper relationship with Mary Magdalene than with the rest of his acquaintances. Their relationship could have been interpreted by an overactive imagination as romantic. But some of the other Gnostic writings such as the Gospel of Thomas suggested almost the opposite. There, women were considered so inferior to men that they could enter heaven only if they first became men.

This unbiblical, dualistic thinking forced the Gnostics to take one of the two positions. Jesus simply couldn't be both spiritual and physical, of both the ether and the material world. Thus, in the Gospel of Mary, he was fleshly and not divine. The Gnostics' other choice was that Jesus was only divine and never material. But the dualistic position, which they held firm, forbade them from philosophically considering Jesus as both. If Jesus was God, then surely no human could have touched him. If he had been touched, then he could not have been God.

Some Gnostics concluded that three levels of humanity existed. The most basic was the physical or material men and women who were little more than animals in human disguise. They had no hope of redemption. The second was psychic forms, meaning those with a soul inside a material body. The possibility of redemption existed for this second group, although most would never seek it because of their material influence. Finally, most Gnostics considered themselves as the *pneumatics*: spiritual people whose bodies weren't material but more of an illusion—vapor, or in modern terms, a projected image. These people were said to be born redeemed, above all others, with a secret and personal understanding, knowledge, or *gnosis* of God. The Gnostics and their writings were eventually rejected by the main Church, but not until after several hundred years of intense struggle. The Gnostic influence, however, lingered—perpetually all the way to Hank's house and beyond.

A remarkably insightful book, *Against the Protestant Gnostics*, by Philip J. Lee (Lee 1993), traces the Gnostic influence from its early origins through to the Protestant Church of the twentieth century. While I don't agree with everything he says, Lee's work is brilliant, clearly requiring much research, knowledge, and thought, and it helped me a great deal in my personal quest.

Gnostic teachings were rejected by the main Church not because they didn't accept the divinity of Christ. It was far more complicated than that. The wise Church fathers recognized that the Gnostics were centered not in a true Judeo-Christian philosophy but in a Platonic and Zoroastrian Dualism.

It is difficult to trace the exact date of the Gnostics' origins. Some of their thinking preexisted Christ by a few hundred years in the form of Jewish and other religious sects such as the Essenes. Lee points out that, during periods of chaos in the real, material world, the Gnostic way of thinking is most attractive. This only makes sense because the main tenet of Gnosticism is that only the heavenly world matters, not the real, material one. At the time of the Essenes, Israel had been recently conquered by the polytheistic Romans, and the physical world was no longer making a lot of sense to these Jews. How could evil win out over good? Because of this disillusionment, their aspirations of an earthly theocracy and Jewish state were evaporating. In that context, mystical thinking was becoming increasingly attractive. They could use their theology to transcend the material world around them. It is far beyond the scope of this book, but a similar story has been plaited into the netting of Islamic terrorism, which rose out of the disillusionment of Muslims being dominated by the culture of Western "infidels" for over a hundred years.

Many of these first Essenes withdrew physically into the wastelands, such as the area where the Essenes lived on a high rocky outcropping above the Dead Sea, a place called Qumran. The pre-Christian, Gnostic sects at Qumran were the transcribers and keepers of the Dead Sea Scrolls for the two centuries prior to Christ. Their famous scrolls not only contained many biblical texts but also writings about their personal beliefs, their customs, and even their daily activities. Some of their extra-biblical writings described their beliefs in absolute dualistic and mystical terms. Several centuries later, some of this thinking was mirrored in the beliefs of Christian Gnosticism.

The people of Qumran believed this world was sharply divided between good and evil. They didn't carry it as far as the Zoroastrians, who believed the spiritual or heavens were likewise divided between the good divine and the evil divine. Later on, some of the Christian Gnostics adopted these Zoroastrian ideas as well, separating the evil Old Testament God from the good New Testament God.

The application of this form of Dualism at Qumran was evident in the Gnostic Jews' civil scrolls. They recorded that they believed in a completely sovereign God. To account for evil in the world, they figured that some people were born evil and others born good. Those controlled by the "Prince of Light" were good, and those controlled by the "Angel of Darkness" were evil. It was not possible for people to have the free will to choose evil on their own. Somewhat like the Zoroastrians, there was no crossing over between these groups—no opportunity for repentance, in other words. To account for the fact that good people sometimes did evil and evil people sometimes did good, they believed this Dualism could be amalgamated. For example, one set of scrolls describes the in-processing of new members. They were literally judged, using percentages of good and evil, by body type and later, once the community got to know them, by their behavior.

The word *gnosis* is simply the Greek word for *knowledge*. However, it is quite different from the gnosis to which Socrates or Aristotle aspired. It was more of a Platonic-Dualistic knowledge that dwelt within the ether. This dualistic knowledge was not obtained through education like any other kinds of knowledge (what some evangelicals would call head knowledge) but came directly from God, fully formed, and articulated. It was a convenient and lazy kind of knowledge.

My experience at Hank's house was a modern example of this super-spiritual gnosis. The deacon at that gathering had knowledge, or gnosis, that came directly from God about Mildred's adultery and my grieving of the Holy Spirit. He had never met me before and probably hadn't known Mildred well enough to have any logical insight into her private life. But that didn't matter; the knowledge came directly from above and didn't need to be processed through the human senses of seeing, hearing, or even thinking.

The frightening thing was that no one could oppose this "knowledge" because doing so would mean opposing God himself. That is why divine gnosis is so powerful, alluring, and treacherous. Regrettably, this ties in with ASW. Hank's self-worth was increased when the reason his bogus healings didn't work was the fault of the one being healed. The deacon scored many ASW points with Hank, the rock star, by creating scapegoats for his failures. Gnosis is handy for those who claim it and are skillful at using it.

This form of super-spiritual knowledge has always been attractive for Christians because it can be used to manipulate others for a person's own gain, allowing them to appear spiritual without exposing the raw intentions of their evil nature, which remain neatly hidden in the troughs of their cellar. A more mainstream use of this kind of gnosis occurs when pastors and other Christian leaders use the method to manipulate congregations to do almost anything they want. All they need to say is, "God says" or "God wants you to do such and such." The more acceptable verbiage in evangelical circles is, "God spoke to me," "God convicted me," or "God showed me." A few guys in my DI group were able to close the deal on engagements to attractive young women using such tactics. It was because I held this belief that I face an impasse when I was given orders by Rod that made no rational sense.

Selfish intent and emotional or social factors are conveniently written out of the equation with gnostic thinking, and the claimer of the gnosis is left without true accountability. Thus the concept of super-spiritual gnosis is a useful tool in the hands of those Christians who happen to also be broken, fallen, sinful, selfish, and sometimes narcissistic—who are dealing with their own ASW. The original Christian Gnostics also found a boost to their ASW, theologically, because they believed they were above all other Christians. After all, they were pneumatics. They had been chosen to be pneumatics by God because they deserved it. In their thinking, they had the right to look down on everyone else in the same way that the caste system of the Hindus allows for a hierarchy of human worth. It was thus tempting to assume that you were a pneumatic, which had a higher value in God's economy.

God Is on My Side ... or Is He?

The first church my wife and I attended together in Michigan, before moving to Egypt, seemed to be a loving place. At the time, its numbers were swelling rapidly, and a point came when we had to choose to either build a new building or have two Sunday morning services. And what happened? This wonderful group of people began to polarize on the issue of whether to build or not to build. The older members, who had built the first building and carried a large debt for a decade, were opposed to building again. The pastor, who envisioned a mega-church on that site someday (and him the superstar-pastor at the helm), led a large group of the younger members who wanted to build and expand.

The climax of this discussion came at a congregational meeting one Tuesday night. It would turn out to be one of the most disappointing events of my young Christian life. The meeting began cordially and then became "spiritual." By this I mean that representatives from each side gave prepared speeches on how God had "spoken to them," telling them that we should either build or not build. Both sides backed their gnosis with tangential scripture. The pastor, who carried a large amount of spiritual clout, shared the gnosis God had provided him with earlier that morning during his devotions. He quoted from Isaiah 54:2: "Enlarge the place of your tent, stretch your tent curtains wide, do not hold back; lengthen your cords, strengthen your stakes." Many of us were ready to build at that point—that is, until Kevin shared.

Kevin was one of our well-respected members and elders. He had been part of the original church congregation who had suffered through a long and draining building program 20 years earlier, and he brought the perspective of a successful businessman. God had also spoken (gnosis) to him that week with two verses. The first one was from Proverbs 22:7: "The rich rule over the poor, and the borrower is slave to the lender." He flipped through his Bible until he came to the New Testament verse 1 Corinthians 6:12: "...I will not be mastered by anything."

Things eventually became ugly—very ugly—leading to a nasty church split and many hurt people. How was it possible that God had given divine gnosis on two sides that were diametrically opposed? As the wise Abraham Lincoln said regarding the Civil War (Christians on both sides were claiming God's gnosis as supporting their cause):

> The will of God prevails. In great contests each party claims
> to act in accordance with the will of God. Both *may* be, and

one *must* be, wrong. God cannot be *for* and *against* the same thing at the same time. In the present civil war it is quite possible that God's purpose is something different from the purpose of either party—and yet the human instrumental-ities, working just as they do, are of the best adaptation to effect His purpose. (Lincoln 1953)

Both men in our church were good men, but each had a personal agenda. Their personal agendas weren't all bad. But, in acceptable fashion, they re-cruited God's gnosis, professing, "God spoke to me" as a kind of nuclear option in a war of words. That night, this culminated in an unstoppable force meeting an impermeable wall—God's gnosis against God's gnosis. Most of the time, unfortunately, it is one-sided. Christians will use this nuke-card to get their way, and their opposition is left speechless and feeling undeserved guilt at having opposed God in the first place. It is an enticing and addictive behavioral tool within Christendom. And these manipulative behaviors are not rare and are sometimes the modus operandi within the business of some churches. The draw of this form of Christianity takes people into its web like psychological cocaine. I have witnessed far too many pastors behave this way through the years. This is why it is always a good idea that the pastor submits to a group of elders or overseers who are more than just his or her hand-picked cronies.

If you were to time-travel back to the first couple of centuries and search for the Gnostics, you might be disappointed. They would not be that easy to find because they were not confined together under one flag in the same way that Mormons or Jehovah's Witnesses are today. In an article about the Gnostics, theologian Arthur Darby Nock, stated, "You could not have found anyone in Corinth to direct you to a Gnostic Church: the overwhelming possibility is that there was no such thing." (Nock 1972). At the same time, the mainline Church had many followers who thought in Gnostic ways. Phillip Lee writes in *Against the Protestant Gnostics*, "Very few Gnostics were to be found outside the main body of the Church." It was difficult to pinpoint Gnostics because they seemed to have been sprinkled from one end of the religious spectrum to the other.

In one area of thought, the Gnostics were highly ascetic, legalistic, and structured. Those groups followed more laws than the Levites could ever fancy; they lived apart from this "evil world" in every way possible. Some ate only bread and drank only water from a special spring or well. Some of them, such as Symeon the Stylite, lived on tall poles for years to separate themselves from the evil world, vertically. In the case of Symeon, he climbed an ancient column from a ruin, which had some piece of a platform at the top, and remained there for the rest of his life. The story goes that the pillar was improved to the point that it started with him nine feet off the ground but was almost 50 feet tall at the time of his death. The concept of self-flagellation, or beating their evil, human flesh almost to the point of death, originated with the Gnostics and was carried into the Middle Ages by the mainstream Church. Even the concept of the monastery—separate from the evil world—has its roots in this line of thinking.

In other places, Gnostics indulged in every sin that was conceivable—some were beyond conception. They had no shame about sexual orgies and festivals of such gluttony that it put the hedonistic non-Christian Romans to shame. Paul may have been referring to these Gnostics in 1 Corinthians 5:1 when he said, "It is actually reported that there is sexual immorality among you, and of a kind that even pagans do not tolerate: A man is sleeping with his father's wife."

So how could these two polar opposites be of the same philosophical breed? Gnostics considered that this physical Earth was not only of lesser value than the spiritual or heavens, but that it was created in an evil state. So if this world, your own body, your physical desires, and your physical life are of no significance at best and evil at worst, you have two options. Like the first group, you can try your best to separate yourself from this world. Or, like the second group, you can view this world as so insignificant that it no longer matters. This second group believed that, as long as your spiritual heart was in God's camp, it didn't matter what your body did. This is exactly the kind of thinking that Paul opposed in his letter to the Romans (Romans 6:1–2): "What shall we say, then? Shall we go on sinning so that grace may increase? By no means! We are those who have died to sin; how can we live in it any longer?"

Some Gnostics, somewhat like the Zoroastrians, went so far as to believe that the Earth was the essence of evil, created by a hateful, evil Old Testament God. A loving, good New Testament God was bringing salvation through an earthly Jesus. So he either had to be less than God, opening the door for this idea of Jesus marrying Mary and having a family in *The Da Vinci Code*, or not physical at all. Simple verses such as John 21:12–14 are important when confronting such heresy. In that passage, even after the resurrection, it is suggesting that Jesus had a real, physical, human body:

> Jesus said to them, "Come and have breakfast." None of the disciples dared ask him, "Who are you?" They knew it was the Lord. Jesus came, took the bread and gave it to them, and did the same with the fish. This was now the third time Jesus appeared to his disciples after he was raised from the dead.

As I've mentioned, the early Church fathers in their wisdom confronted this Platonic Dualism that had found its way into many parts of the Church. Through the Council of Nicaea (325 A.D.), a good attempt was made to put it to rest, but the horse was already out of the barn. Gnostic Christians were a minority within the Church, but a significant minority with a majority-sized influence. When their brand of theology was confronted by the main Church, rather than disappearing, it simply was absorbed, like a lot of Roman polytheism, into the Church culture. The Gnostic air was already in their lungs, including the lungs of some very influential people.

AUGUSTINE THE PLATONIST

There is little debate that Augustine of Hippo was the greatest Christian theologian of the Church's first thousand years. Some would argue the greatest ever. There is no way to overestimate his influence on the thinking and shape that the young Church took.

He was born in 354 A.D. in the small village of Tagaste, in the area of Hippo-Regius in what is now part of Algeria. The ancient name meant the place where Numidian kings often resided with their horses. Augustine's mother, Monica, had a great influence on her son and was a confessing Christian. To further his education, his parents sent the teenager off to Carthage, the Roman capital in North Africa, which was only a two-day journey away. There, he greatly increased his knowledge of philosophy and Christian theology and, as well, sowed a few wild oats. One of the seeds he sowed came back as a son named Adeodatus, who Monica helped raise. However, since Augustine was of a higher class than his mistress, she eventually left him so he would be free to marry a woman of his statue. This was difficult for both Augustine and his mistress. He wrote that she had more courage than he did because she had taken the brave step of leaving.

Besides being enticed by the beauty of the women of Carthage, Augustine was also enticed by different schools of spiritual thought, especially Manichaeism. He became deeply engrossed in this Christian Gnostic cult for the next nine years of his life, even converting his father to this faith upon his return to Tagaste. If not for his mother's contempt for his newfound religion, he might have never returned to the mainstream Christian fold.

Manichaeism was a Christian sect, although most Christians would not consider it Christian at all. It followed the teachings of Mani of Persia, a wild man who wore a brightly colored coat, traveled throughout Persia and western Asia with his walking stick, and preached with great charisma. His flamboyant style may have given root to the term *maniac*, which in Latin meant "a crazy person" or at least "someone with great enthusiasm." It also may be that this man was called Mani as a nickname because he was so enthusiastic. Many of these interesting characters in human history probably did suffer from conditions such as bipolar disorder (the older name for this was "manic-depressive disorder").

Mani drew strongly from Zoroastrianism, the main religion of Persia at the time, as well as from Gnosticism. This Gnosticism included the type of Gnostic-Judaism that existed at Qumran, although Mani considered himself a Christian. Some reliable evidence exists that he also traveled as far as India and China and had an exchange of ideas with some Buddhist thinkers, but other scholars disagree.

Augustine was able to break the spell of Manichaeism only through the prayers and nagging of his beloved mother and the fact that the cult relied heavily on superstitions and even astrology. As he matured intellectually, it became difficult for Augustine to continue to hold to such irrational beliefs. After his studies advanced, he returned to Carthage to teach rhetoric. Then, to further his studies and continue his own internal journey, he sailed for Rome.

As the emerging capital of Christianity, Rome didn't offer Augustine the safe haven from Manichaeism that his mother had hoped for; it, too, was infiltrated heavily with the sect. Later, he moved north to Milan to work as a rhetoric professor. There he met Ambrose (340–397), one of the Church leaders, who had been a faithful follower for years of another Gnostic cult, Marcionism. This cult held the premise that the Old Testament God was evil and different from the New Testament, good God.

It was still difficult for Augustine to embrace Christianity fully. He considered himself somewhat "tutored" into the Christian faith from dualistic Manichaeism by Plato's Dualism, helped along by a semi-ex-Gnostic, Ambrose. As Augustine fully embraced Christianity for the first time, he also, in some ways, exchanged his Manichean Dualism for Platonic Dualism, which he thought would be more compatible with biblical Christianity. This was not so strange because, as I've mentioned, some Christian theologians at the time and in later centuries considered Plato to be a kind of de facto Christian saint. They did not seem to grasp that Plato appeared so congruous with Christianity because the Christianity of the fourth century had already been tainted by Platonic teaching during the Greek and Gnostic conversions of the previous three centuries. It was akin to, for example, meeting your father for the first time as an adult but not realizing he was your father. You might say, "I really like that guy for some odd reason." You like him because he looks much like you and you have some characteristics in common.

Raised Protestant, I didn't know much about Augustine prior to my personal journey except that a charming old city in Florida was named after him. As I traced the influence of Plato and the Gnostics in early Christianity, I noticed how the influence seemed to deepen and congeal after the creeds and before the period leading into the Dark Ages. Through my study of Church history, for the first time I began to realize how profound an influence the deep thinking of Augustine had on this period of Christian history and on the subsequent thousand years. Of course, many of his ideas had a positive influence on the development of the Church. Still, I had a great inkling that Augustine had something to do with this further absorption of Platonic ideas within the mainline Church, even though he made a strong stand against the more severe positions of Mani.

After reading Augustine's pivotal work, *The City of God*, which was written soon after the Visigoths sacked Rome in 410 A.D., my suspicion was quickly confirmed. In his writings, Augustine makes clear his great respect for Plato. He also acknowledges, as I discovered myself, that it was the dualistic influence of the mathematician Pythagoras that made Plato stand out from other Greek philosophers. Quoting from *The City of God*, Book VIII, chapter four:

> Of the pupils of Socrates, Plato was so remarkable for his brilliance that he has deservedly outshone all the rest ... Socrates excelled in practical wisdom; Pythagoras favored contemplation, and to this he applied his whole intelligence. It is to Plato's praise that he combined both in a more perfect philosophy ...

In chapter five, Augustine adds:

> If, then, Plato defined a philosopher as one who knows, loves and imitates the God in whom he finds his happiness, there is little need to examine further. For, none of the other philosophers has come so close to us [meaning Christians] as the Platonists have, and, therefore, we may neglect the others [but not the Platonists].

Augustine begins chapter six with:

> The Platonic philosophers, then, so deservedly considered superior to all the others in reputation and achievement, well understood that no [material] body could be God and, therefore, in order to find Him, they rose beyond all material [physical] things.

Later in chapter six, he adds this profound summary:

> [The Platonists] argued that whatever exists is either matter [physical] or life [spiritual]; that life is superior to matter; that the appearance of a body [soma] is sensible, whereas the form of life is intelligible. Hence, they preferred intelligible form [spiritual] to sensible appearance [physical].

We call things sensible which can be perceived by sight
and bodily touch.

Augustine ends chapter nine praising both Plato and Pythagoras again, this time because they looked to the higher, spiritual realm. Then, in a fascinating twist, he starts chapter 10 of book VIII with the same scripture verse I used in the previous chapter from Colossians 2:8 warning Christians against being taken captive through non-Christian philosophies. Thus he acknowledges the risk of flirting with Greek philosophy, yet he believed Plato was the exception. He adds later in the same paragraph that the apostle writing Colossians meant we needn't reject all secular philosophies because God had manifested himself to some (implying Plato) even though he lived before Christ. Interestingly, he never mentions Colossians 2:9: "For in Christ all the fullness of the Deity lives in bodily form." This verse is opposed to Platonic Dualism. But, as I later recognized, Augustine saw the similarities of fifth-century Christianity with Platonic thinking because the fifth-century Church had already been greatly influenced by Plato.

I agree with Augustine, in a way, that there is sometimes great merit in the observations of secular men and women. God has made many truths in this world self-evident. However, the error of the nonbeliever—and often of the believer—is in the conclusions they reach. Without a humble studying of scripture, along with the guidance of the Holy Spirit, our corrupted reason can easily reach wrong conclusions. Because our reason, different from what Aristotle believed, is indeed defiled, we must be cautious about becoming dogmatic over issues that are not blatant.

In summary, Augustine had repented from the troughs of Manichaeism and its radical Gnostic-dualistic thinking, but still, almost ghostlike, some of its influence continued to haunt him for the rest of his life. This is typical of many of us. I still see the world through my Bible Belt southern culture, even if I'm not so fond of it anymore. Augustine's view of the universe was forever tainted. He made further statements in *The City of God* that reflect this ghostly remnant. He wrote of the physical life as inferior and not fulfilling. As well, he wrote of how, when man reaches heaven, he will no longer be weighed down by his "animal flesh," which is a profoundly dualistic way of looking at the world and in complete opposition to how N. T. Wright describes our future in his book, *Surprised by Hope: Rethinking Heaven, the*

Resurrection, and the Mission of the Church, as living on in new, resurrected bodies living in a more perfect material world. We must remember that the Bible is clear that our future is not in Heaven, suspended in a mystic vortex of bliss. It is living in our rectified, material bodies on this concrete earth for all of eternity.

You can track Dualism's later historical journey from the post-Reformation Church all the way up to my little white Baptist church and to my DI experience. The snarly path would lead all the way to the imitation-bamboo table and the black hole of confusion that materialized in its center. With this historical information, I knew that I would be able to solve the riddle of that rabbit hole that almost consumed me. However, it wasn't a simple task to sort it all out. The traces of Platonic Dualism of the Gnostics and Augustine, the Neoplatonic Dualism of the Medicis of the Renaissance, and the Aristotelian influence of Averroes are entwined like long spaghetti noodles accidently spilled across a terracotta, Florentine, kitchen floor. I will now carefully craft those complicated strands into simple bundles and make them relevant for our present age. In the end this all had to result in just a personal resolution and by finding a way that we can all return to a natural Christianity.

CHAPTER SEVENTEEN

---◆---

A Divided Present

In the opening scene of the film adaptation of John Osborne's play *Luther* (Osborne 1961), the reformer is standing in a cathedral-turned-church when a man comes down the aisle with a dead man in a wheelbarrow. The man pushing the wheelbarrow lashes out at Luther, saying something like, "This man's blood is on your hands." In the scene, Luther stands distraught, in anguish over the violence that his thesis has unleashed. Overall, the play and movie present a non-historical version of Luther, one in which he is wishy-washy and plagued by constant doubts.

In real life, the Catholic-versus-Lutheran bloodshed was terrible. It began before Luther died in 1546 and must have been difficult for him, a peaceful man, to bear. Before long, the bloodshed became a three-way fight that included the Calvinists. There were many conflicts throughout Europe, but one of the most notorious and bloody was the Thirty Years' War, from 1618 to 1648. In those three decades, it is estimated that casualties, dead and wounded, were over 10 million. The violence, using period weapons, was no less than what we see between the Shiites and Sunnis in Iraq, the warring factions within Syria, or the periodic brutality in Darfur. Some of my evangelical friends remark that Islam is a religion of war and death and Christianity is of life and peace. Those friends don't know history.

The reasons behind the Thirty Years' War, and the subsequent lesser wars for 10 times that period, were more political than religious, with power struggles between the major European countries. Some viewpoints suggest that the conflicts were entirely political because the concept of an authentic Christian war is an oxymoron (Christ himself being the great peacemaker).

However, it is safe to say that the Thirty Years' War began with a theological disagreement and that type of conflict was sustained, at least on an emotional level.

The three main offshoots—scholastic Catholicism, Lutheranism, and Calvinism—had one thing in common. While, like all of Christendom, they had a Platonic-Dualistic heritage, these three in particular were also highly influenced by Aristotelian ideas through the influence of Thomas Aquinas (mentioned in chapter 15). The northern Europeans clearly had strong scholastic ties, and Luther and Calvin came out of that same line. When you—falsely—believe that you can obtain absolute and precise truth via the use or your reason, it creates a conceit of theological certainty. This is where you're confident that your precise theological positions are the correct ones. You begin to feel a higher personal value because, in your eyes, you are on God's side and the others are not. Therefore, those who don't agree with you deserve the worst you can muster.

MAKE LOVE, NOT WAR

With so much death and destruction in the aftermath of the Thirty Years' War in the seventeenth century, the pendulum once again moved in the other direction during the eighteenth century. Many small house churches and other Christian groups began to spring up. In those churches were Christians weary of intellectual debates about theology and rational certainty. They rightly recognized that the highest biblical virtue was love, not reason. Thus, before long, the pendulum swung quickly to the opposite direction, back toward a Platonic-Christian Dualism, where reason was antagonistic to faith. Reason was thrown back to the inferior side of the dualistic divide and faith elevated as its righteous opposite. This new way of Christian thinking was called the Piety movement. Frustrated with the decades of religious wars, unimaginable cruelty, and the constant splitting of theological hairs, Philipp Jakob Spener, considered the father of Pietism, proposed a "heart religion" to take the place of "head religion" in the late seventeenth century.

Spener's godson, Nikolaus Ludwig von Zinzendorf (1700–1760), was one of the main apostles of the movement, helping it to spread from Moravia to other parts of Europe and directly influencing John and Charles Wesley

(1707–1788) and eventually the founding of the Methodist Church. The Methodists strongly influenced the Second Great Awakening, which created the Bible Belt and many parachurch organizations such as DI.

I have neither the space nor the knowledge to discuss the continuing evolution of both Christian and secular Western thinking for the remaining three centuries up until the imitation-bamboo table. The story becomes increasingly complex through those centuries, and it would take hundreds of pages to do it justice. Philip Lee, in *Against the Protestant Gnostics*, does a scholarly job of covering this material. I will add a few generalities here.

In the previous chapter, I made the analogy that the roots to modern Christian and secular thinking might resemble strands of spaghetti randomly dropped across a floor. But that is an understatement—spaghetti noodles are well-defined strands that keep their shape unless they are overcooked, like I've been known to do. A better word-picture might be confluent rivers running into the sea. But these wouldn't be ordinary rivers; they would be brightly and variously colored, like streams of paint. Once they flowed into the giant sea of modern Western culture, they would mix and interact. In some places, they would blend uniformly into a dull gray, while, in other areas, small streams of pure colors would venture far out into the sea or combine with only one or two other colors.

Starting from the Thirty Years' War, four main Christian headwaters led to this sea. These were the Catholic, Lutheran, Calvinistic, and Pietistic movements. From these factions came several lines of secular thinking as well. However, because I am mainly interested in the roots of American evangelicalism, I'll focus on the latter two. For expediency's sake, I'll have to ignore other voices that had enormous impact on both Christian and secular thinking, including men such as John Locke (1632–1704), Immanuel Kant (1724–1804), Søren Kierkegaard (1813–1855), Charles Darwin (1809–1882), Friedrich Nietzsche (1844–1900), and Sigmund Freud (1856–1939).

The First Great Awakening in America was the fruit of the Calvinists. With their high regard for reasoning, being greatly influenced by the Enlightenment, this movement had an emphasis on learning the classics and sciences and resulted in some of the best Christian expressions of theology, art, and music in North America. However, when a movement places too high a value on reason at the expense of emotion, the movement often goes to seed and eventually becomes a dead orthodoxy. This is exactly what happened with many of the churches at the heart of the First Great Awakening. These huge stone structures still stand, like pigeon-dunged monuments to a forgotten time, in the heart of every major North American city. Some of them still have services, giving lip-service to an absentee land-lord God that no one knows and is now defined by pantheistic interpre-tations. Others have been converted to private homes or office buildings. Others have become community centers where new-age spiritual groups, Transcendental Meditation, and yoga, Pilates, and Zumba classes are held.

THE SECRETS OF VICTORIA

The height of the Calvinists going to seed corresponded with the reign of Queen Victoria of England, from 1837 to 1901. The Victorian culture of the time was not actually a reflection of the queen herself, of course, but of the post-Calvinistic age. She was a product of the culture just like everyone else in England and North America was at the time. The Victorian age was a period when precision of behavior was at its peak. Some historians refer to this age as the "cult of respectability." The standards for Christian gentlemen and ladies were impossible for anyone to achieve. It was in this crazy time that Lewis Carroll wrote his story about Alice falling down a rabbit hole and finding a world of chaos and irrationality. The land of wonder was the antithesis of the Victorian world above—and in some ways far more real.

It is no accident that the best-selling book was written by Reverend Charles Lutwidge Dodgson (pen name: Lewis Carroll) who was a clergy-man of the English High Anglican Church. The adventures he wrote about were inspired by a real girl, Alice Liddell. It is intriguing that Alice's father was the dean of Christ Church at Oxford, which some would consider the "bull's-eye" of Victorian England. Alice, as an adult, even became a romantic interest of Queen Victoria's youngest son.

To add a troubling dimension to the story and a real twist, there were rumors that Dodgson's relationship with the 10-year-old Alice, or possibly with her 14-year-old sister Lorina, was more than platonic. Something hap-pened in 1863, in the middle of writing *Alice in Wonderland*, which caused an abrupt and ugly breakup between the houses of Dodgson and Liddell.

Letters were found written by Dodgson that suggestively expressed his love of little girls. He, being a professional photographer during a period of his life, also had a large collection of photos of young girls, some were nudes or sexually suggestive. Others, who had studied his life closely, have strongly denied this and explained that there was an innocence in his admiration of children. I have no idea who is right. Many of these issues about Dodgson are discussed thoroughly in Morton N. Cohen's book, *Lewis Carroll: A Biography* (Cohen 2002) and Katie Roiphe's book, *Still She Haunts,* (Roiphe 2002).

Skulking around the edge of gossip, it may be imagined that if Dodgson had molested one or both of the girls, at that time of Victorian prudence and propriety, no words would have been spoken outside the families, and no involvement of the police would have occurred that would implicate anything but a perfect Christian veneer. But if this speculation was true, the complexity is that Dodgson had lured Alice Liddell's interest by creating a story in which she, as the fictional character, escapes the world of pretend-Victorian perfection into a real-world of chaos and confusion. If indeed Dodgson did molest her or her sister, he lured them from their perfect Christian world into a real, ugly, confusing world and a reality that everyone had to pretend didn't exist as if it really were behind a looking glass. Perhaps Dodgson lived in that dark hole himself. It is no coincidence that Dodgson was also an accomplished mathematician, and the fictional worlds that he created, in many ways, represented mathematical antitheses.

In contrast with the Calvinists and Lutherans, the Pietists moved in the opposite direction, elevating emotions in exchange for reason, which they devalued. In pure Platonic form, the Pietists considered raw emotions to be on the dark side of the divide along with all other functions of the brain. Thus, to enjoy the emotions as God had intended for them to be experienced, the Pietists relabeled their emotions with spiritual names such as "joy" or "being moved by the Holy Spirit." This was a profound and pivotal development within the American evangelical Church.

Emotions would never have had to be relabeled if the Church had not, falsely, considered them as opposing faith, on the wrong side of the dualistic divide. So rather than being angry, they were "grieved" (a spiritual experience). Rather than feeling euphoric, manic, or giddy, they were "joyous" (a spiritual fruit). Or to have total inhibition of emotions, they were "slain in the Spirit." This gave them permission, albeit a dishonest permission, to show real emotion, even in extreme forms. Within mainstream evangelicalism, if a church worship service could stir up a lot of emotions, it was interpreted as the work of the Holy Spirit. But if the service was referred to as "very emotional" rather than "very spiritual," that would not go over so well with many Christians. Pietism's powerful influence eventually made its way into the thinking of the Wesley brothers, John and Charles, who were "richly warmed" by the Spirit.

A Secular Faith

Before concluding these ideas, I will leap across to the secular world briefly to point out a parallel transposition of the emotions but for a slightly different reason. In modern times, secularists have elevated their concept of emotions to a more spiritual level but as defined by a pantheistic rather than a Christian perspective. Instead of *spiritual*, the buzzword has become *energy*. This neutral word can make the spiritual secularist as well as the secular atheist feel comfortable.

Some atheists standing on the rim of the Grand Canyon would fall into the similar dualistic trap as some Christians. They would not be able to see the grandeur of the magnificent landmark pulling at us emotionally, which is a brain function. Instead, they would substitute the term *spiritual Earth* or *feeling the Earth's energy*. This is religious terminology that tries to inject meaning back into the nihilism that must accompany all true atheism. This has little to do with real energy in the sense of the science of physics, except for the electrochemical energy of impulses moving down brain neurons. At this point, the atheist cheats, trying to make meaning where there can be none. Some Christians can't accept a simple and pure emotion because they see all meaningful events as rooted in the spiritual. Some atheists can't accept simple emotions because that would mean there is nothing else in this cold universe except brain function that we feel as emotion. There atheists are trying to say there is something here but nothing there. However, if there is really nothing on the other side of human life ... there can be nothing on this side.

Hankering for Love

I began chapter 16 with a story about toupeed, leg-stretching, Hank, and I'll end this one with its sequel. One day, a few months after the experience at Hank's house, Steve came down to my dorm room, asking if I had any clothes to wash. He was going to his parents' house five miles away to do a load of laundry. "Wanna come?" he asked.

"Sure," I said, always eager for an opportunity to save a little money. I grabbed my musty-smelling duffle bag stuffed with dirty jeans, shirts, and underwear and followed him down to his car. In a few minutes we pulled up in front of a typical middle-class ranch-styled home. "Hmm," he muttered. "Mom's car's here."

I had met Steve's mother only once, on the night of the Full Gospel meeting. If I were honest, I would have to admit I found myself attracted to one of my friends' mothers for the first time in my life. It was creepy. But there was no question she was a beautiful woman. She was thin, with olive skin, cobalt-blue eyes, and long dark hair. I knew she was "old"—nearing 40—but her tanned, fit body could have passed for that of a 28-year-old.

We trekked through the house as Steve shouted, "Mom? Mom?" Secretly, I was hoping she would be home so I could catch a glimpse of her striking face. When there was no response, Steve opened the door down to the laundry area in their unfinished basement.

Once we had the washing machine loaded, we sat down to talk. I perched on a five-gallon paint can and Steve on top of the dryer. He spoke of looking into a Catholic monastery that was "full gospel" located near Ann Arbor, Michigan. I asked whether he really was ready to commit to life-long celibacy. Being the kind of classical nerd who had almost never talked to the opposite sex—save his own mother, celibacy didn't seem as if it would be that hard.

About that time, we heard a creak in the upstairs hardwood floor, then another one just in front of it. With a puzzled look on his face, Steve pushed his glasses up on his nose, jumped off the dryer and said, "Mom must be home. I bet she's in bed with a migraine."

We jogged up the basement steps. To our shock and dismay, we saw—or caught—Steve's mother and Hank tiptoeing out of her bedroom in their sock feet. Hank was in his usual white dress shirt, but it was untucked, and he carried his brown oxfords under his arm. Steve's mom looked embarrassed and made little eye contact. Clutching two long-stem wine glasses in her right hand, she had her white blouse neatly tucked into her navy skirt on one side, but it was out on the other, and her hair was a mess.

They were like two deer caught in the headlights. While Steve's mother seemed humiliated, Hank, in his confident—guiltless—style, immediately spoke as if nothing was wrong. "Hi, boys," he announced. "Nancy and I were just spending some time on our knees praying for the lost in our city. I always start my prayer time with a little wine and bread—a communion with Jaeeeesus before I get down to business. Isn't God great?" He beamed with an ear-to-ear smile. His personality was so compelling that I recall wanting to smile back and say, "He sure is. Thank you, Jaeeeesus!"

Hank was the embodiment of Dualism, as he saw only the Christian spiritual as relevant. Such overemphasis on the heavenly reality caused him to be totally blind to his hypocrisy in this material and real world. When you lose sight of the meaning of real things in this real world the conclusion is always moral failure. It was a moral failure in the murderous Thirty Years' War, in mindless church splits, and in a Victorian world where surface re-spectability was paramount, at the expense of personal debauchery.

Steve seemed even more discomfited than his mother about catching Hank and her in the bedroom, and we quickly returned to the basement to finish our clothes. I didn't say a word, allowing the figurative elephant to sit quietly with us. Steve certainly said nothing more—at least not at first. It wasn't until we were pulling into the gravel parking lot behind our dorm that he said, "I know that looked funny. You know ... with Hank and Mom alone in her bedroom during the day when Dad's at work. But you've got to understand ... Hank is the godliest man I've ever known. He's full of the Holy Spirit. Mom considers him her best friend, but it's a Jesus-centered relationship ... strictly platonic."

CHAPTER EIGHTEEN

The Summit Ridge

I've done a lot of hiking and some mountaineering in my life—in the Appalachians, Rockies, Alps, and Himalayas, and even through some unnamed dry and rugged mountains in Oman and Sinai that looked as if they had been imported from the surface of the moon. Now I do most of my hiking or climbing in the North Cascades in Washington State, whose ruggedness is awe-inspiring. Their abyss-like valleys of avocado-green velvet, cascading spikes, and ice-accented crags give the appearance of mythical castles and cathedrals of such grandeur that even J. R. R. Tolkien would be awestruck. When you climb nearby glacier-clad Mount Baker and are alone on the high glaciers, you are surrounded by enormous geographical features that makes you feel like a flea on the spine of a Seismosaurus.

I love all mountains; however, if I had a favorite, it would have to be the Matterhorn, which straddles the Swiss–Italian boarder. I have only had the opportunity to dream about climbing that mountain, but I have studied it so much I feel as if I know the route to the top very well. The Hornli ridge is the most popular route and involves hiking, bouldering, scrambling, rock climbing, and just a little crampon-required ice ascending. There's a few fixed ropes over the most difficult parts. An ice axe is only useful near the very top and to transfer between the "Swiss Summit" (14,691 feet above sea level) and the "Italian Summit." (14,686 feet above sea level). It is one of the deadliest mountains on the earth (over 500 have died trying to climb it) due to its allure, accessibility, and technical difficulty.

A 300-foot-long, knife-edged icy ridge is suspended between the two summits. The width of the ridge is only about six inches in places and the—almost vertical—wall going down on each side is over 5,000 feet to the bottom. The path is this poor mixture of rock and ice. If it were all ice, crampons would give you an advantage. If it were only rock, friction shoes or boots would be the preference. But the mixture makes whatever you wear—the wrong choice. With the typical high winds at the summit, the crossing gives even a seasoned alpinist some angst.

As a climber, you are usually roped to a partner. During the crossing of the summit ridge, if one climber starts to slip over the edge, the only way the roped mountaineers can be saved is if the other climber—counterintuitively—leaps off the opposing side. This leap has to be done instantly. Each climber is left dangling in a counterbalance, with one climber hanging over Switzerland on the north face and the other over the Italian south face.

The summit ridge of the Matterhorn is a great metaphor, which I will use in this chapter to explain the influences of the two great Greek philosophers. Italy is a country that has been heavily influenced by Plato, in some form, since his visit to the peninsula (c. 399 BC). You can see it clearly in the sensual experiences of their visual and culinary arts. Switzerland, on the other hand, has been heavily influenced by the teachings of Aristotle through the writings of Averroes of Spain and Aquinas of Paris in the twelfth and thirtieth centuries and then Calvin of Geneva of the sixteenth. You can see the impact in the rigid precision of Swiss engineering, where a train two minutes late into the station is a national scandal.

THE PHILOSOPHICAL TIGHTROPE

In chapter 13 I introduced the painting, *The School of Athens*, by Raphael. I believe this is the most important painting ever created by a human being, certainly within the Western Hemisphere. Maybe the Lascaux paintings were second in historical significance. Raphael's fresco was painted on the wall of Pope Julius II's private study in his apartment complex at the Vatican about the same time that Michelangelo was painting his, far more familiar work, on the ceiling of the Sistine Chapel nearby. The fact that Raphael depicted Plato and Aristotle standing at the center of the painting (encircled by many other important thinkers and movers) was no coincidence. These two philosophers represent the two cliffs on each side of the narrow path of Western civilization for the past two and half centuries.

Lurking just over the edge of the south side of the ridge is Plato and his Dualistic view of reality and over on the north side is a sharp tumble into an infallible Aristotelian reason, a reason based utterly on empirical observations. The history of Western civilization can be easily explained as us silly humans walking the summit ridge, like two tethered drunks, falling off one side then the other, back and forth, over and over again—without pausing at the path of equilibrium in the middle. In other words, on one side is the Platonic notion that this material world has no value, whereas the only value is found in the far more real—unseen world. This unseen world has been interpreted at various times in different ways. It was the *heavenly* for the medieval Church and *sensual* (meaning here of course "of the senses" and not just sexual) for the Renaissance and *energy* in the postmodernists. In Raphael's painting, Plato is not only pointing upward to the ether but is wearing red, representing fire, which is immaterial, and violet, which is the color of the sky or what he considered the ether.

Aristotle, on the other hand, is pointing downward toward this material Earth, wearing brown to represent dirt and blue to represent water. He believed that you could always reach truth through the logical interpretation of what your senses told you about the material world. However, in some ways opposite of Plato, if your senses couldn't observe it, then it was not real. This was simply an arbitrary conclusion by Aristotle's successors that had profound implications on later Western civilization.

We Christians have fallen off the Platonic side several times in history. It happened first with the Gnostics of the first century. We struggled to climb back onto the path through the efforts of the early Church fathers and Church councils but we never quite made it and stayed over that edge throughout the medieval period. Then we toppled further backward, way over the same edge as Pietists and eventually as evangelicals.

Secular society has been the Church's roped-up climbing partner in this tango on the ridge, taking turns in leading and following. The secularists went over the Platonic edge with the early Greek mystics, pulling the Church with it, and again with the Medicis' Renaissance. Despite all of its wonderful glory, the Renaissance could not be sustained on an underpinning of human-sensual experience alone. If it had been built on a more biblical concept of the honest enjoyment of a glorious, material world created by God, I think it would have been a different story.

North of the Matterhorn, the Church took the lead, being lured over the Aristotelian side of the cliff slipping on the ice of the Scholastics. The secular culture, roped to the Church, followed, falling into the Enlightenment and the Age of Reason. The Scholastics and the Enlightenment, just like the Renaissance, made many admirable contributions to our culture but, with a basis on the certainty of an Aristotelian reason it would, inevitably, lead to despair.

It was after the age of despair—culminating on the battle fields of the twentieth century wars—that the secularists took the lead again, this time sauntering back over the Platonic cliff into the abyss of postmodernism and the age of anti-reason. Roped-in, with their carabiners locked in place, the American evangelical church soon followed in the plunge with a new irrational spirituality and a flirtation with the ambiguous god of pantheism. Once over the edge, both the secularists and Christians could sit down in total agreement on the relativity and personalization of truth without ever having to turn a page. Truth becomes certainty because you feel it is true or, like the Gnostics, God spoke truth to you and only to you.

The path of balance in the philosophical realm is to simply include the respect of the material world, along with the spiritual. This means esteeming human reason and sensual perceptions of the real world but without the Aristotelian certainty. A proper view of the Fall of Adam would deny such a confidence. I will further illuminate this dilemma of balance in very real-world terms in my closing chapters.

THE PSYCHOLOGICAL TIGHTROPE

Walking the summit ridge is also a great simile for how we see ourselves on a psychological level. I've described the ASW as the basic principle of human behavior. When we look at this issue of self-worth, three choices emerge, only one of which is healthy. On one side of the knife-edge path is the attitude that it is our responsibility to earn God's pleasure and that of others. However, on that side you get enough of a glimpse at the contents of your cellar that you live in a chronic state of shame. You could say that this emotional perspective parallels the Platonic devaluation of the material because we sense that our worldly failures have contaminated us and tainted our hopes of having spiritual value.

The dangerous cliff on the other side of the summit ridge represents the emotional concept that it is our responsibility to earn God's pleasure, but, in this case, we have a sense we've done pretty well at it. This side parallels the Aristotelian view that we can look with our senses at what we have accomplished in the material, i.e., good deeds and showing kindness, financial success, and reaching the logical conclusion that we are pretty good fellas. With this group, it is a requirement to sweep your failures and limitations into the cellar, quickly closing the door and throwing a heavy rug over it. The thinking goes, if our senses can't perceive it, then it isn't real. This is the way I handled the rage from my childhood when I first became a Christian.

A more graphic illustration of this kind of self-deception comes from a TV documentary I watched about 15 years ago. It was about a FBI sting to catch people who were trying to hire hitmen. Each encounter was videotaped by several secret hidden cameras. One woman, whom I will never forget, was a gospel singer in a group with her husband and two other men. Sitting in a white pickup truck in a strip mall parking lot in Las Vegas, she spoke with an undercover FBI agent who she thought was a hitman. The agent was prodding her to be explicitly clear because he knew the video would incriminate her in a court of law. She had already communicated through a middleman that she wanted her husband killed. The following is their conversation, which I'm paraphrasing:

Agent: "Ma'am, what do you want me to do?"

Gospel singer: "I want you to kill my husband dead—but make him suffer first. Can you run over his legs with your truck and break them, then drag him down the street and let him lie and suffer for a while before you finish him off by running over his ugly face?"

Agent, shaking his head: "Why do you want him dead so badly?"

Gospel singer: "I'm in love with Bill, another singer in our group. We're having an affair now, but we want to get married. We feel guilty about sleeping together while not being married."

Agent: "Why don't you just divorce your husband and marry Bill?"

Gospel singer, with a sweet, angelic smile on her face: "You don't understand. We're strong Christians, and we don't believe in divorce."

When Christians with these attitudes are caught in any sort of compromising situation, they appear to be in great distress, crying and professing repentance. Even though God knew about their sin all along, and they knew that he knew, it didn't bother them then. The woman couldn't divorce her husband without others finding out about it, but she could have him killed in secret. It is horrifying for all of us to have our cellar doors thrown open for the whole world to see inside. Their entire empire of false self-worth can be annihilated in a second.

When I was in the Chinese restaurant, Rod and I were equally at fault—Rod for using guilt manipulation and me for allowing it to perpetuate. Each of us had our own demons in our cellars that made us the way we were, demons we both denied. Prior to my fall, I thought I had succeeded at being saintly in all of my thoughts. It wasn't until the murderous dragons of anger and hate raised their foul heads did I get a glimpse of my inner man.

Besides living in guilt, and being immune to guilt, the only healthy choice is the third one: the narrow route down the middle of the ridge. That path is the knowledge that, in Christ alone, God finds us acceptable, and his acceptance is total, comprehensive, and planted entirely in grace. Jesus is the perfect hybrid of the totally spiritual and fully material. This was why he created so much controversy in the early Church because they were trying to force him into a Platonic mold where you could only be material or spiritual, but never both.

On the Aristotelian side, we could also erroneously conclude that Christ's redemption isn't enough. We need some observable (empirical) evidence that we are redeemed such as through correct church membership, good works, business success, or some type of behavior. However, we need to be careful to not to stumble too far in the other direction and fall into the error of thinking on the Platonic side that, except for Jesus and his redeeming work in us, we are worthless garbage because we are material. This idea is expressed in such hymn lyrics as, "which saved a wretch like me." I don't know why this grace path in the middle is the narrowest and most difficult to maintain … but it is.

A RAW SANCTIFICATION

Sin entering into the world greatly affects the material side of the Dualistic divide. If the Fall of Adam has roots in the concrete, then true change is possible, but it may come at a pace more consistent with a glacier than a waterfall. Human behavior can change and attitudes can transform, but following the laws of brain biochemistry and physics—which God beautifully created—they occur slowly at best.

When a sharp contrast exists between what you believe about sanctification and reality, only two options are available: change what you believe or construct a veneer that is consistent with what you believe and superimpose it over the inconsistent reality. This is what the Pharisees did. In Matthew 23:27, Jesus called them "whitewashed tombs, which look beautiful on the outside but on the inside are full of the bones of the dead and everything unclean." This is what the Gospel singer was trying to do by murdering her husband in secret so she could marry the man she really loved without the stain of going through a divorce. This *veneerization* is what I believe many Christians have done for ages.

It was a harrowing but at the same time liberating revelation to know that I, too, had been constructing this veneer. This masquerade was the Christian world I had been living in prior to my fall down the abyss. I wish that I had seen things more clearly, before I had become a father, so that I could have been a better example to my children of living Christianly with candor. I am still hopeful that it is not too late.

In the year 2002 we uprooted the family one last time and moved here, to the beautiful San Juan Islands of Washington State. We found this place to be our personal Garden of Eden. For me, it has been an inviting place where I could harvest my thoughts, the fruits of my study, and organize them into this book. It has also been a place where we have watched the methodical launch of each of our children out the safety of our nest and out into the world.

Our oldest, Bryan, is married and has two sons and is finishing a PhD program in Minneapolis. He was only five when we landed in Cairo. Daniel, who suffered so much during those two years and who I was certain we were losing during one prolonged illness, is also finishing up a PhD at the University of Washington. He still suffers from the mysterious illness that started as a small boy in Egypt. Tyler, who was born in Cairo, is the only child who has settled nearby, enjoying his work in carpentry. Amy, born in Duluth, Minnesota, during our first year back, has now returned to Minnesota where she is attending graduate school. Ramsey, our youngest, born at K.I. Sawyer Air Force Base in Marquette, Michigan, just moved to Manhattan this week, where he is working as a mathematician and programmer with an Internet start-up company.

During the past decade, I've had the opportunity to revisit my original dream, which was to spend my life living and bringing health care to the most remote areas of the world, although this time in only brief nibbles. I still feel a great grief of what could have been. I returned to NW Pakistan in 2006 to help after the terrible earthquake in Kashmir. In 2008 I was able to visit Cairo again for a time of final closure, this time taking Amy and Ramsey for their first visit. On the trip, I found several old Egyptian friends, however; I could not find the Chinese restaurant where the fall all began. I think where it stood may, ironically, be a real crater ... a new construction zone. In 2010 I spent time on the Nepalese–Tibetan boarder providing health care. I also have been lucky enough to be taken around the world by my pursuit for the answers to those questions born in the dusty streets of Cairo in 1988. I've spent many hours studying, contemplating, and writing in teahouses in Asia and over cappuccinos in the Middle East, North Africa, and Europe.

Corresponding to our move from Rochester, the expedition out of my crater and through the post-evangelical wasteland was also finding closure. Then, for the first time in over a decade, things were starting to make sense again. With a systematic study, God had granted me the grace to find the answers to the questions of why and how. The pinnacle of this task now, besides just telling my story, is to answer for others the final supposed question of so what? How do we change our thinking and what difference does it make if any? The closing chapters will resolve these final questions.

CHAPTER NINETEEN
So? The Philosophical Question

Somewhere along the shore of the Black Sea, three thousand years before Christ, some ingenious artisan, with relatively little effort, molded and carved a beautiful sculpture from a block of beeswax. Then he packed clay around the wax figure. Next, the clever fellow heated the clay form in a hot oven until the clay baked and the wax melted and ran out through a drain hole he had made in the bottom of the mold. Taking a mixture of tin from Afghanistan and copper from Cyprus, he melted it on hot, billowed coals and poured it back into the baked-clay mold. Once it was cooled and solidified, the clay was broken away with a rock or hammer. Presto, the world's first bronze sculpture appeared!

When I first entered the Egyptian culture over 25 years ago, we were cut off from most American influences. Soon, the American-Western culture began melting and running out through my pores, just like the wax draining from the clay mold, leaving only a kind of universal, human culture. Many things I had taken for granted as rational, good, natural, and maybe even Christian began to melt under the constant questioning of my Egyptian neighbors and friends, who saw things differently. Many of them were Christian Egyptians (Coptic Christians) who saw things from a very different perspective than myself with my American-evangelical upbringing. The soft wax aspects that drained out of me were only American, after all, and not necessarily Christian.

As we try to establish new ways of thinking, we have to allow many cultural things to melt away before we can pour in new ideas that are worth considering. It's a challenge, but it's not impossible to do. Phillip Lee points out in the concluding chapter of *Against the Protestant Gnostics* that if Ambrose could escape the years that Marcionism held him in its grip and Augustine could escape the troughs of Manichaeism, surely we can escape Dualism's influence in the twenty-first century Church. My goal in this book is to provide a framework for that change.

If I've failed to translate these important, but sometimes abstract, ideas into practical applications as to how we should think and act, my efforts may have been in vain. My intentions were much deeper and nobler, I'd like to think, rather than walking through the Christian world causing chaos, like a John Deere tractor pulling a plow through untilled ground, I will be planting something new and giving real hope.

A METAPHYSICAL REPENTANCE

What would a non-Platonic-Dualistic Christianity—or what might be called a material Christianity—look like? We can start with fundamental metaphysical considerations, specifically creation itself. Plato placed a dualistic curtain between the material world and the unseen world (ether); moreover, he set them on a tiered system. This is an artificial division. In what I think is a true biblical perspective, the material world is not the antithesis of the spiritual; rather, each is a part of creation as a whole. Both the material and the unseen, although they are different, still create a uniformity of God's stuff. It is close to what science fiction writers, or even some within mainstream astrophysics, see as parallel universes.

The real antithesis of creation is nothingness. This is where the great divide actually occurs, with the metaphysical curtain dropping precisely at this point. Without God, there was nothing. No matter, no space, no time, no quarks, no dark matter, no big bang—absolutely nothing. With God there is all that is, seen and unseen. Before God spoke, there was only empty space with a capital E.

To take that thinking one step farther, everything this side of the point of creation is a miracle or supernatural. This is a profoundly new way to think. Miracles include all the things that happen within the laws of physics, cause and effect, biological systems—all are covered with God's fingerprints and are miraculous. It is difficult to permit this cultural connotation of the word *miracle* to melt and run out and start fresh. But this is exactly the point

Albert Einstein was making when he said, "There are two ways to live your life. One is as though nothing is a miracle. The other is as though everything is a miracle." (Hinshaw 2006). Einstein said what I'm trying to say. Either the universe is a complete fluke and has no meaningful value, purpose, or intention, or the universe was created by God, and everything within it is from God and thus a miracle.

The real intellectual dilemma of humankind is the fact we are here. The presence of something—rather than nothing—begs the question, *Why?* I respect atheists and agnostics greatly because the way out of this labyrinth is not easy, and I know that I could have easily ended up in their camp once again. Yet arrogance is prevalent on both sides. The worst choice is to sit and think nothing, be consumed by "living in the moment," or to keep yourself so entertained that you don't have to think about the big questions.

NEURONS OR DEMONS, TAKE YOUR PICK

While I was still living in Cairo in 1989, I received a desperate call from an American missionary mother, Andrea, who lived in a flat a few miles from us. Her son, who had epilepsy, was having a seizure and was not recovering from it. I ran the whole way to their apartment. As I passed a pharmacy, I ran inside and demanded a bottle of diazepam and a syringe. The pharmacist handed it to me without question, and I continued on to Andrea's apartment at full speed. When I arrived, her son, Andrew, was in bed and still going in and out of a seizure. His long, thin body would stiffen and shake before relaxing, then stiffen and shake again. Another American man, Chad, was present, whom I had never met before. Later I learned he was a missionary with the same organization as Andrea.

As I administered the diazepam into the boy's small vein, Chad announced that the boy was being attacked by demons and that he needed to perform an exorcism. He began to pray loudly that the demon would leave the boy's body. In about a minute, the typical time for diazepam to take effect—enhancing the brain's production of gamma-amino butyric acid (GABA, a neurotransmitter) and quieting the rapid-firing brain neurons—the boy stopped shaking and started to wake up. Chad suddenly began praising God for delivering the boy from Satan's influence. In the conversation that followed that event, Chad confidently took credit for casting out the demon that had been terrorizing the boy's soul and warned Andrea about looking out for demonic influences in their family. They should look for and throw out things such as a Michael Jackson cassette tape or Rubik's cubes, he insisted.

Having spent my medical career in neurology, I had a different explanation, but I made my argument with less force than Chad, who was exhibiting an overconfident personality behavior. I explained that the boy suffered from generalized tonic-clonic seizures (formerly known as grand mal seizures). Being aware of his long complex history, I was sure his seizures were caused by hypoxemia of his brain during birth. When the brain sustains an injury, especially if that injury is in seizure-prone areas of the brain such as the temporal lobes, the neurons there have a tendency to misfire, causing seizures.

Because Andrew's seizure was so prolonged, it put him in real danger. This was especially true living in a place like Cairo where the concepts of ambulances and emergency rooms were outside their realm of thinking at that time. I recommended to his mother that he be put on medication to prevent future seizures.

Chad seemed irritated at my suggestion. With even more confidence in his voice, he replied that I wasn't "looking at it from a spiritual side." He told Andrea she must choose to follow either "God's way or man's way," adding he would not put his son on "worldly drugs," but, as a godly man, he would use prayer to protect him from Satan. Andrea and her husband, with a sincere desire to follow and obey God, chose Chad's way. My view seemed trite and unchristian to them—as I did as a person from that day forward.

Chad, like many American evangelicals, lived in a Christian-Platonic world, where the curtain of Dualism came down sharply, dividing the seen versus the unseen worlds. Neurophysiology, and the wonderful, miraculous brain God created, were on the inferior, worldly side of the equation. To put the situation in the upper-story, unseen world was much more consistent with godliness than taking drugs. This included drugs created by smart men and women with wonderful minds who were created by a wonderful God and who used the principles of biochemistry that God originated.

If we purge the Platonic view from our thinking, Christians then don't have to embellish their stories by proving that God did something, outside natural laws, to give them more merit. It seems to me that God would find rejecting the natural systems of cause and effect, the system that he created, highly offensive. Also, I believe he, as a God of truth, dislikes lying, especially lying for him. Yet lying for God is widely accepted in Christian society as a good thing, although those who do so would never admit it.

Because I no longer submit to indiscrete "god-talk" and am skeptical of many of the bigger-than-nature workings ascribed to God, I have had Christians suggest that I am no longer a spiritual person or that I'm trying to remove the "mystery of God." I must strongly disagree. The universe is filled with so much mystery that it blows the mind. These are mega-mysteries, like quantum physics and dark matter (to name one of thousands) and weirder things. The fact that we exist is a paradox. This whole issue of causality is a mystery, where cause and effect is real in this material world, but God's sovereignty is as well. My point is, we should not lie, and we should not reduce the creator of the universe down to an elf in your pocket who can make a leg grow or the rays of a sunlight look like a cross. If he chooses to work outside of his creation, it appears to be uncommon ... but never trite. As I've said before, because God dwells within reality, the more contact we have with raw reality, the more contact we can have with God.

A SUBSTANTIAL HISTORY

There's still another example of evangelical logic, which becomes so absurd that it would be fitting conversation around the table at a tea party with the Mad Hatter and March Hare. Some evangelicals would say that every event, from running into Marge at the bakery to a huge disaster in which thousands are violently killed, is a divine appointment, and this is somehow mixed up with the sovereignty of God. The cliché "everything happens for a purpose" sends the message that events have meaning only if they are anchored in the unseen world via God's puppeteer strings. This type of determinism can become suffocating to a culture.

Dualism, when taken to its logical conclusion, always ends with determinism. Determinism means that we are just cogs in the machinery of the universe or, in the case of us theists, the machinery of God's will. In this case, it is the will of God that steamrolls through history, which our own actions or will cannot foil. If nothing in this world has meaning unless it is attached to puppeteer strings from the unseen world, then the unseen world controls everything, and we have no free will. If you take on a new, non-Dualistic frame of mind, where history is material and meaningful, then there is a profound opportunity for change … but where risks are also real.

THE PARADOX OF THE DIVINE ASSASSIN

One of the most blatant examples of this quirky circular reasoning, when it comes to risks, happened when I was working in the emergency room at the air force base in Marquette, Michigan. A four-year-old boy, Sam, had managed to push open the screen door of his house and run across the backyard to be with his father, who was on a riding lawnmower. Not seeing his son, the man backed over him. Horrifyingly, Sam's precious little head was sliced into pieces, and he died in our emergency room soon after.

Sam's parents, Bob and Clare, were members of our church. In the midst of our grief, the next Sunday one of my fellow elders announced to the congregation from the pulpit that "God doesn't make mistakes!" Loud amens followed. Then he added, "This event had an ecclesiastical purpose—to teach Bob and Clare, and all of us, to depend on God!" With this mindset, God must be a veritable sadist.

But does that really make sense to anyone with a rational mind? What kind of God do we serve if he slices the brains of four-year-old boys to bits and murders them—just to teach his parents something like patience? This God sounds worse than Hitler, or an ISIL operative. It doesn't surprise me that so many of our churched young people abandon Christianity as soon as they have the freedom to do so. It also doesn't surprise me that non-Christians want no part of a God like that. As Christians, we have painted ourselves into a metaphysical corner with this bizarre reasoning.

And somehow this great ecclesiastical lesson for Bob and Clare eventually failed anyway. They never recovered from Sam's tragic death but eventually blamed each other to the point of divorce. It begs the question: if God butchered Sam to teach his parents something, but they remained untaught, how did God—who knows the future—not know that they would remain untaught? Thus, it can only be concluded that God's cruel act was all in vain. Moreover, God knew it would be in vain. Mad Hatter, please pass the jelly!

So how can we explain little Sam's awful death in non-Dualistic terms that would make sense in a world created by a loving and sovereign God?

These kinds of questions have plagued Christians since the days of Christ. The goofy answers given to these questions has hidden God from countless people over the centuries.

In the wonderful world that God made, when a child pushes a screen door with a certain force, that door moves in the direction of the motion. Then the child uses the wonderful brain God has given him to visualize his daddy and to want him. Then that child's brain allows him to walk in an upright position. Each stage of the accident could be described in terms of physics and human physiology, but my point is clear. An honest mistake like leaving the door unlatched has real consequences in the real world God has made. I will say again, the world is real and therefore not completely safe. Does God still reign sovereign over these events? Absolutely. The final destiny is in his loving hands. God will eventually remedy all the messy mistakes of this life and the brokenness of nature.

You could follow a similar play-by-play account of two men in a Chinese restaurant in Cairo, Egypt. Each with a unique set of emotional baggage and a systemic theology that was deeply flawed. Crap happens in this world, it is the way it is, because the world is real. Not having a Dualistic perspective takes away the psychological need to blame God. This need to blame has been the ruin of many good people.

Does prayer have no value then? What does the Bible say about prayer? To me, prayer definitely has value, far beyond simply relaxing us like meditation might do. It is not an exercise to drift, transcendently, out of the soiling of this material into a pantheistic bliss. Instead, it is the act of petitioning God to step into the material, which he has made—but which has become broken, and to fix it now. God didn't just wind up the universe like a clock before going on vacation to Belize, where he's dozing in a hammock with a Corona. He walks through the material world, not as an absentee landlord but a hands-on one, and he does step in and act directly. But God apparently only rarely works outside his natural laws. This isn't a theological position but a simple and honest observation of the real world as it exists without delusional or wishful thinking.

It's difficult to completely grasp this harmony between real cause and effect and a loving and sovereign God. Perhaps it's like a decorative quilt, with sparkly bells, stars, and beads that tinkle and spin and are chaotic but are sewn to the backing of flat, stable fabric. The real, dynamic cause and effect of our lives is somehow sewn to the stable backdrop of God's endless love and overwhelming sovereignty. And that is the great mystery and beyond my ability to grasp or explain.

NATURE: FINDERS KEEPERS, LOSERS WEEPERS

Another way that purging ourselves of Dualistic thinking, which would have an impact on us and our Christianity, is our view of nature itself. I believe that Christians should be the greatest tree huggers of all. As well, they should be animal huggers, stream huggers, Newton's laws huggers, and huggers of the cosmos. This is all God's stuff, made for his and our good pleasure, not for us to abuse.

However, the view of nature in Western civilization is now based on two powerful, non-Christian, influences. The first of these is the pantheistic view that nature is valuable because it is god or because their abstruse god dwells amidst it. The second influence is from the Swiss philosopher, Jean-Jacques Rousseau (1712–1778).

In the eighteenth century, due to a Dualistic influence, Christianity had a very low view of nature. Rousseau rebelled against his Calvinistic upbringing, with its low view of nature, and sought to make the natural world important again. To do this, he rejected the Christian-Dualistic notion of nature being created malicious and then made even worse by sin entering into the world. He replaced it with the opinion that nature is basically perfect ... unless people interfere with it. This is exactly why the terms "Natural, Nature and Organic" are so popular today. Those terms don't mean what we think they mean. They are actually referring to—from Rousseauian theory—things that have not been interfered with by humans ... and are therefore intrinsically better. He also applied his natural view to political philosophy with the main tenant that people thrive when they are not interfered with by other people (Church and state). With this view, he became the chief philosophical architect of the French Revolution. He promised a utopian world ahead, but instead the dystopian world of Hugo's *Les Misérables* (Hugo 1862) came in the revolution's wake. Ironically, the only place that Rousseauian theory could apply is that humans should not insert human ideas into basic, natural Christianity, but they always have ... including Rousseau.

But the Christian, without a Dualistic view of nature, would give nature the glory that God intended. Yet, a biblical Christian view would have the understanding that nature is not perfect, due to the influences of third-person sin. We would also see ourselves as instruments of change and with the potential of improving nature (the gardeners of Eden), an idea that Rousseau, as well as most of our current culture, would have strongly rejected.

The only place that the Rousseauian theory would apply is in the Gospel itself. It is the one thing that always diminishes when humans add to it. As I have alluded to in the subtitle of this book, without intention, I eventually found myself on the trail of finding the simple and pure, natural Gospel.

THE LOSS OF PLATONIC AND ARISTOTELIANISM CERTAINTY

Nature is not perfect in the biblical story, and we humans are part of that imperfection. We definitely have faults in our morality but also in our perceptions and ability to reason. The simple premises of Aristotelian philosophy require a perfect perception of the world around us and an impeccable ability to process that information with our logic. If we turn from the Aristotelian influence toward a more biblical model, we must lose our rational confidence.

We also must avoid falling off the other side of the crag by adopting a Platonic or mystical certainty. This is an alluring path, as we live now within this post-modern age of anti-reason. This search for truth is based on emotional feelings, but for the Christian at least, those feelings have been rebranded as "spiritual" to make us feel better about them.

One example of this spiritual confidence, which I first heard in the Billy Graham movie *Time to Run* (World Wide Pictures 1973), was the idea that we can know God is there with conviction because we each have a God-shaped hole or void in our hearts that only God can fill. There has been serious philosophical discussion about this idea, such as by Christian philosopher/mathematician Blaise Pascal (1623–1662); however, I believe that most people use this term in its most simple, apathetic, and superficial way. To take this Platonic way of thinking into an even more sinister place, as I have suggested before, you justify all your actions or personal positions (often it involves manipulating others to do things you want) by saying "God spoke to my heart." For me personally, it was a leader who said that God told him that I was to make my family move to Yemen. I also know there are many times that I had taken actions or manipulated others and passed it off as God's notion. We must remember, as I mentioned in the chapter 13, the Bible says we can't trust the human heart.

Almost everyone is familiar with René Descartes' (1596–1650) statement, "Cogito ergo sum," which translates to "I think, therefore I am." This is probably the most famous quote in philosophy. Few understand the content ... that he was one of the first rationalists to reject Aristotelianism theory of certainty. He, rightly, did not trust the senses to lead to total truth. The fact that we reason at all must prove that we exist ... and that is the only certainty we can know. Post-modern philosophers even challenged that one point of certainty.

To most American evangelicals, losing certainty sounds atrocious. It feels so appalling because we have lived so long under the influence of Aristotelian rationality and Platonic mysticism that we don't recognize it as an extra-biblical view of epistemology. As a good Christian, our culture obligates us to have total confidence, not only in acknowledging God's existence, but having the right church, the right doctrines, precise interpretation of science, correct political party, and the perfect position on all moral issues. This view of certainty is the wedge that creates all Christian divisions. Once daylight between positions has been established, the lever can be inserted and you lift yourself up, scoring a better ASW ... or so you think.

I am sure that there are many things in this book that hardened evangelicals will find offensive, but this acknowledgement of uncertainty will undoubtedly offer the worst offense. They believe that if you don't have certainty, then you can know nothing at all. That is absolutely not correct. I am also not saying that theological doctrines are not important or relative. They are extremely important and absolute, but we just cannot know them absolutely all the time. We don't give up because of this problem. We study harder and we listen with a real learner's heart.

True discipleship is not memorizing the established answers and then being smacked on the back of the head every time we deviate from the rote. It is a lifetime of journeying, circling closer and closer to reality, the place where God dwells. Jesus' 12 friends all knew reality much better at the end of their little adventure than when he first requisitioned them out of the Galilean normalcy. At the end, they knew that sexual fantasies about their friends' wives were no different than adultery except for the fear of getting caught. They knew that hate was of the same cast as murder, without the public consequences. They also learned that all their attempts of righteous living in a Jewish society were trifling at best and still required the clemency of God. If they had lived by a blind faith in a—predigested—irrevocability they would never had left their nets or purses to follow this man of contradictions. The first step of discipleship is a quam toward one's present course, especially if that course is not working.

As with nature in general, we Christians must respect reason as God-given, without exaggerating its clarity. Certainty is not the opposite of doubt. Doubt is a psychological phenomenon where a person waivers back and forth between two possible conclusions or, more literally, between two minds of thought. Certitude is an illusion that no mortal person can obtain and to demand it leads us to a position of arrogance that is inconsistent with substance. As Socrates pointed out, critical thinking always starts with deliberate doubt. We live by faith, a moral position, and faith is expressed best where certainty cannot be fully obtained. Reason is not faith's nemesis, as I had been taught, but they are comrades, each buttressing the other in time of need.

We are now living in a pragmatic age, where part of our Western culture is committed to reason and science, yet others (sometimes the same person) will also revel in a post-Aristotelian (a.k.a. postmodern) age of non-reason with a pantheistic flair. Thus, a Christian must be very careful at this juncture of repentance. If he or she is willing to give up certainty, then that person must not exchange reason for a post-modern relativism or pantheistic mysticism, relabeling it as Christian spirituality. That would be a direr mistake and a more lethal stumble off the other side of the ridge. I will restate once more that reason is good, reliable most of the time, and God given. It does not reside on the inferior side of some philosophical divide. However, as fallen men and women, our reason cannot take us the whole way to certainty about God or anything but can reach a high probability ... and that is enough. Before the fall of Adam, I do believe that certainty was self-evident ... but not now.

CHAPTER TWENTY

※

So? The Spiritual Question

ON PLATO AND THE SOUL

Throughout Greek—and later Church—history, the psyche and the soul were considered one and the same. The Greek translation of the word *soul* is "psyche." Ironically, it was only when Pythagoras came up with the concept of metempsychosis did the soul start to be viewed as a ghostly mist that inhabits but has no concrete relationship with the physical body and brain. An example is a steam pipe where the steam inhabits the pipe but has not physically bonded to the steel (like rust) and can exist freely without the pipe containing it. Plato's concept of the soul was shaped at Pythagoras's school in Italy. Centuries later, through the continued Platonic-Dualistic influence within the Church, the modern concept of psychology and spirituality was further split. Psychology (the study of the psyche) was relegated to the inferior, material brain and spirituality assigned to the superior, unseen soul. Just as metaphysics (the study of existence) is core to the study of philosophical systems, so the study of the human soul is central to any study of theological systems. The first in proper thinking is to reunite the subjects of psychology and spirituality.

ON ARISTOTLE AND THE SOUL

Different from the Platonically influenced Christians, Aristotle, being pre-Christian, of course did not have a view of original sin but asserted that our reason—interpreting information from our senses—was without flaws, leading us to truth every time. I must say at this juncture that to be fair to Aristotle, some of the things that I attribute to him were actually interpretations of his writings by later thinkers inside and outside the Church over the past two millennia.

In an oversimplified view of Aristotle's views of psychology, based on his writings in *De Anima* and the *Parva Naturalia*, he suggested that within the human psyche is a conflict between the urges and reason. When the urges win, the resulting consequences could be what we know as mental illness. However, the infallible reason of the mind is able to conquer these impulses and bring good mental balance and health. This idea was a foreshadowing of Freud's concept of psychoanalysis where he considered that the rational superego was in charge of the primal urges of the id.

AMERICAN EVANGELICAL VIEW OF SPIRITUALITY

The idea of original sin bringing a curse to all of humanity and nature is a foundational doctrine of all Christian sects and, in many ways, separates it from many other major religions. However, assessment of the level of this curse varies from church to church and individual Christian to individual Christian. American evangelicalism has taken the position on the far end of the spectrum, where this curse has totally decimated all of humanity, leaving nothing but shapeless crowds of fallen wretches.

American evangelicals also have adopted the Pythagorean-Platonic view of the soul, metempsychosis. The essence of who we are, in that view, is a soul with no connection to the material brain. Our character is therefore fluid and changes with a simple act of the will. So, in their opinion, while we start as total wretches, we can be completely fixed. Because this is not consistent with reality, "fixed people," will always disappoint us, and, if we imagine that we are "fixed," we will ultimately disappoint ourselves.

American evangelicals also hold the view that simple spiritual exercises such as morning devotions, prayer, and fasting can hasten that change, moving us far along that spectrum toward our original pre-fallen state of godliness. Of course, many will incorporate the working of the Holy Spirit as a catalysis that can expedite that change to an instantaneous level. As I've stated in chapter eight, when a detachment develops between our level of perceived godliness and the harsh reality of who we really are, it gives opportunity for pretense.

A New View of the Soul and Spirituality

My new understanding rejected all Aristotelian and Platonic influences on Christianity, trying to see it in its natural form. Unlike Aristotle, as I mentioned several times, our senses, while often correct, can make mistakes. Also, different from Plato's perspective, I now see the human psyche as intimately connected both to our material bodies and nature where we live.

If we can acknowledge that our emotional selves are part of our material brains, subject to all the good and bad of self-deception, including our mystical (emotional) interpretations, we can embrace truth with great humility. We must understand that our will—the master of our behavior—is good and powerful, but it comes with flaws, too. God has given us the ability to feel, but that feeling also come with inaccuracies. Because we are material, the brokenness is never completely untangled in this world because it is real and organic. There is a real hope of change, but like I said in chapter 18, it is methodical and with frequent setbacks. We are to love everyone but never fully trust anyone—and certainly not ourselves.

Raw, or what you call natural, spirituality is simple. The central Christian doctrine is that we have congenital guilt from a fallen world. We contribute to that guilt through our own, wrong actions. Jesus came to acquit us of that guilt, with a total exoneration. This notion, if fully understood—and no one really gets it—is profound. All of our longings for the positive appraisal for our self-worth has been totally satisfied in Christ. We are now set free. The great masquerade ball is over … the last step of the final dance movement ends where the cross penetrates the dirt. More precisely, where the iron nail penetrates the material flesh of God. Regarding sanctification, the simple law is God's gift to his people, telling them the best way to live consistently with how we were created. It is never about penance but to bring us contentment and to society, peace. It was never about ASW. As the Church, we have been given the fantastic opportunity of bringing that peace to a fragmented world. We are the commissioned crack-repairmen and women. This is the real Gospel for us all because it solves the two quandaries of life: finding value and purpose.

CHAPTER TWENTY-ONE

So? The Question of Community

THE COMMUNITY OF CHRISTIANS

I am not a church service person. I know to say such a thing is offensive to many, and I'm sorry about that. This is a personal preference; it's not for any theological or philosophical reason. While many Christians enjoy the Sunday morning tradition, I know I'm an aberration. My life would be much easier if I honestly enjoyed Sunday morning church service, but I don't. My attitude possibly dates back to my early upbringing when the church service was a farce, was terribly boring, and going each Sunday only served as an act of self-atonement. As well, my tendency toward social anxiety doesn't make large crowds especially gratifying.

I currently attend a church, here in the San Juan Islands, with a female pastor. Many of my old evangelical friends assume I've gone over to the dark side because of her, as they have certainty that women should never be in leadership roles. Her candor and talent for making precise points has made her one of the best pastors I've ever listened to ... and I have listened to many. For centuries, the Sunday morning service has been seen as the primary avenue of Christian worship and that has never been so true as in modern evangelicalism. Romans 12:1 states the following; "Therefore, I urge you, brothers and sisters, in view of God's mercy, to offer your bodies as a living sacrifice, holy and pleasing to God—this is your true and proper worship." In my reading of this verse, I believe that New Testament worship is something very different, organic and practical. Ture worship involves a deep personal commitment and not just an emotional experience.

I do like interacting with people on a one-to-one basis, even though on Sunday mornings that interaction can only occur within two dimensions at best. But I deeply crave honest, Christian friendship and fellowship in the same way as a man crossing the Sahara on his knees craves water where there is virtually none. Such true fellowship is rare and very hard to find. It is not possible during a typical Sunday morning church service where a smile and a handshake are as far as the interaction can go. Perhaps in a well-led Sunday school class, a little true fellowship can be found, and in small groups even more.

I'm sure many people enjoy Sunday morning church services, and I completely respect that. However, I wonder how many attend, imagining they enjoy it because they believe it is what God wants them to do or going out of guilt or penitence. I've talked to many teenagers who candidly share that this is a common feeling among them.

CHURCH DEFINED

At this juncture, I'd like to raise the issue of semantics when discussing the Church. I hope to explain my vision of what a non-Dualistic Church would look like. But it's best to avoid the word *church*, a word loaded with connotations, many of which have nothing to do with the original biblical intent.

The Greek word for *church* in the New Testament is spelled (in the English alphabet) *ecclesia* or *ekklesia*. It describes a group of people, not an institution, and simply means "those called out for a purpose." A modern example would be something like Congress or even the Army. It is where people from all walks of life come together for a common goal. Over time, however, the word *church* has come to mean a place, a service, or an institution, anything but a group of people. In the old biblical sense, you can't "go to church" any more than you can "go to family" because *ecclesia* was never a location or an event. Thus, it can be said that the real church is a collection of Christian people; henceforth I'll usually refer to this group using the more neutral term *Christian community*. This is not to downplay the immense importance of this community in God's plan. It is the Christian community that is the bride of Christ, not some man-made institution. One influence of the Gnostics, which has had a continuing influence on North American Christianity, is the personalization of the Christian faith. The Gnostics considered Christianity to be a personal matter between you and your God. True biblical Christianity is more than that. I really think that God was sovereign, working through the great ecumenical councils and fathers to keep the Church from going even farther off course.

If you read the New Testament without wearing Dualistic glasses, you will see that the mandates for the Christian community's form or shape are few. There are historical examples of how it functioned in different areas. When I first arrived in Marquette, I spent at least six months studying early Church history in the Ante Pacem period (meaning "before the peace," referring to the era before Emperor Constantine in 312 A.D.) and learned that it took many natures during that period. Some Christians met daily, some hardly met at all. Some groups had elders, some deacons, or both. But with Dualistic glasses on, these descriptions in the Bible of church forms have no longer have earthly historical meaning but are spiritualized as absolute laws or mandates. The belief is that, if these mandates are not followed precisely, as with Levitical law, God will be displeased. Similarly, the snake handlers in the Appalachians took the example of handling snakes and not getting bitten as a biblical mandate. The precise interpretation of the presumed forms has been the catalyst for many church splits over the past three hundred years.

One of the few real mandates can be found in Hebrews 10:24–25: "And let us consider how we may spur one another on toward love and good deeds, not giving up meeting together, as some are in the habit of doing, but encouraging one another—and all the more as you see the Day approaching." Thus the opposite of "not meeting" isn't simply meeting for the sake of meeting but encouraging one another as the Christian community was meant to do. Encouraging one another was especially significant to the Christians within the Roman Empire during the first few centuries. As a minority that went through constant discrimination and cycles of outright persecution, they were subject to great discouragement. But it is hard to encourage one another if we don't know one another. And it is hard to know one another when we live in a Christian community where we each pretend that we are much better than we really are, and we don't dare show a sign of weakness, and where much of our real lives are subterranean, in carefully sealed cellars.

Good friends from every sort of church denomination would argue vehemently with me about my oversimplification of this community and about the great freedom of church in its raw and natural form. Each friend promotes his or her own church form as the only true "biblical" structure.

We have many people leaving the Church out of disillusionment. They need to understand that they have the freedom to create forms that serve the mission of the Church for them better. It is better to be a "freelance" Christian alone than to leave Christianity altogether. It is healthier to have a small group that meets in a house, coffee shop, or bar than to freelance it. It is preferable to have a church with seasoned elders than a small clan with no elders, especially a clan with one dominate leader. Sometimes you may be forced to choose between a church with theological flaws and a church with impeccable doctrines—in your opinion—but with a pastor who has a caustic personality disorder. In that case, the former may be better.

Christian aspirants also must know that they have the freedom to not be Republicans, political conservatives, patriots, certain skin color, American, or any other label that has been associated by some with being a good Christian. But, ideally, we should strive to create that place where people leave each meeting encouraged rather than a place that is a spiritual beauty pageant where members compete for who has the greatest ASW. I do believe strongly that churches must have a plural leadership. Those dominated by one person-ality eventually fail and take a lot of people down the sewer drain with them.

The other great "permission" that many must embrace and that is American evangelicalism is not the only game in town. You can be a won-derful Christian and immerse yourself in other great traditions. I know that this is true because I've met those good people. They appear in the Catholic, Orthodox, Coptic, and other great cultural interpretations of Christianity. Might some of them be wrong in their theology or, may God forbid, have an unscrupulous church history? Of course they do. They all do. Even cham-pion thoroughbreds require constant shoveling, or their stalls will fill with shit. We are ALL wrong on some points, but that should not stop us from meeting. However, this plasticity should never be an excuse for trivializing important theological doctrines or attempting to revise the corrupt history of our particular church movement to make us feel better. We often worry that we—or worse, our friends—might be wrong on some important theo-logical point. However, what really should keep us awake at night is the fear of becoming certain about a view that is absolutely wrong. As long as we know there is a chance we might be in fault … we are safe.

A PERILOUS SEARCH FOR THE AUTHENTIC CHURCH

When we first returned from Egypt in 1990, I wasn't at all sure I was still a Christian. I was suffering from clinical depression to the point that I was seriously considering suicide, so seriously that I had a specific plan for hanging myself in our barn … and I had a rope. I took long walks at night along icy Hermantown Road in Duluth. Such walks had always been a special time of prayer for me, before my fall. But on those lonely nights, when I was searching in desperation, the sky, the billions of brilliant stars, seemed cold and empty. I felt I was suffocating beneath an impenetrable blanket of dense, woven rage. I remember begging the emotionless, dead universe, "God, if you are out there somewhere, please find me!" Was he hiding somewhere within the Large Magellanic Cloud, or playing hide-and-seek behind the Cat's Eye Nebula, or was he never there in the first place? I really didn't know at that point.

During this difficult time of reentry, with Denise's prodding, I attempted to take my family back to church, but I almost reached a point where I couldn't stomach it any longer. We tried many churches in the Duluth area, but it was always the same façades and platitudes in each—something like a KFC franchise serving the same three-piece-original recipe box in Biloxi as in some remote village in China's Gansu province. If anyone spoke to us, and it was usually with good intentions, the conversation would go like this:

"Are you folks new to town or just visiting?"

"We're new."

"Where did you come from?"

"Uh … Egypt."

"Egypt! Were you in the military?"

"Uh … no … we were, uh, missionaries."

"Missionaries! Praise God; that must have been a blessing."

"No, it was hell."

At this point, the person would either quickly move away or give a canned response like, "You must not have trusted God because God never fails."

I was always amazed at such comments because I hadn't said anything about God failing us. I hadn't been trying to make any theological statement about God's sovereignty. I was just being honest about my emotions.

However, the person, consistent with the Dualistic view, felt obligated to hastily make a connection of my state of mental health to some significance in the immaterial realm.

The lowest point came when we started attending a large evangelical church in a nearby city, whose ranks had been growing quickly under the guidance of a charismatic pastor named Randal. One Sunday morning while I was sitting on a pew in the vestibule, Randal came in and took a seat next to me. He looked me in the eye and smiled. "Hey, Michael. How's life treating you?"

Not recognizing he intended it as only a shallow, meaningless greeting, I answered sincerely, "I'm very depressed right now." I felt this was a fair statement—it was during the period in which I was being besieged by thoughts of committing suicide—feeling so hopeless that suicide seemed it might be the only road out of the perpetual swamp I was mired in. In my honesty I was, indeed, begging for help. But the tall, thin pastor just smiled—and didn't speak another word to me. Had he heard me? I would soon learn that he certainly had.

A few moments later, we were seated in the huge auditorium along with 500 fellow churchmen and women. After a lively choir performance, Randal took the podium, looked out over his congregation and at me, and loudly proclaimed, "I'm sick and tired of Christians telling me that they are depressed. It makes me sick to my stomach! Do we serve a depressing God?"

"No!" came the cry from a few deacons in the front row.

I have rarely felt so alone and desperate in my life as I did at that moment, like a malignant absence within the soul. If I hadn't already known it from my experience the night of the rabbit hole, I then knew for certain that neither Randal nor DI—and maybe no one—gave a damn about me or my family. Perhaps Randal and others like him cared only about their ability to score religious points with other Christians in their personal quest for a greater ASW. The inaudible message screaming in my ear was, "Do it!" The hanging that I thought I had deserved for stabbing Larry in the head at age seven was now long overdue. "You are a hopeless loser. Do it today!" It was again brought home to me that Randal was living in the same evangelical world I had been living in for 15 years, before I went to Egypt.

Before my fall down the rabbit hole, faced with a Christian claiming to be depressed, I would have reacted in a similar fashioned as this pastor. For a Christian to suffer or fail had to be his or her own, first-person spiritual failure. Cause and effect in the seen world would have no value at all, so it had to be spiritualized as a simple moral and, therefore, spiritual failure of the one depressed.

THEN I MET DAVE

But in the midst of my despair, eventually there came a glimmer of hope who went by the simple name of Dave.

Once again Denise insisted that I not give up on the Church, even though I was sure that I could never darken the door of Randal's church again. We tried a new one, a small church on Arrowhead Road in Duluth. It was the same thing all over again, strangers standing in the vestibule, wearing plastic nametags and drinking coffee in Styrofoam cups. One by one they greeted us and asked who we were. When a newspaperman, Dave Peterson, asked me about my time as a missionary in Egypt, and I responded, "It was hell," he didn't bat an eye, just smiled softly. Putting his hand on my back in a kind of man-hug, he added, "Hey, I want to hear ALL the details. Can I bring the pastor, and we meet at Burger King after church?" He was immediately ready to drop all of his personal plans for the day, just for me … a complete stranger.

That afternoon, I sat with Dave and the pastor for two hours over a Whopper and fries, as big snowflakes tumbled, like Lilliputian acrobats, out of the grey sky and onto windshields of the cars in the parking lot. Through the birch trees, which lined the highway, you could see the whitecaps of a churning Lake Superior a few hundred yards away. I had been back in the States for six months, and Dave was the first person to sincerely take an interest in our experience.

For the first six weeks after we got home from Egypt, we were staying with friends in Ann Arbor, Michigan, which was near our home before we moved to Egypt. These friends were great hosts, letting us crash in their basement while we got our feet on the ground. But John, the husband, said the pastor, our former pastor, had told him to avoid discussing our experience in Egypt because it may be too painful to talk about. But I was dying to talk about it if anyone would just listen. Certainly the DI missionary department wasn't interested in our story. We did have friends, the Wilsons, who had been on staff with DI in Ann Arbor. I'm sure they would have listened, but they had moved away during our long absence abroad.

That afternoon in Duluth, I didn't hesitate to tell Dave our entire Egyptian story while sitting in that slick, fiberglass booth. It had been pent up for six months with virtually no audience. I felt as if the saga had been stuffed inside me for so long and so hard, as if into a tightly sealed jar, that once I removed the lid it might explode like a snake-in-a-can prank. And I was ready for that.

Dave was a stocky man, about 40 years old, and the pastor, coincidentally named David, was about 28, thin, and five-foot-seven at best. I will never forget stocky Dave's face. He sat like a statue, intently listening, and elbows on the table with his chin set firmly on his two fists. Maybe that was the talent that made him a good newspaper reporter. About 45 minutes into the story, the most amazing thing I had ever witnessed occurred. It was as if I'd just had 10 years of therapy rolled into one second. What was it? It was simply a huge, sincere tear, tumbling down Dave's silent face, dripping from his cheek onto his fist. He wiped it off with a paper napkin and kept listening. His tears were a validation of my hurt ... and that was all I ever needed.

Until that point, I'd assumed that Dave, like everyone else, wasn't even paying attention to me. I figured he'd been daydreaming, off fishing somewhere out amidst the whitecaps. With the sight of the tear, I froze in confusion, followed by a strange kind of delight—and immeasurable relief. I became choked up, as if a 50-pound turkey was being pulled up my esophagus by a rope. I couldn't speak anymore—but I could cry. The dams burst in my own eyes, and for the first time I began to sob uncontrollably until my French fries became a soggy blur. It may have been the first time I had cried in 15 years. Real men, especially Christian men, don't cry. They only see the glory in the ether. I hadn't cried at my friend Karl's funeral. But, after that day with Dave, I cried for weeks or maybe months. At least once a day, I had to get alone in private and sob. When the crying would take a reprieve, I would clean off my face and go about my business of working in my clinic and being a father and husband. But it wasn't a crying that was spiraling downward, drowning me in grief. With each session of tears, I felt I was swimming closer to the surface with glimpses of daylight starting to filter down to me. It was a mystery ... but it was like the salty water itself carried away some of the toxins of pain, rage, and perpetual sadness.

But that day, I finally had an ear, and that's all I had wanted. I didn't necessarily want the answer, or a cliché, or a Bible verse. I knew all the Bible verses. I didn't want someone listening only to the first sentence out of my mouth before interrupting and trying to make some idiotic meaning out of it by connecting it to something in the unseen world—God teaching me a lesson or things being my fault because I had not been obedient. I didn't want to watch someone squirm in social awkwardness because I wasn't putting a positive spin on everything, like Christians are supposed to do. Lastly, I didn't want someone glancing at their watch within 30 seconds of the story, like many busy pastors do.

I can't remember what happened after Dave's tear and the tears that followed. It really didn't matter. I can't recall what he or David said to me that day; maybe they said nothing at all. But I do know that, prior to that meal at Burger King on Skyline Drive in Duluth, Minnesota, I'd felt hopeless, so hopeless that I was certain I would commit suicide before a few more weeks passed. Dave had "spurred me on to love and good deeds" without saying a word ... but by his unassuming behavior. Afterward, sitting in the fast-food parking lot under a windshield now covered in new, soft blanket of snow, I knew that someday I would find God again, and I would be well. On that day, I also found the real Church once more.

On a personal level, my ideal church would be a group of people, most of whom are believers, but nonbelievers, or people seeking God, also would be welcome. As deep and honest thinkers, we would meet regularly at a coffee shop or bar, and, during our times together, we would share honestly about our lives and encourage one another. None of us would carry the belief that we had the corner on the only precise way to think and that our mission was to convert the other people to that higher way of thinking. We would discuss deep theological questions in a respectful atmosphere and welcome all the tough questions of life. As a group, we also would be involved with service projects, bringing redemption to a broken world ... being a band of "crack-fillers." We would have a high appreciation for art in all its forms. We also would spend many hours laughing, joking, and simply enjoying one another's company. These are some of the qualities that characterize my taste in church, but it is an elusive church that I've yet to find ... yet ... but for which, I still have hope.

The Community of non-Christians

Isn't anyone tryin' to find me?
Won't somebody come take me home
It's a damn cold night
Trying to figure out this life
Won't you take me by the hand
Take me somewhere new
I don't know who you are
but I, I'm with you …

These are the closing lyrics are from Avril Lavigne's song *I'm With You*, which was released in 2002, the year we moved here to the San Juan Islands. It could be the heart-cry for this generation. I believe that the non-Christian society has a natural, intense desire to know Christ—the raw Christ—or at least what he is offering, but they don't realize this. It is their natural inclination to want to be reunited with the one who made them and the only one who loves them deeply and accepts them unconditionally. They are begging for this type of help, acceptance, and reunification. So, with a world that is hungry for God, why does it seem as if people desire anything else but him?

The tool of lies is the maker of the greatest evil. Like a cloaking device, lies have worked to obscure the true, wonderful Gospel from those who desperately seek it. Dualism has been one of the biggest utensils of that deception, but there have been many others.

Good Guys and Bad Guys

Because Dualism's destiny has been to separate the material world from the immaterial world, the tendency has been to carry that separation into the lives of men and women by defining them as worldly men and women versus heavenly men and women. We want to separate the good guys from the bad guys with sharp lines of demarcation. This is connected to our basic ASW; as I said in chapter five, the first step is to create a separation between us and others. The second step is to use the others for comparison and leverage our own value.

When Christians see the world dualistically, the worldly people—whose king Christians believe is Satan—stand in total opposition to the people of God. The non-Christians thus become their foes in a kind of great culture war. Like Peter in the Garden of Gethsemane, Christians want to draw their righteous swords and go to battle with these "nasty" people, whom evangelical Christianity often sees as the enemy. You know who I mean: gays, transgender people, whores, drug dealers, Islamists, evolutionists—and yes, even Democrats—all those whom American evangelicalism opposes within this conflict.

But Jesus made it clear that his kingdom wasn't of this world (John 18:36). We cannot so easily separate the world we live in into the good guys versus the bad guys. In the parable of the wheat and tares, Jesus makes the point that we shouldn't try to separate the two groups. With this in mind, carefully read the following passage from Matthew.

> Jesus told them another parable: "The kingdom of heaven is like a man who sowed good seed in his field. But while everyone was sleeping, his enemy came and sowed weeds among the wheat, and went away. When the wheat sprouted and formed heads, then the weeds also appeared.
>
> "The owner's servants came to him and said, 'Sir, didn't you sow good seed in your field? Where then did the weeds come from?'
>
> "'An enemy did this,' he replied.
>
> The servants asked him, 'Do you want us to go and pull them up?'
>
> "'No,' he answered, 'because while you are pulling the weeds, you may uproot the wheat with them. Let both grow together until the harvest. At that time I will tell the harvesters: First collect the weeds and tie them in bundles to be burned; then gather the wheat and bring it into my barn.'" (Matthew 13:24–30)

Relating to the Summit Ridge metaphor, mentioned in chapter eighteen, there is also a dichotomy in the way a Christian culture chooses to handle the greater, non-Christian pluralistic society. On one side of the cliff the Church falls into the temptation of pantheism. If you have a theological system that affirms the view that all rivers (religious ideas) run into the same ocean, then it is easier to accommodate people of different cultures and different faiths. This type of religious tolerance is built on relativism of truth for the sake of peace. Hinduism, the first such view, was likely born (and for the same reason) when multiple cultures were blended in the northern Indus Valley after the Aryan invasion around 1800 BC. Within American Christian groups, the mainline Churches have been most vulnerable to this pantheistic temptation.

On the other side of the cliff, when faced with cultural pluralism, the Church falls into the temptation of kneading American nationalistic and conservative political ideas into their Christianity. Within this framework, the differences between people are accentuated in order to enhance one's sense of self-worth and personal peace at the sake of a broader, more inclusive peace. It is to state that he or she, alone, has absolute truth in all religious and cultural matters. Because others do not believe these same truths, they are inferior and worthy of disdain. The American evangelicals have been most vulnerable to this temptation of mingling conservative nationalistic ideas within their faith. This problem was never clearer than in the 2016 presidential election. The greatest danger here, is if you take this path too far, you end up on the outskirts of Fascism. It has been reported, but not proven, that Sinclair Lewis, the first American Nobel Laureate in Literature, said, "When Fascism comes to America, it will be wrapped in the flag and carrying a cross." (Illinois State University 2012)

The first approach borrows, loosely, from the Platonic view of the other-worldly, ideals. The Church redefined these ideals as the mystical or spiritual. In that model, it is easy to adjust your concepts of the spiritual, because they are not material. The second approach is underpinned by a theological and cultural certainty. This level of assumed certainty is only possible if you have adopted the arrogance of an Aristotelian type of infallible reason. It would simply state that I know that my subculture is superior to all others because we have figured out the truth and no one else has. We have figured out the truth because we are more superior in our reasoning and morals than the others.

The right approach for the Church is to maintain the near-certainty of the simple theological essentials, yet, promoting a comprehensive peace. This peace is not based on agreement, but on the moral directive of the gospel, that we love all people immensely, in spite of our differences. We must avoid mixing all other philosophical views within Christianity, including pantheism or American nationalistic views.

BEING HUMAN

We were flawed men and women before we were Christians, and we are no better now. The non-Christian community is not hungry for phonies; if they were, there would be a great influx of them into our churches. They are hungry for the Dave Petersons of the world. The real people who do really care about them, who cancel their plans at a moment's notice ... just for them. How can we say we love the world when some Christians are advocating abandoning the war refugees in the Mediterranean (or anywhere for that matter)? How can we say we are full of love when many in the evangelical community want new state laws that give them the freedom to be mean and discriminate against non-Christians or Christians who have a differed view on some social issues? It is bizarre. I think Jesus, if he were a modern businessman, would cater to the most rejected of society, including transgender people or Muslims. He felt safe within his purpose and own value ... which gives a severe liberation.

This current age, the post-postmodern time, is sometimes referred to as the period of Authenticism. I do think this is an idealism of hope, but it's not reality, just another illusion. While those born after 1980 want truth or total candor, in time I'm afraid that idealism will fail them. However, their intent is to be respected. This generation is acutely suspicious of pretentiousness, and the Christian must put great emphasis on candor if they want to be taken seriously. This generation is tired of the deception of the older ages. However, we must remember that, in The Catcher in the Rye, J. D. Salinger (Salinger 1951), created his teenage protagonist Holden Caulfield back in 1951, a man-child who was disgusted by the phonies of his world. So Authenticism really isn't a new concept.

Dr. Francis Schaeffer and his wife Edith are my greatest Christian heroes. I had the chance to be acquainted with Edith through L'Abri Fellowship in Rochester. Some find it odd that I loved the book written by their son Frank, Crazy for God (F. Schaeffer, Crazy for God 2008) because he exposes, graphically, his parent's human frailties. I also enjoyed his Calvin Becker Trilogy

(F. Schaeffer, Zermatt: A Novel (Calvin Becker Trilogy) Reprint 2004), (F. Schaeffer, Saving Grandma: A Novel (Calvin Becker Trilogy) Reprint 2004), (F. Schaeffer, Portofino: A Novel (Calvin Becker Trilogy) Reprint 2004), which were fictional books, but thinly veiled autobiographical stories of living at L'Abri in Switzerland. I love the books because they make the Schaeffers human, and I just adore humans! I feel closer to my heroes when they fumble and fail because I fumble and fail all the time. I am skeptical of those who appear too good to be true. My heroes are not super.

THE RESORT AND THE LANDMARK

In the 1960s, Gatlinburg, Tennessee, was a small stop for gas and a sandwich on the way into the scenic Great Smoky Mountains National Park. As a kid we would take leisurely Sunday drives down there in the summer, with Dad at the helm of his Oldsmobile. Over the years, Gatlinburg was discovered by the rest of the world, and it grew in leaps and bounds. That growth moved farther west into the towns of Pigeon Forge and Sevierville, where hotels sprang up, followed by shopping centers and outlet malls. Then people starting coming just for the shopping, so more hotels opened to accommodate the out-of-town shoppers. After that, Vegas-type shows began to appear to catch the eye of the rising flow of traffic, and in a chain reaction, more hotels were built to give the show-goers a place to stay.

The result? What used to be a quiet, two-lane highway in the little mountain hamlet of Gatlinburg has now become a bumper-to-bumper four- or six-lane traffic jam. On both sides of the boulevard are tall hotels, bright lights, and billboards so dense that the beautiful Smoky Mountains have become obscured in the background. It's likely that some visitors now come for the shopping and the shows, unaware the mountains even exist.

This is the path that non-Christians must travel into God's kingdom. The raw beauty of his total acceptance and love is now obscured by many add-ons to Christianity—the rules, condemnation, doctrines, politics, and culture wars that have much more to do with the American evangelical subculture's mores than with anything divine. It is human nature to highly esteem one's own culture. It seems clear that these Christians often place a greater value on their American evangelical subculture than they do on the simple Christian doctrines. Yet they mix that subculture with biblical concepts, and while it seems they are defending those biblical truths at all cost, they are actually defending their own culture at all cost. It is at this juncture that neutral, equivocal issues—those that are neither good nor bad—move toward becoming a hindrance to spreading word of the good of God's grace and forgiveness.

HONEST QUESTIONS DESERVE HONEST ANSWERS

When I was reconsidering Christ in high school, I had frank questions. I didn't understand why there was suffering in this world. I didn't understand how the world could be only six thousand years old. And I couldn't understand how I could be confident, philosophically, that God was really there when he seemed silent. When I asked my Christian leaders these questions, they made it clear that Christianity was about faith, not reason. Then they would throw in meaningless but ego-stroking clichés such as "God said it, I believe it, and that settles it."

This separation of reason and faith is based on the Dualistic view that the mind is inferior to the spirit. It was too huge a pill for me to swallow, to bury all my questions and accept Christ, not on a biblical concept of trust, but on a Dualistic, mystical, anti-rational faith. Now, in the twenty-first century, even the secular world is living in a post-reason culture. Now Christians have even more license to ignore the hard questions, exchanging a pantheistic mysticism for rational answers. We can't let that happen anymore.

In the evangelical mode of belief, no honest doubts about God are allowed, and, if expressed, these doubts are perceived as a sign of spiritual immaturity, and the person is shunned. I know this firsthand, having taught some high-school-level Sunday school classes over the past few years. In an effort to reverse Dualistic thinking, I try to welcome such doubts and questions. Despite my efforts, however, old ideas are difficult to dislodge. The few kids who are honest enough to express their doubts are often disrespected by their Christian peers. In one case a pastor yanked me from being a teacher because I was allowing kids who doubted to express their doubts publicly.

But if Christians can't or don't answer young people's questions adequately in the safety of their churches, non-Christian professors will be happy to answer them, with their hollow certainty, in the secular environment of the college classroom. If Christians wish to prevent the majority of the children of evangelicals from eventually leaving the faith, they need to embrace the idea of a non-Dualistic Christianity. Guilt manipulation about dress code, church attendance, music, or tattoos will only work for so long before youth and young adults eventually run for the hills of secularism.

Christians have the job of tearing down these obstacles and making the path to a naked and honest Christianity clear and unhindered. For many, this means a total reboot of how they think Christianly. This new, non-Dualistic way of thinking may completely revolutionize how Christians see the world. That's what it did for me. When encountering those outside the faith, we Christians should be reflecting God's acceptance and love, not obscuring them. This is true evangelism. This is how Christ did it. Once that path is clear, those in desperation, as described in Avril Lavigne's lyrics, will be able see the way home.

A journey that started in a pit of despair in an out-of-the-way Chinese restaurant in Cairo, Egypt, took me through many paths for over 15 years. I traversed through mine fields of personal psychological development that required a frightening level of frankness. I navigated through dark halls of Western history taking me back at least 3,000 years. In countless coffee shops spread across four continents; in pup tents, airplanes, park benches, and in my own bed on many of nights—by the light of a headlamp—I devoured books written by thinkers and explorers from many walks and times of life. By thought and prayer I bushwhacked my way through many confusing emotional conflicts and intellectual question of the post-evangelical wilderness, until I came to a clearing ... a glade where I found peace once more. But far more than just a personal recompense, I think I may have inadvertently discovered an idea that could revolutionize and help restore all of Christianity to a far more authentic and natural form. Beneath all the butterflies of pretense and above the crypts of scheming serpents, there really is a balm of healing for all of the ills of this world.

INDEX

A

abuse 62, 63, 66, 92, 95, 200
Adams, Jay 94
Air Force 24, 25, 191
Alexander 122, 151
Alice in Wonderland 81, 180
American evangelism 99
Anderson, Irvine H. 100
Ann Arbor 183, 215
anxiety 55, 66, 81
anxious 63
Appalachians 29, 91, 103, 185, 211
Aquinas, Thomas 155, 178
Arab 2, 4, 6, 155
Aristotelian 147, 153, 155, 156, 158,
    175, 178, 187, 188, 189, 190, 201,
    202, 203, 207
Aristotle 118, 129, 133, 147, 149, 150,
    151, 152, 155, 156, 157, 165, 174,
    186, 187, 205, 206, 207
Arminius, Jacob 158
ASW
    (Appraisal of Self Worth) 50, 52,
        53, 54, 69, 81, 166, 188, 202,
        207, 212, 214, 218
atheism 182
atheists 48, 70, 182, 195

Augustine 170, 171, 172, 173, 174,
    175, 194
Averroes 155, 175, 186
Awakenings
    (referring to the First and Second
        Great Awakenings) 100

B

Baptist 30, 35, 39, 43, 70, 78, 80, 83, 85,
    108, 159, 175
Berlinghiero 135
Bible xiii, 12, 26, 30, 35, 41, 45, 46, 47,
    48, 57, 58, 69, 70, 72, 74, 75, 77,
    78, 80, 83, 84, 86, 88, 90, 91, 94,
    102, 103, 108, 110, 115, 124,
    159, 160, 167, 174, 179, 199, 202,
    211, 217
Bible Belt 30, 35, 41, 45, 46, 47, 48, 57,
    69, 70, 77, 78, 80, 83, 86, 91, 108,
    124, 174, 179
Biblical Counseling Movement 94
Bradford, William 92
brain 51, 78, 90, 93, 94, 95, 96, 101, 103,
    151, 181, 182, 191, 195, 196, 199,
    205, 206
Buddhism 46
Buddhist 171
Byzantine 13, 145, 147, 148, 149

C

Cairo 2, 3, 4, 6, 7, 8, 10, 11, 12, 16, 18, 19, 27, 48, 58, 66, 191, 192, 195, 196, 199, 224

Calvinism 157

Calvinist 73

Calvinists 78, 177, 179, 180, 181

Carroll, Lewis 180, 181

Catholic 46, 92, 123, 135, 144, 145, 148, 155, 157, 159, 177, 179, 183, 212

certainty 178, 188, 201, 202, 203, 209, 223

Chalcedonian Creed 138, 139

Chaucer, Geoffrey 135

Christ 12, 13, 31, 39, 40, 47, 69, 72, 78, 79, 84, 85, 99, 100, 101, 111, 112, 117, 122, 128, 129, 135, 136, 137, 139, 146, 164, 174, 177, 180, 190, 193, 199, 207, 210, 218, 223, 224

Christendom 13, 14, 83, 84, 102, 112, 143, 149, 168, 178

Christian 1, 9, 10, 12, 13, 14, 15, 16, 17, 18, 21, 22, 23, 24, 26, 27, 34, 36, 37, 39, 40, 44, 45, 46, 48, 51, 54, 58, 59, 70, 72, 73, 74, 77, 78, 79, 80, 82, 83, 84, 85, 87, 88, 89, 91, 93, 94, 96, 97, 100, 101, 102, 104, 107, 108, 109, 110, 111, 112, 119, 120, 122, 124, 127, 128, 129, 131, 134, 136, 138, 139, 140, 145, 146, 147, 149, 154, 155, 156, 157, 159, 161, 163, 164, 165, 166, 167, 169, 170, 171, 172, 174, 177, 178, 179, 180, 181, 182, 184, 189, 191, 193, 194, 196, 197, 200, 201, 202, 203, 205, 206, 207, 210, 211, 212, 213, 214, 216, 218, 221, 222, 223

Christian fatalism 109

Christianity 6, 14, 22, 23, 29, 30, 34, 35, 46, 47, 51, 73, 77, 80, 84, 101, 105, 108, 112, 113, 115, 123, 124, 128, 136, 147, 149, 152, 153, 154, 157, 168, 171, 172, 174, 175, 177, 194, 198, 200, 207, 210, 212, 219, 222, 223, 224

Christian psychology 59, 94

Church 1, 14, 17, 21, 22, 24, 26, 30, 31, 32, 33, 34, 35, 36, 37, 39, 40, 41, 42, 44, 45, 46, 47, 48, 50, 51, 69, 70, 72, 73, 80, 83, 84, 85, 86, 89, 100, 104, 113, 118, 122, 123, 124, 127, 128, 129, 130, 131, 132, 133, 135, 136, 137, 138, 139, 140, 141, 143, 144, 145, 146, 147, 148, 149, 151, 153, 154, 155, 157, 158, 159, 163, 164, 166, 167, 168, 169, 170, 172, 174, 175, 177, 179, 180, 181, 184, 187, 188, 190, 194, 198, 200, 202, 205, 206, 207, 209, 210, 211, 212, 213, 214, 215, 217, 224

Cohen, Morton N. 181

Constantinople 137, 138, 144, 145, 146, 148

Cosimo 144, 145, 146, 147, 149, 153, 154

Cotton, John 92

Crusade 144, 145, 148

Cyprus 2, 3, 7, 9, 10, 14, 15, 17, 193

D

Dark Ages 134, 135, 137, 140, 152, 172

Darwin, Charles 179

Darwinism 53

The Da Vinci Code 85, 163, 170

De Anima 206

de' Medici, Averardo 144

de' Medici, Cosimo di Giovanni 144

de' Medici, Giovanni di Bicci 144

demon 96, 195

demon possessed 96

denomination 128, 211

depression 22, 23, 26, 58, 79, 81, 96, 213
Descartes', René 202
DI
    "Disciples Inc." 2, 3, 7, 9, 10, 11, 12,
        13, 17, 18, 23, 24, 25, 26, 72,
        75, 78, 79, 80, 81, 85, 88, 92,
        93, 102, 103, 105, 107, 108,
        166, 175, 179, 214, 215, 216
Disciples Inc
    "DI" 2
dispensationalism 99, 100
Dodgson, Charles Lutwidge 180, 181
doubting 22
Dualism 83, 84, 85, 87, 88, 91, 92, 94,
        97, 99, 100, 102, 105, 107, 112,
        113, 115, 116, 118, 120, 121, 122,
        123, 124, 127, 134, 136, 137, 138,
        140, 153, 155, 158, 163, 164, 165,
        170, 172, 174, 175, 178, 184, 194,
        196, 197, 218
dualistic 84, 86, 92, 95, 96, 100, 103,
        109, 113, 115, 119, 124, 129, 133,
        136, 137, 143, 157, 163, 165, 172,
        173, 174, 178, 181, 182, 194
Duluth 21, 22, 24, 25, 191, 213, 215,
        216, 217

E

ecclesia 210
ecumenical 211
Edwards, Jonathan 100, 101
Egypt 2, 3, 4, 6, 7, 11, 13, 17, 22, 24, 25,
        27, 58, 72, 82, 121, 166, 191, 199,
        213, 214, 215, 224
Einstein, Albert 195
Eldredge, John 51
emotions 4, 7, 14, 50, 78, 89, 90, 93, 94,
        96, 97, 130, 133, 154, 156, 158,
        181, 182, 213
Enlightenment 134, 156, 157, 179, 188
eschatological 99, 100, 124, 146

Eschatology 99
Essenes 164
Eupalinus 117, 119
evangelical 21, 22, 24, 49, 58, 78, 83, 86,
        87, 89, 91, 100, 101, 105, 128, 129,
        130, 131, 166, 177, 181, 188, 192,
        193, 197, 209, 214, 219, 221, 222,
        223, 224
evangelicals 47, 48, 77, 84, 86, 87, 92,
        112, 124, 128, 134, 165, 187, 196,
        197, 202, 206, 224
exorcism 96, 195

F

faith 3, 9, 13, 14, 30, 37, 41, 47, 58, 60,
        72, 74, 77, 78, 84, 85, 91, 93, 95,
        108, 115, 129, 131, 162, 171, 172,
        178, 181, 203, 210, 223, 224
Fall of Adam 52, 62, 95, 120, 150, 155,
        188, 190
Florence 143, 145, 146, 149, 152, 153,
        154, 157
Florentine Council 145, 147
foundations 77, 146
Francis Schaeffer 75, 127, 134, 153, 221
French Revolution 156, 200
Freud, Sigmund 72, 179
Full Gospel 159, 183

G

Gale, Bob 107
Gemistos 146, 147
Gnostic 133, 136, 137, 163, 164, 165,
        168, 170, 171, 172, 174
Gnosticism 136, 138, 164, 165, 171
Gnostics 134, 135, 136, 137, 155, 159,
        163, 164, 165, 166, 168, 169, 172,
        175, 179, 187, 188, 194, 210
God 3, 14, 16, 18, 19, 21, 22, 25, 34, 35,
        36, 37, 39, 40, 41, 42, 44, 45, 48,

50, 51, 53, 73, 74, 75, 79, 80, 85,
86, 87, 88, 89, 90, 91, 92, 94, 96,
99, 100, 103, 104, 105, 107, 108,
109, 110, 111, 112, 115, 117, 119,
122, 124, 127, 128, 129, 130, 131,
134, 135, 136, 137, 138, 139, 146,
148, 150, 152, 154, 155, 160,
161, 162, 163, 164, 165, 166, 167,
168, 169, 172, 173, 174, 178, 180,
181, 184, 187, 188, 189, 190, 191,
192, 194, 195, 196, 197, 198, 199,
200, 201, 202, 203, 207, 210, 211,
213, 214, 217, 218, 219, 221, 222,
223, 224
godly 10, 36, 79, 89, 90, 196
Goldman, MD, Robert 54
Gospel of Mary 163
Gospel of Thomas 163
Graham, Billy 78, 201
Grant, Robert M. 136
Great Awakening 80, 83, 100, 179
Great Depression 36, 37, 62
Greece 116, 118, 137
Greeks 118, 119, 121, 136, 144
guilt 39, 40, 41, 112, 130, 168, 190,
207, 210
Gulf War I 86, 102

H

Harvard, John 101
healing 24, 25, 59, 161, 162, 224
heaven 29, 36, 89, 91, 100, 109, 119, 120,
122, 124, 136, 137, 138, 140, 163,
174, 219
hell 18, 39, 40, 42, 70, 88, 213, 215
Hellenistic 120, 122, 138
Hinduism 46
Holy Spirit 41, 146, 162, 165, 174, 181,
182, 184, 206
Hudson Taylor 24
Hugo 200

humanism 152, 153, 155, 156

I

Irenaeus 136
Islam 46, 48, 124, 149, 177
Islamists 144, 146, 219

J

Jesus 13, 17, 23, 43, 45, 46, 69, 72, 73,
74, 79, 84, 86, 99, 101, 102, 125,
131, 136, 137, 139, 146, 148, 154,
161, 163, 169, 170, 184, 190, 191,
202, 207, 219, 221
Jews 129, 148, 164, 165
Jim Elliot 24
Judaism 46, 171
Justification 78

K

Kant, Immanuel 179
Kastro 115, 116, 117

L

Lascaux paintings 186
Lavigne, Avril 218, 224
Lee, Philip J. 164
Leonardo of Vinci 152
Liddell, Alice 180, 181
Liddell, Lorina 180
Lincoln, Abraham 167, 168
Lindsey, Hal 102
Local history 85, 108
Locke, John 179
Luther 141, 143, 177, 178
Lutheran 46, 177, 179
Lutheranism 157, 178
lying 36, 40, 90, 131, 197

M

Mad Hatter 23, 44, 81, 197, 198
Mani 137, 171, 172
Manichaeism 137, 171, 172, 174, 194
Manichean 172
Manzoni, Piero 111
March Hare 44, 197
Marcion 137
Mark of Ephesus 146
Marquette 24, 25, 26, 66, 82, 125, 130,
    133, 191, 198, 211
material
    (as in the physical world) 26, 44,
        51, 52, 78, 84, 85, 87, 88, 91,
        95, 100, 105, 108, 109, 121,
        134, 135, 138, 146, 150, 152,
        153, 155, 163, 164, 173, 175,
        179, 184, 187, 188, 189, 190,
        194, 197, 198, 199, 205, 206,
        207, 218
math 70, 94, 118, 120
Matterhorn 185, 186, 188
maturity
    (spiritual maturity) 12, 13, 58,
        80, 81
Medici family 143, 148, 149, 152, 154
medicine 54, 88, 94, 101
Medicis 143, 147, 148, 149, 175, 187
meta-history 85, 86, 127
metaphysical 47, 85, 112, 116, 150,
    194, 198
metaphysics 85, 118
metempsychosis 205, 206
Michelangelo 152, 186
Middle Ages 128, 135, 140, 155, 169
Middle East 2, 3, 26, 87, 93, 100,
    102, 192
miracle 36, 194
Mirandola, Giovanni Pico della 152
mission 16, 18, 26, 123, 212

missionaries 2, 14, 16, 24, 72, 88, 213
molesting 33, 73
Moravians 158
Mount Baker 185
Mount Olympus 119, 120
Musgraves, Kacey 46
Muslim 1, 2, 9, 13, 17, 125, 145, 149, 155
Muslims 4, 6, 9, 16, 48, 149, 164, 221
mysticism 120, 152, 202, 203, 223

N

Natural 200
Neoplatonism 154, 157
Nicene Creed 137, 146
Nietzsche, Friedrich 53, 179
nihilism 48, 182
Nock, Darby 168
Noll, Mark A. 86
nouthetic counseling 94, 96
nouthetic counselor 96

O

Oration on the Dignity of Man 152
Orthodox 129, 145, 146, 149, 212
orthodoxy 179
Osborne, John 177

P

PA
    "Physician Assistant" 4, 6, 102
Palaiologos, John VIII 145, 146
pantheistic 91, 180, 182, 199, 200,
    203, 223
Parva Naturalia 206
Pascal, Blaise 201
Paul
    (Apostle Paul) 18, 103, 119, 122,
        129, 150, 169, 214, 215
penance 35, 36, 207
Pharisees 45, 191

philosophical 27, 75, 77, 79, 82, 84, 85, 93, 99, 107, 118, 120, 121, 122, 133, 135, 137, 143, 144, 147, 151, 152, 154, 156, 157, 169, 188, 200, 201, 203, 205, 209

philosophies 84, 122, 127, 129, 132, 139, 155, 174

Phoenician 116

Physician Assistant "PA" 4, 101

Piety 178

Plato 51, 120, 121, 122, 124, 129, 133, 134, 136, 143, 147, 149, 150, 151, 152, 153, 154, 155, 156, 157, 172, 173, 174, 186, 187, 194, 205, 207

Platonic 120, 121, 124, 134, 137, 138, 140, 146, 147, 149, 150, 151, 152, 153, 154, 155, 156, 157, 158, 163, 164, 165, 170, 172, 173, 174, 175, 178, 181, 187, 188, 190, 194, 196, 201, 202, 205, 206, 207

Platonism 143, 147, 153, 154, 157

pneumatics 163, 166

Pollock, Jackson 111

Polycrates 117, 118

polytheistic 118, 119, 120, 129, 164

Pope Eugenius IV 146

Pope Julius II 152, 186

Pope Leo X 152

postmillennial 146

post-postmodern 143, 221

post-tribulation 99

prayer 12, 16, 17, 48, 88, 90, 160, 162, 184, 196, 199, 206, 213, 224

premillennial 99

pre-tribulation 99, 102

Protestant 35, 78, 80, 157, 158, 164, 168, 172, 179, 194

Protestants 128, 135

psychological 27, 41, 48, 49, 55, 59, 77, 81, 82, 111, 112, 148, 168, 188, 199, 203, 224

psychology 50, 59, 70, 71, 88, 94, 96, 205, 206

Puritan 44, 92, 93, 101

Pythagoras 117, 118, 119, 120, 121, 122, 173, 174, 205

Q

Queen Victoria 180

questioning 37, 46, 48, 75, 127, 129, 131, 193

Qumran 164, 165, 171

R

rabbit hole 1, 11, 49, 59, 75, 107, 111, 175, 180, 214

rage 11, 18, 27, 48, 49, 56, 58, 63, 64, 189, 213, 216

Raphael 151, 152, 186, 187

reason 25, 27, 31, 36, 40, 41, 44, 46, 50, 53, 56, 58, 59, 65, 66, 74, 75, 78, 88, 91, 92, 93, 102, 129, 131, 133, 140, 147, 148, 150, 151, 155, 156, 157, 158, 166, 172, 174, 178, 179, 181, 182, 187, 188, 201, 202, 203, 205, 206, 209, 223

redemption 163, 190, 217

Reformation 128, 143, 155, 157, 175

relativism 203

Religion 46, 168

Renaissance 141, 143, 151, 152, 153, 154, 155, 156, 158, 175, 187, 188

Republic 150

Republican
    Republican Party 95

Rivera, José 92

Rochester 127, 130, 132, 133, 145, 158, 192, 221

Roman Empire 148, 149, 211
Rousseauian 200
Rousseau, Jean-Jacques 200

S

Salinger, J. D. 221
Samos 116, 117, 118, 120, 141
sanctification 79, 81, 111, 112, 191, 207
Schaeffer, Edith 221
Schaeffer, Frank 221
Scholasticism 155
Scholastics 157, 188
The School of Athens 149, 151, 186
science 45, 72, 94, 143, 156, 182, 194,
        202, 203
Scriptures 53, 138
Second Great Awakening 30, 80, 83,
        100, 101, 179
self-esteem 52, 57
sex 37, 40, 41, 93, 152, 183
sin 37, 45, 47, 79, 80, 90, 91, 92, 94, 95,
        96, 111, 139, 162, 169, 189, 200,
        201, 205, 206
Sistine Chapel 186
six thousand years
        (Assumed age of the Earth by some
        evangelicals) 72, 73, 223
Skinner, B. F. 72
social anxiety 56, 66, 70, 79, 209
Socrates 120, 165, 173, 203
soul xiv, 1, 11, 18, 27, 50, 63, 72, 78, 93,
        94, 97, 99, 103, 120, 121, 134,
        135, 139, 153, 163, 196, 205,
        206, 214
sovereignty 108, 128, 197, 200, 213
speaking in tongues 160
Speusippus 150
spiritual xiv, 13, 17, 18, 22, 24, 39, 40,
        41, 50, 51, 58, 60, 69, 78, 81, 85,
        86, 87, 88, 89, 90, 92, 93, 94, 97,
        102, 103, 104, 105, 108, 113, 116,
        119, 122, 124, 129, 130, 134, 135,
        136, 137, 138, 139, 140, 141, 146,
        152, 154, 159, 163, 165, 166, 167,
        169, 171, 173, 174, 180, 181, 182,
        184, 188, 190, 194, 196, 197, 201,
        206, 212, 215, 223
spiritualized 87, 127, 135, 211, 215
suicide 23, 50, 58, 96, 213, 214, 217

T

Tennessee 25, 83, 88, 222
terrorist 102
Thirty Years' War 177, 178, 179, 184
Tolkien, J. R. R. 185

V

Victorian age 180
Villa Medici at Careggi 147, 152, 153
Voltaire 134

W

war xiii, 2, 23, 37, 42, 86, 87, 132, 144,
        168, 177, 219, 221
Webb, Charles 34
Western civilization 118, 134, 141, 153,
        186, 187
worldly 85, 86, 88, 90, 91, 92, 93, 94, 99,
        101, 122, 188, 196, 218
Wright, N. T. 51, 174

Y

Yemen 9, 202

Z

Zemeckis, Robert 107
Zoroaster 122, 123, 124, 136
Zoroastrian 124, 129, 147, 164, 165
Zoroastrianism 124, 147, 171
Zoroastrians 165, 169

BIBLIOGRAPHY

Back to the Future. Directed by Robert Zemeckis. Amblin Entertainment, 1985 Film.

Anderson, Irvine H. 2005. *Biblical Interpretation and Middle East Policy: The Promised Land, America, and Israel.* Gainesville, FL: University Press of Flordia.

Aristole. unknown. *Metaphysics.* Athens, Greece: Unknown.

Bradford, William. 1736. *Of Plim⁻oth Plantation.* Plymouth, MA: Personal manuscript.

Brown, Dan. 2003. *The Da Vinci Code.* New York, NY: Doubleday.

Cohen, Morton N. 2002. *Lewis Carroll: A Biography.* New York: Vintage Books.

Ed., Anna-Teresa Tymieniecka. 1997. *Passion for Place Book.* Rotterdam: Springer Netherlands.

Eldredge, John. 2011. *Wild at Heart.* Nashville: Thomas Nelson.

Elliot, Elizabeth. 1981. *Through the Gates of Splendor; Rev Upd ed.* Carol Stream: Tyndale Momentum.

The Motorcycle Diaries. Directed by Walter Salles. FilmFour, 2004. Film.

Goldman, Robert. 1992. *Death in the Locker Room II: Drugs and Sports Updated Edition.* Chicago: Elite Sports Medicine Publications.

Grant, Robert M. 1967. *Gnosticism and Early Christianity Revised ed.* New York, NY: Columbia University Press.

Hinshaw, Robert E. 2006. *Living with Nature's Extremes: The Life of Gilbert Fowler White.* Boulder: Johnson Books.

Hugo, Victor. 1862. *Les Misérables.* Paris: A. Lacroix, Verboeckhoven & Cie.

Illinois State University. 2012. *The Sinclair Lewis Society.* Accessed November 25, 2016. http://english.illinoisstate.edu/sinclairlewis/.

Lee, Philip J. 1993. *Against the Protestant Gnostics.* Oxford: Oxford University Press.

Lewis, C. S. 1970. *God in the Dock: Essays on Theology and Ethics.* Grand Rapids: Eerdmans.

Lincoln, Abraham. 1953. *The Collect Works of Abraham Lincoln.* New Brunswick: Rutgers University Press.

Lindsey, Hal. 1970. *The Late Great Planet Earth.* Grand Rapids, Michigan: Zondervan.

Mather, Cotton. 1681-1708. *Personal Diary of Cotton Mather.* Boston, MA.

Nock, Arthur Darby. 1972. *Essays on Religion and the Ancient World.* Oxford: Oxford Press.

Noll, Mark A. 1995. *The Scandal of the Evangelical Mind.* Grand Rapids, Michigan: Wm. B. Eerdmans Publishing Company.

Osborne, John. 1961. *Luther.* Performed by Albert Finney. Theatre Royal, Nottingham. June 26.

Regarding Henry. Directed by Mike Nichols. Paramount Pictures, 1991. Film.

Parks, Tim. 2006. *Medici Money.* New York, NY: W. W. Norton & Company.

Roiphe, Katie. 2002. *Still She Haunts: Reprint.* Crystal Lake: Delta Publishing.

Salinger, J. D. 1951. *The Catcher in the Rye.* Boston: Little, Brown and Company.

Schaeffer, Francis A. 1985. *A Christian Worldview; (5 Volume Set).* Wheaton, Illinois: Crossway.

Schaeffer, Francis. 1968. *Escape from Reason.* Downers Grove, IL: InterVarsity Press.

—. 1972. *He Is There and He Is ot Silent.* Downers Grove, IL: InterVarsity Press.

—. 1968. *The God Who Is There.* Downers Grove, IL: InterVarsity Press.

Schaeffer, Frank. 2008. *Crazy for God.* Boston: Da Capo Press.

—. 2004. *Portofino: A Novel (Calvin Becker Trilogy) Reprint.* Boston: Da Capo Press.

—. 2004. *Saving Grandma: A Novel (Calvin Becker Trilogy) Reprint.* Boston, MA: Da Capo Press.

—. 2004. *Zermatt: A Novel (Calvin Becker Trilogy) Reprint.* Boston: Da Capo Press.

Taylor, J. Hudson. 1987. *Hudson Taylor (Men of Faith) 2nd Ed.* Bloomington: Bethany House Publishers.

Tim LaHaye, Jerry B. Jenkins. 1995-2007. *Left Behind (series of 10).* Carol Stream, Illinois: Tyndale House.

The Matrix. Directed by Lana and Lilly Wachowski. Warner Brothers, 1999. Film

Webb, Charles. 1963. *The Graduate.* New York: Washington Square Press.

What is Nouthetic Counseling. 1999. Web. October 20, 2016. http://www.nouthetic.org/about-ins/what-is-nouthetic-counseling.

Time to Run. Directed by James F. Collier. World Wide Pictures, 1973. Film.

Wright, N. T. 2008. *Surprised by Hope: Rethinking Heaven, the Resurrection, and the Mission of the Church.* New York: HarperOne.

—. 2011. *The Kingdom New Testament: A Contemporary Translation.* New York: Harper Collins.

Made in the USA
Monee, IL
21 December 2019